Robert B. McCormick is Associate Professor of History at the University of South Carolina Upstate and Chair of the Department of History, Political Science, Philosophy and American Studies.

CROATIA UNDER ANTE PAVELIĆ

America, the Ustaše and Croatian Genocide
in World War II

ROBERT B. MCCORMICK

I.B. TAURIS

LONDON · NEW YORK

New paperback edition published in 2018 by
I.B.Tauris & Co. Ltd
London • New York
www.ibtauris.com

First published in hardback in 2014 by I.B.Tauris & Co. Ltd

ISBN: 978 1 78831 087 1
eISBN: 978 0 85773 671 0
ePDF: 978 0 85772 535 6

A full CIP record for this book is available from the British Library
A full CIP record is available from the Library of Congress

Library of Congress Catalog Card Number: available

Typeset in Garamond Three by OKS Prepress Services, Chennai, India

To Cindy, Mary, and Anna. My girls.

CONTENTS

LIST OF FIGURES

Figure 1 Reverend Krunoslav Draganović was not only key to organizing and operating the Ratline in the late 1940s but, as the playing card attests, he remained an American contact for many years afterwards. Courtesy of the National Archives.

Figure 2 Ante Pavelić speaking in Rome during his first trip to Italy after being named Poglavnik. Note the Nazi and Italian flags, the hastily assembled uniforms, as well as the Ustaše 'U' on the soldiers' caps. Courtesy of the National Archives.

Figure 3 Although the NDH's end was near, Ante Pavelić is greeting German Ambassador to Croatia Siegfried Kasche and General Edmund von Glaise-Horstenau in 1944. Courtesy of the National Archives.

Figure 4 King Aleksandar and Foreign Minister Louis Barthou pictured only moments before their assassination in Marseilles. Courtesy of the *New York Times*.

Figure 5 The funeral procession in Belgrade for King Aleksandar was sombre. The assassination failed to generate a Croatian revolution in Yugoslavia as Ante Pavelić had wished. Courtesy of the *New York Times*.

Figure 6 Wallace Murray as head of the Division of Near Eastern Affairs for the State Department during the 1930s was an early voice

ACKNOWLEDGEMENTS

I am indebted to countless people who have helped me complete this project and the following list is in no way comprehensive. A great deal of thanks is owed to Dr Jerry Augustinos, Distinguished Professor Emeritus of the University of South Carolina, who not only introduced me to Ante Pavelić when I was a graduate student, but also taught me how to be a historian. He made valuable contributions to an earlier version of the manuscript. The late Dr Owen Connelly of the University of South Carolina was always a source of inspiration and continues to be so for me. Over the years, many colleagues have offered me insight, encouragement and assistance. They have endured many of my discussions about American and Yugoslav history. Dr Carol Loar, Dr Paul Grady and Dr Dwight Lambert of the University of South Carolina Upstate were particularly noteworthy for their friendship and assistance. The late Dr Randall Austin of Chadron State University and Dr Cheryl Golden of Newman University helped immeasurably on this project when it was in its infancy. The conversations we shared about Pavelić and Yugoslavia went a long way in forging the basic outline for the project. The list of people who helped with suggestions and advice is too numerous to list, but they all in many ways offered invaluable help.

As with all projects of this nature, it could not have been completed without help from numerous members of staff at libraries and archives. The staff of the National Archives, the Public Record Office, the Dwight D. Eisenhower Presidential Library and the

Harry S. Truman Presidential Library were particularly helpful. They often steered me to sources that I otherwise would have missed in my research. I am grateful for grants provided by the University of South Carolina Upstate that helped fund necessary research. Noteworthy assistance on this project was provided by the always helpful, cheerful and talented Mary Kay Gault of the University of South Carolina Upstate Library. Mrs Gault secured important materials from around the country for me without which this project would have languished for years to come. In the final stages, John Brenner of the University of Missouri Press was especially helpful with editorial suggestions that greatly improved the manuscript. His unending enthusiasm and support for this project strengthened it immensely. I am exceedingly appreciative of the editorial staff at I.B.Tauris, in particular Tomasz Hoskins and Allison Walker, for supporting and improving this manuscript. Any flaws or omissions are purely my own.

On a personal note, my most heartfelt thanks are extended to my mother, Rene Cary. Throughout the life of this endeavour she has been a font of encouragement, love and support. I have never had a greater advocate. These meagre words do little justice for what she has done. Even though my father, the late Reverend Robert L. McCormick, did not see any of this project, he taught me the greatness of history and inspired my love of the discipline. I am forever grateful to my wife Cindy for her patience and understanding, especially for the countless hours required to research and write the manuscript. To my daughters Mary and Anna, many thanks for allowing me time to be alone to finish 'daddy's book' when I knew very well that all you wanted to do was play.

ABBREVIATIONS

ACC	Allied Control Commission
ADP	Alex Dragnich Papers
AFHQ	Allied Forces Headquarters
CIC	Counter Intelligence Corps
DDEL	Dwight D. Eisenhower Library
DP	Displaced Persons
FRUS	Foreign Relations of the United States
G-2	Military Intelligence
G-5	Assistant Chief of Staff
HSS	Croatian Peasant Party (Hrvatska Seljačka Stranka)
HSTL	Harry S. Truman Library
IMRO	Internal Macedonian Revolutionary Organization
IRR	Investigative Records Repository
MTOUSA	Mediterranean Theatre of Operations United States Army
NAMP	National Archives Microfilm Publication
NARA	National Archives and Records Administration
NDH	Independent State of Croatia (Nezavisna Država Hrvatska)
OKW	Oberkommando der Wehrmacht
ONZA	Department for the Protection of the People (Odjeljenje Za Zaštitu Naroda)
PRO	Public Record Office
RG	Record Group
SACMED	Supreme Allied Command Mediterranean

CHAPTER 1

ANTE PAVELIĆ AND THE EMERGENCE OF THE USTAŠE

The United States neglected Yugoslavia and the Balkan Peninsula for most of the 1920s and 1930s.[1] The economic boom in post World War I America and the consequences of the Great Depression focused Washington's attention on domestic affairs and relations with countries with whom the United States had a significant economic interest. Otherwise, isolationism ruled from coast to coast. No matter how hard politicians tried, however, they could not completely separate America from international affairs. Due to its large immigrant population, even distant and seemingly remote countries such as Yugoslavia were to attract Washington's attention from time to time. Since the United States had a large population of Croatians, Serbians, Macedonians and other Balkan peoples, any turmoil between ethnic groups in Yugoslavia had the potential for major repercussions within the United States. While America was looking inward, Yugoslavia experienced a series of crises, both internal and external, which ultimately led to the German invasion in April 1941, and the creation of an alleged independent Croatia, an Axis satellite. Some of the turmoil was triggered by Ante Pavelić. A remote, mysterious and almost unknown figure to the State Department for much of the 1930s, Washington reluctantly became interested in Pavelić and the activities of Croatians within the United States, some of whom were sympathetic and supportive of the Ustaše.

American diplomacy

As the United States emerged as an industrial giant in the late 1800s, even relatively obscure areas such as the Balkans necessitated some official American presence. Serbia hosted an American mission as early as 1882; however, it was considered a far-flung distant posting, without any real significance. By the time the United States placed permanent representatives in Yugoslavia in 1919, little had changed. Like most Balkan capital cities, Belgrade was viewed as a backwater.[2] In the 1930s, America's staff at the mission 'consisted of one minister, one secretary-of-embassy, and a part-time military attaché who "covered" several Balkan countries simultaneously'.[3] There were various other staff members, but this certainly was a skeleton crew. Besides the office in Belgrade, there was a consulate in Zagreb, established in 1920, which was staffed by two department officials. Washington deemed a larger presence in Yugoslavia unnecessary, primarily because America had little economic or national interest in the new kingdom or the region. Throughout the 1930s, the United States never imported more than $6.7 million of goods from Yugoslavia in a single year. Likewise, American exports had an equally small share of the Yugoslav market, peaking in 1937 at $7.2 million. To place this in perspective, American trade with Czechoslovakia was several times as much.[4]

Within the State Department of the 1930s there were few people who knew much about Yugoslavia or Balkan affairs in general, therefore postings in Belgrade or Bucharest usually came with a good deal of freedom to mould American policy. Foremost among those ignorant of the region was Secretary of State Cordell Hull, a man with little experience or interest in international relations, who became the longest-serving secretary of state in history, holding the post from 1933 to 1944. Hull was mostly a figurehead for President Franklin Roosevelt, who preferred using his own hand-picked men for gaining information and advice on foreign affairs. Hull was heavily dependent on his staff for policy decisions and leadership. As historian Martin Weil commented, 'Documents went out under his name, but they rarely reflected his own independent opinions, which were few'.[5] Throughout his tenure in office, the Tennessean allowed the bureaucracy of the State Department to run day-to-day affairs. American relations with Yugoslavia and the rest of the Balkans were managed by a Kentucky native, Wallace Murray, since 1929, the head of the Division of Near East Affairs.[6] Murray's experience with Eastern Europe was extremely limited, having only served as secretary to the American legation in Hungary from 1920 to 1922. The Middle East was an area of greater interest for him. Neither Hull nor Murray concerned themselves much about Yugoslav politics. Historian Vladimir Petrov noted that 'months and sometimes years passed without a single Department message to the legation in Belgrade requesting specific information related to a particular episode or a comprehensive analysis of the situation as a whole'.[7] What is perhaps most striking is the State Department's lack of interest in how Balkan countries fitted into the context of European politics. There was much attention paid to following Italian or German affairs, but little was focused on the role Balkan states played in the plans of these expanding fascist countries. Yugoslavia was a faraway country with no one in the State Department very much interested in or capable of understanding its complicated political landscape. It would take terrorist violence and a world war to begin to alter this situation.

Yugoslav politics

Regardless of American isolation, major events were changing Yugoslavia in a profound and dramatic fashion. The late 1920s brought significant domestic turmoil to Yugoslavia, as political rivalry between nationalist parties reached a fever pitch. The Yugoslav government was permanently crippled by its inability to develop a national political party that could draw large numbers of votes from various nationalities. Instead, politics focused on ethnically divisive parties who forged deeper ethnic hatreds in order to solidify their political power among their constituents. Most Croatians, especially the peasants, endorsed the Croatian Peasant Party (Hrvatska Seljačka Stranka, HSS), which had gained prominence under the leadership of the Radić brothers, Ante and Stjepan. Throughout the 1920s and 1930s, the Peasant Party fought for, at most, an independent Croatia and, at minimum, a Croatia with a great amount of autonomy within Yugoslavia. Serbians looked to Nikolai Pašić and the Radical Party as the mouthpiece for their interests. Neither party even pretended to cooperate with the other. This was never more apparent than in debates that surrounded the ratification of the 1921 Constitution, a strongly centralist document dictated by the desires of the greater Serbia faction of the Radicals. The constitution was approved without the support or participation of key Croatian leadership, making it a major point of contention throughout the 1920s. In effect, the constitution created a centralized state under Serbian authority which provided the King, a member of the Serbian royal family, with considerable power. Consequently, Croatians never fully accepted the document or the Yugoslav government under it, believing that neither represented Croatian interests or the country as a whole. Croatian leadership saw the constitution as a Serbian document only exercising jurisdiction over Serbs.

By the mid 1920s, Premier Pašić's dominance, enforced by the police and censorship, became more precarious as trade agreements with Italy faced serious opposition from the independence-minded Croatian Peasant Party now led by the surviving Radić brother, Stjepan. The Croatians were concerned about growing Italian interest in the Dalmatian Coast and had no faith that the Radicals would protect them from Mussolini's ambitions. At the Paris Peace Conference of 1919, Italy was denied most of its territorial claims, including much of Dalmatia, promised by the 1915 Treaty of London. Pašić's death in 1926 damaged the cohesion of the Radical Party by depriving it of its long-term anchor, and moved Yugoslavia towards even more instability. The political quagmire allowed King Aleksandar to flex his muscles. This was especially true after the elections of 1927 failed to provide the country with anything more than the continued divisive political formations of the previous years.[8]

By May 1928, the Skupština (Yugoslav Parliament) faced gridlock. The particular issue was the Italian trade treaty; however, the deep-seated problems were nationalistic. The government, led by Prime Minister Veljo Vukičević, did not include even one Croatian; attempts to attract Stjepan Radić to join had failed. It was unfortunate for Croatian interests and hopes for Yugoslav unity that the Croatian Peasant Party championed an ill-fated policy of non-participation. Croatian abandonment of the political arena on several different occasions meant that the Serbian dominated Skupština was able to move forward with a Serbian platform. Although Radić returned to the Skupština in June 1928, Croatian and Serbian mistrust continued to burn. The rhetoric on both sides had been heated, with talk of violence which occasionally spilled over into fist fights in and around the parliament. These were only minor disturbances compared to the events of 20 June 1928, when a Radical Montenegrin deputy, Puniša Račić, mortally wounded Radić on the floor of the parliament. Radić lingered, at times seemingly on the road to recovery, until his death on 8 August.

Croatia erupted with demonstrations and violence, as the cause of Croatian independence now had a new martyr, while some Serbians hailed the assassin as a hero. The Yugoslav government had reached a point of grave crisis. By 6 January 1929, King Aleksandar, seeing no opportunity for the Skupština to function, dissolved the 1921 Constitution and proclaimed his dictatorship. He had little choice in the matter since the Croatian Peasant Party, now led by the politically-challenged Vladimir Maček, refused to abide by the constitution, which they argued was never approved by Croatians and did not recognize Croatian rights. Indeed, many Croatians viewed Aleksandar as more of a foreign monarch than the king of Yugoslavia. Some believed the dictatorship was the final manifestation of a carefully crafted strategy of Serb dominance in Yugoslavia. Since Serbs were not about to allow Croatia a significant amount of autonomy, the country's politics had ground to a halt. Appreciating the threat of a potential civil war if firm leadership did not unite Yugoslavia, the King proceeded to grasp full control over his kingdom. Aleksandar rapidly moved to quash unrest. All political parties were banned and press freedoms were curtailed. He changed the name of the country from the Kingdom of Serbs, Croats and

Slovenes to the Kingdom of Yugoslavia, an act designed to de-emphasize ethnic divisions in the hope of creating a common national identity.

Ustaše origins

Irritated by Croatian political impotence, angered over Aleksandar's grasp for power and eager to champion the cause of Croatian independence, Ante Pavelić founded the Ustaše, a political and paramilitary organization, in Zagreb on 7 January 1929.[9] He had no stomach for a dictatorship led by a member of the Serbian royal family, a family he considered foreign and imperialistic. Pavelić had been moving towards a break with Yugoslavia for years, but especially after being elected to the Skupština in 1927. As a deputy representing Zagreb, he enjoyed a prominent pulpit from which to preach his vitriol-laced message of Croatian independence.

The origins of Pavelić's beliefs rest in his early life in the ruggedly beautiful region west of Sarajevo. The future leader of Croatia was born in the small village of Bradina, Herzegovina on 14 July 1889, the son of a railroad worker on the Sarajevo–Metković line. His early life was spent in an ethnically mixed, rural area that included large numbers of Muslims. Extreme nationalists typically emerge in areas where there is constant and appreciable contact with another ethnic group, and such was the case with Pavelić. He received a good education, attending schools in Travnik, Senj, and Karlovac. In 1910, he travelled to the capital of Croatia – a heady experience for this small-town young man – to attend the University of Zagreb. The University was a centre of Croatian nationalism and Pavelić became an adherent almost immediately, joining a nationalist group called Young Croatia. He earned his stripes in 1912, being arrested for demonstrating in favour of Croatian separatism. Although already a political activist, Pavelić did not shirk his law studies and graduated in 1915.[10]

The newly-minted attorney was a staunch supporter of the nationalist Party of Right, being elected general secretary in 1918. He embraced the strongly nationalist foundation of the Party, refusing to recognize Croatia's inclusion in Yugoslavia. In 1922, he took time away from his political agenda to marry Marija Lovrenčević in Zagreb. The couple had three children, two daughters and one son. By 1927, Pavelić, now vice-president of the Croatian Bar, was elected to the national assembly as a deputy from Zagreb with the aid of an alliance with Ante Trumbić, one of the grand old men of Croatian politics. Pavelić's biggest supporters were students, strongly influenced by romantic notions of the nation and its heroic past. His position with students and nationalists was further entrenched when he defended Macedonian students affiliated with the Internal Macedonian Revolutionary Organization (IMRO) during a trial in Skopje. With this devoted base of followers, his plans for establishing an independent Croatia were already well advanced.

To Pavelić, independence was the only policy for Croatians, who, in his opinion, had suffered for generations under foreign regimes such as the Habsburgs and at present the Karadjordjevićs. Though he was an unknown politician to the Americans, he had emerged in Yugoslavia as a voice for Croatian independence, a champion of Croatian interests who drew his message from earlier Croatian nationalists. Pavelić's political inspiration stemmed primarily from two Croatian politicians, Ante Starčević and Josip Frank. Starčević was a contemporary of Bishop Joseph George Strossmayer, the intellectual father of Yugoslavism. The son of a Catholic father and an Orthodox mother, Starčević championed Croatia's historical right to be an independent state, arguing that Croatians had never abandoned their independence, regardless of Habsburg or Ottoman domination. As leader of the Party of Right, his hatred of Habsburg dominance gained a large following among Croatians who had long been weary of Hungarian hegemony. In opposition to South Slav unity as outlined by Strossmayer, Starčević worked to undermine Serbian identity by aggressively arguing that Serbians were Croatians who had converted to Orthodoxy. Such statements were blatantly offensive to Serbians and helped set the table for future ethnic tension between Serbian and Croatian camps. Starčević, however, was not a proto-fascist. As Sabrina Ramet notes, Pavelić and his followers altered Starčević's reputation to fit their fascist desires 'by denying that the 19th century liberal had ever believed in human equality, ignoring his championing of women's equality, and endeavouring to portray him as a prototypical racist'.[11]

As Starčević grew older, his party suffered from a lack of leadership which, in turn, forged factions. Josip Frank, a popular German-Jewish lawyer and follower of Starčević, was a committed Croatian nationalist who became the leader of the Pure Party of Rights, a splinter of Starčević's party, from 1898 until his death in 1911. Frank, Starčević's son-in-law, reversed a key component of Starčević's beliefs. Seeking to become prominent in Croatian politics, he supported the Habsburg monarchy, hoping to elevate Croatia's place in the Empire and reduce traditional Hungarian power over Croatians. He continued, however, to embrace a hatred for Serbs, a position which was useful for rallying Party supporters. With Frank, a man who believed that Orthodox Serbs were a degenerate force, the seed of anti-Serbian feeling germinated. Though he despised Hungarian dominance in Croatia, his ultimate goal was the establishment of a Croatia in the fashion of Hungary after the Ausgleich of 1867. In other words, Croatia would become an autonomous political entity within the Habsburg Empire, enjoying extensive rights over its domestic affairs.

As years passed and optimism faded, especially after the collapse of the Habsburg state, Frank's party retreated into the safety of its vehemently anti-Serb and anti-Orthodox dogma. Having failed in achieving its aims, it directed its frustration towards the Serbs. After the creation of Yugoslavia, the Party stood in opposition to the state and the 1921 Constitution, both of which worked against Croatian autonomy and independence. To the Party faithful, full independence seemed the only legitimate policy, although it appeared a distant dream. This did not, however, discourage a small core of Croatians who accepted that independence was a lengthy process, having already consumed hundreds of years. Consequently, Frank's followers emerged as Croatian zealots who did not seek accommodation with the Serbs but favoured violence, as the only option left to achieve their aims.

The Ustaše

Those in tune with Frank's strongly anti-Serb positions were left without a unifying voice until Ante Pavelić emerged as leader of the Ustaše. But Pavelić's ability was not obvious to all. After the Ustaše's founding, it took about two years for him to be recognized as the movement's point man. Although he lacked the oratorical proficiency of Mussolini or Hitler, Pavelić had political skills and wanted to develop the Ustaše along the lines of revolutionary and terroristic organizations such as IMRO. From the organization's inception, the Ustaše was violent and revolutionary. Members' beliefs were a collection of seemingly disparate ideologies bound together in one movement. In Ustaše ideology, one could be a proto-fascist while at the same time a deep believer in Catholicism. At its ideological core was a fervent, mystical belief in the holiness and sanctity of the Croatian state. As Ustaše architect, Pavelić maintained that Croatians had established a state 1,400 years earlier and that over the centuries they had never abandoned their right to independence. Regardless of the Ottomans, the Habsburgs, or the Karadjordjevićs, Croatia had always existed. Pavelić's chief goal was therefore the resurrection of an independent Croatian state with borders which corresponded to earlier manifestations of Croatia. This objective was only achievable through the destruction of Serbian – foreign – influence within Croatia, which, in turn, necessitated the annihilation of Yugoslavia. Correspondingly, the wellbeing of the state was of such significance that individual rights ran a distant second to the establishment and maintenance of Croatia. Pavelić's fascist tendencies were apparent.

In their desire to demonstrate the distinctiveness of their people, the Ustaše deemed Croatians of pure peasant stock a separate nationality from their Balkan neighbours. By World War II, Ustaše ideologues would proclaim that Croats were Goths and therefore of Germanic stock, far removed from the inferior Slavic Serbs.[12] Any myth could be used to separate Croatians from Serbs. Like the Nazis, the Ustaše placed the peasant on a pedestal, extolling his virtues of clean living and hard work. The peasant was nearly incorruptible and there was much discussion of establishing a peasant republic. Even

Nazi and Croatian currency during World War II featured images of the solid and pure peasant. Pavelić, though he believed in the virtues of the peasant, was a clever politician who judged that such a picture would attract disenchanted peasants to his cause while weakening the Croatian Peasant Party.

Another key aspect of Ustaše ideology was an unmistakably close association with Catholicism. As a devout Catholic, Pavelić reckoned that the Croatian peoples had been chosen by God to defend Catholicism against assaults from both Orthodoxy and communism. This religious zeal held by some Ustaše, which demanded no tolerance for Orthodoxy, helped give a mystical and almost Biblical quality to the Ustaše movement. According to Pavelić and his minions, Croatians had been warriors and martyrs for Christianity and needed to continue the good fight for their independence, which would only strengthen them as the 'bulwark of Christianity'. This fervour enabled Pavelić to successfully demonize Serbians. Pavelić did not despise Serbs only because they were a different ethnic group, one which had exercised power over all of Yugoslavia for the past decade. He also condemned them because they embraced Orthodoxy, a foreign faith, which, the Ustaše believed, was encouraged by the Serbian-dominated Yugoslav government as a method for stamping Serbian identity on Croatian citizens. Thus Orthodoxy was viewed as a tool for smashing Croatian national identity. Likewise, communists, who were on the march in the 1920s and 1930s, were mortal foes of Catholicism and had to be stopped. To the Ustaše, Croatians faced both political and religious enemies who were determined to destroy Croatian culture, its traditions, its language, its political life and its religion. In other words, Ustaše ideology encouraged some aspects of a holy war.[13]

Perhaps the best description of Ustaše sentiment came during World War II from a Lieutenant Miloš, an Ustaše guard. Miloš was speaking to Vladko Maček, his prisoner, about the terrible murders being inflicted upon the Serbian people. Miloš justified his and the Ustaše's actions saying that, 'I am perfectly aware of what is in store for me. For my past, present and future deeds I shall burn in hell, but at least I shall burn for Croatia.'[14] Such extreme nationalistic zealotry was the foundation for a loyal core of Ustaše.

Tactically, Pavelić believed that only through violence, conducted by his revolutionary vanguard, the Ustaše, could Croatia break free from Yugoslavia's tentacles. Croatia was at a critical juncture in its life which necessitated military action. But Pavelić was fearful of the Ustaše being labelled as just some petty terrorist organization. He realized that the Ustaše needed to operate like a legitimate military force, carrying out actions against its enemy, if it had any hope of being seen as an acceptable political option. He was all too aware of how IMRO had rarely been perceived as anything but a terrorist organization, and one often weakened by factionalism at that.

Though emerging as the recognizable head of the vanguard in the Croatian independence movement, Pavelić did not look the part of a dynamic political leader. Fitzroy MacLean, the famed adventurer and Winston Churchill's representative and confidant in wartime Yugoslavia, wrote that Pavelić was 'a plain, gloomy-looking lawyer with flat features and large ears'.[15] Most pictures show him as a humourless figure, looking stern and unbending. He was depicted often in military uniform and jackboots. A smile is never seen on his face, and he appears stiff and serious, more like a party bureaucrat than the future Poglavnik (head or leader). Nonetheless, he had the characteristics necessary to lead a violent terrorist/revolutionary organization.

In light of King Aleksandar's coup in January 1929, Pavelić, fearing arrest, fled Yugoslavia and proceeded to organize the Ustaše. Although Pavelić was little more than a novice in covert methods and planning, he designed the Ustaše to operate as a paramilitary organization. In 1929, Pavelić travelled to Vienna and Sofia looking for émigrés eager to join his movement or willing to support it financially. His recruiting efforts, coupled with his publicly admitted goal of overthrowing the Yugoslav state, compelled Belgrade to convict him of treason and hang a death penalty over his head. Not in the least deterred, Pavelić used pageantry and secrecy to attract members. Hoping to create absolute loyalty and *esprit d'corps*, he required all members to swear allegiance to himself and to the independence of Croatia in an elaborate ceremony which included a knife, a revolver and a crucifix. The Ustaše's motto, 'Za Dom Spremni' (Ready for the Fatherland), was meant to rally his followers into fighting for an independent Croatia. Pavelić's recruiting efforts, however, achieved modest results, since most Croatians were repelled by his radical demands and his willingness to use violence. Unable to recruit many followers, the Ustaše remained a fringe operation with little support within Yugoslavia. It survived by attracting thugs, the highly impressionable and the unemployed. By 1934, Pavelić had amassed an army of perhaps 500 to 600, mostly disenchanted ne'er-do-wells. Though its numbers were small, Pavelić had established an organization of men willing to sacrifice their lives for the Ustaše cause.

The majority of Croatians followed the Croatian Peasant Party leader, Vladko Maček, who, although lacking glamour, was seen as the only realistic option for gaining Croatian autonomy. In the Ustaše's early years, Pavelić and Maček showed signs of cooperation, although Maček played a cagey game of avoiding public knowledge of their contacts. By 1932, Maček chose to divorce the Croatian Peasant Party from Pavelić's Ustaše on the grounds that Pavelić sought only a violent conflict with the Yugoslav government. Maček was willing to negotiate with Belgrade and accept some type of accommodation for Croatia instead of only demanding complete independence.[16]

As the leader of a fledgling movement exiled from its homeland, Pavelić knew that he needed friends within Europe and among Croatian emigrants in the Americas. He recognized that Italy and Hungary could be natural allies, considering that both wished to alter the territorial decisions of the 1919 Paris Peace Conference. His Ustaše needed foreign assistance to help spread its message, because the Croatian Peasant Party had not only the ear but also the allegiance of the vast majority of Croatians. Pavelić was lucky in that Yugoslavia was bordered by many enemies seeking revisions to the agreements forged at the Paris Peace Conference. Budapest continued to bristle over the loss to Yugoslavia of the Vojvodina, a multi-ethnic region with a substantial Hungarian population. Hungary's Regent,

Admiral Miklos Horthy, was interested in backing any organization which would destabilize Yugoslavia and thus allow Hungary to reclaim some of its lands lost after World War I. As tensions were high between Yugoslavia and Hungary, the Ustaše found a compliant Budapest which would allow them to organize a training and staging camp in Hungary near the Yugoslav border.

The camp at Janka Pusta, like many others in Hungary and later in Italy, masqueraded as a farm, but its real purpose was to train Ustaše terrorists for attacks on Yugoslavia. Janka Pusta, established by Pavelić's close associate, Gustav Perčec, became a staging ground for Ustaše terrorist attacks, including a daring 1932 rebellion on a police station in Brušani, Lika, Yugoslavia, a region known to be sympathetic to Croatian independence. The Lika Uprising was significant in that it was the first major attempt by the Ustaše to strike against the Yugoslav government.[17] In essence, it signalled their arrival on the political scene. This revolutionary uprising, however, was quickly smashed by Yugoslav troops forcing the Ustaše to concentrate on attacking trains travelling to and from Yugoslavia, especially on the Belgrade–Vienna line. All of these attacks, regardless of their actual success rate, caused serious disturbances and were a provocation that Belgrade could not ignore. Yugoslavia harshly punished any Ustaše they captured, but they were unable to eliminate Pavelić or destroy his band of terrorists. Bombings of government buildings and political assassinations became a normal part of life for Yugoslavs in the early 1930s.

Like Hungary, Italy too sought revision to decisions rendered at Paris in 1919. Hoping to expand its interests in the Adriatic and gain territory promised to it by the 1915 Treaty of London, Rome demonstrated considerable interest in Pavelić's cause. Potentially, the Ustaše's agenda fitted nicely with Mussolini's desire to re-establish the Roman Empire. His plans would be greatly furthered if he could move across the Adriatic and capture Dalmatia, or at the very least reduce Yugoslav strength. In this way, Italian influence in the Balkans would take a great leap forward and so, accordingly, would Mussolini's reputation. Il Duce determined that Pavelić was an acquiescent tool who could be used to destabilize Yugoslavia and perhaps forge a separate Croatia under Italian suzerainty. Mussolini, with more resources than the Hungarians, went well beyond Admiral Horthy and generously provided Pavelić with funding and numerous bases for operation. Pavelić enjoyed a villa at Pesaro, compliments of Mussolini, and was given carte blanche in training his followers. Despite this, Pavelić and the Ustaše were often out of favour with Mussolini's regime. To some in the Italian government they were seen as a poorly organized and insignificant group who were more of a political liability than anything else. Throughout the 1930s, Pavelić usually enjoyed tacit acceptance by the Italians, while sometimes benefiting from their financial and political support. But neither side was entirely comfortable in this relationship.

Pavelić found other friends in Bulgaria among the members of IMRO. Since its founding in 1893, IMRO had sought an autonomous Macedonia, but opposed its full absorption into the Bulgarian state. This goal remained fairly constant until 1932, when they began demanding complete independence for Macedonia and enlarged the proposed borders of the Macedonian state to ridiculous proportions. Throughout the 1920s and early 1930s, IMRO used their base in the small city of Petrich to launch raids into Yugoslavia, seriously disrupting Yugoslavian–Bulgarian relations and damaging any hope that Bulgaria would be accepted as a supporter of the status quo in the Balkans. After the military coup of 19 May 1934, IMRO was under siege from a newly-formed Bulgarian government. The Bulgarian army attacked IMRO strongholds, forcing the organization to operate in a far less vigorous manner and permanently reducing its influence in Bulgarian politics.[18] IMRO's desire for independence and its violent tactics dovetailed with the Ustaše. Both sought the collapse of Yugoslavia and needed a bold stroke to restore their lagging prestige.

The assassination

Pavelić achieved notoriety as an international terrorist in 1934, by masterminding the assassination of King Aleksandar I of Yugoslavia and Foreign Minister Louis Barthou of France. Though the Ustaše had been involved in attacks upon rail lines and bombings of government buildings, they theorized that only a major blow to the Serbian community within Yugoslavia would change Croatia's status. Pavelić presumed that such an audacious attack would create momentary chaos within Yugoslavia, thus allowing the Croatian independence movement to exercise its muscle and lead Croatians toward the establishment of an independent Croatia. There was no greater target than King Aleksandar. To the Ustaše, he symbolized all that they hated in Yugoslavia. He was a Serbian who dominated the state and opposed any movement towards devolution and Croatian autonomy or independence. Aleksandar had proclaimed the Constitution of 1931, a document that the Ustaše reviled, which placed authority heavily in the hands of the monarch while reducing the power of political parties and local government. Any hope of Croatian independence, at least for the time being, had been throttled. Even support from Italy and Hungary seemed shaky, as long as the Ustaše only served to irritate Aleksandar's regime. The Ustaše needed a big score to forge recognition for their cause. Aleksandar's assassination would at best lead to the collapse of Yugoslavia, allowing for the establishment of an independent Croatia. At worst, Yugoslavia would face a grave crisis which would only serve to strengthen the calls for a separate Croatia.[19] As events demonstrated, Pavelić did not have his finger on Yugoslavia's pulse.

In early 1933, Pavelić and the Ustaše developed plans to assassinate King Aleksandar. On 16 December 1933, at least three Ustaše operatives, perhaps more, stepped into action. While the King was celebrating his birthday in Zagreb in a gesture of goodwill to the Croatian people, an Ustaše operative, Petar Oreb, was to throw a bomb at the King's car as it passed on its parade route through the city. Young Oreb, only 22 years old, seeing that his escape path was blocked, never hurled his bomb and Aleksandar passed unharmed. Later in the evening, the bungled plot was discovered by Yugoslav police, who were usually well informed about Ustaše operations. Arrests were made. The Ustaše did not have an opportunity to redeem themselves with an attack on the King when he visited Zagreb's grand cathedral later in his tour.

The subsequent trial attracted some American attention to the Ustaše for the first time. Reports from Belgrade and Rome established, to the surprise of the State Department, that Ustaše camps had found a safe haven within Italy.[20] It was becoming clear that Italy not only tolerated the Ustaše but had also offered some form of assistance in the assassination plots. The State Department showed little interest in the Ustaše, but was intrigued by the Italian chicanery. They had little knowledge of Pavelić or other personnel in his organization. Even Oreb's trial, reported in great detail by Ambassador Charles Wilson, did little to register as more than a blip in Washington. Wilson wrote that during the trial Borgotaro, Italy was declared to be a training ground for the Ustaše and that it was 'often visited' by prominent Ustaše supporters such as Mile Budak and Branimir Jelić.[21] The State Department, however, was disinterested to the point of almost ignoring the assassination attempt and Italy's involvement with Pavelić and the Ustaše.

Regardless of the State Department's attitude, the Italians, as we have seen, had gone to great lengths to support Pavelić, who had held meetings with both Il Duce and Count Galleazo Ciano, Mussolini's foreign minister and son-in-law. Mussolini had provided him with a house in Bologna and thrown lira behind his cause. Pavelić was allowed to operate camps and train his Ustaše with impunity from Yugoslav protests.[22] The future leader of Croatia was gaining everything he needed, money and quarter; however, he was now dependent on the fickle graces of Italy. Italian interests came first and Pavelić knew that his masters needed to be impressed if the Ustaše cause was to flourish.

Not easily discouraged by the failed assassination attempt, Pavelić immediately began planning another, more serious, effort on Aleksandar's life. For this attempt, he called upon IMRO's expertise as Europe's most notable terrorist organization. IMRO had been a thorn in the side of Balkan peace since its founding in 1893 and its members were known throughout Europe as trained killers. To Pavelić, IMRO, led by Ivan Mihailov (Vance or Vancho), was a natural ally, because both organizations possessed similar goals and had a common enemy. IMRO fitted nicely with the Ustaše ideology, for it too did not hesitate to use violence in achieving its aims. As early as 1930, Pavelić had enjoyed fruitful contacts with IMRO's leadership, having visited with its leaders at their headquarters in Banka, outside of Sofia. With IMRO's assistance Pavelić was introduced to the world of terrorism.

Though the attempted assassination of 1933 ended in failure and not a little embarrassment, Pavelić persevered. With financial assistance from Italy and expertise from IMRO, Pavelić and Eugen Kvaternik, his trusted ally and the son of Slavko Kvaternik a significant Ustaše supporter and well-known advocate for an independent Croatia, began planning another attempt on Aleksandar's life. The plans for this much more professional effort were put into motion in late September 1934, with the goal of murdering the King while he was on a state visit to France. Pavelić was intimately associated with the scheme, having delivered, with his close ally Eugen Kvaternik, weapons and money to the assassins. Aleksandar's trip to France, which was to begin on 9 October, appeared to offer the best chance for killing the King, partly because the Ustaše could move around France with relative impunity. The state visit was designed to forge closer relations between France and Yugoslavia, partly to thwart Italian designs in the Balkans and European revisionism in general. French Foreign Minister Louis Barthou hoped the visit would strengthen the Little Entente, in light of the growing fascist threat. Soon after leaving the destroyer *Dubrovnik*, Yugoslavia's most modern warship, anchored in Marseilles harbour, a smiling and waving Aleksandar, dressed in the uniform of an admiral, and Barthou climbed into a car and proceeded down the parade route. The IMRO trained killer, taking advantage of the slow-moving vehicle and a startling lapse in security, leapt onto the running board and killed both Aleksandar and Barthou with gunshots. The assassin, Vladimir Gheorghiev Tchernozemsky, a Macedonian known as Vlado, was cut down by a sabre blow from Lieutenant Colonel Jules Piollet and died shortly thereafter.[23]

News of the assassination was met with outrage throughout Europe and within the United States. The *New York Times* and other American newspapers spent weeks reporting the story in great detail.

Their correspondents closely covered the return of the King's body to Yugoslavia, the long train journey to Belgrade and the state funeral. They often scooped the State Department, whose information channels were painfully slow and ill-equipped to respond to Balkan events. Within Yugoslavia, Serb and Croat put aside their disagreements, if only for the moment, to express their common grief over Aleksandar's death. Much to his disappointment, Pavelić's hope that the assassination would create momentary chaos and calls for Croatian independence never materialized. As grief consumed Yugoslavia, Prince Paul, the King's brother, stepped forward to lead a regency for the young King Petar II, then only 11 years old. Petar was to assume full power when he turned 18.

It was at this moment that the State Department became interested in Pavelić for the first time. Expressing its condolences to Belgrade and realizing that it was too early to fully appreciate the gravity of the crime, the State Department was interested in who had committed the assassination as well as who had masterminded and been involved in the previous year's assassination attempt that had garnered such little interest in Washington. As the State Department's interest in Yugoslav affairs grew, it became obvious that officials had ignored communications from Belgrade that pointed to an undercurrent of nationalist unrest among Croatian extremists who were associated with the ambitions of Italy and Hungary. The mission in Belgrade and the Zagreb Consulate had made these issues clear as early as January 1931, when they began sending reports to Washington that not only discussed Pavelić's role in the campaign for Croatian separatism, but also discussed his relationship with the governments of Hungary and Italy as well as IMRO.[24] Having paid little attention to these reports or Yugoslav politics, Wallace Murray, using information collected from Petar Oreb's trial, in a State Department memo, concluded that the December assassination attempt had been carried out by an organization called the 'Ustasha' who trained in the safety of a camp near Borgotaro, Italy.[25] Murray surmised that because of the, 'unrefuted charge that Italy has fostered a band of Croatian terrorists on Italian soil for the specific purpose as assassinating King Alexander, it will not be surprising if the strain in Italo-Yugoslav relations, already acute, increases as a result of the tragedy in Marseilles'.[26] Two days later, Murray learned from the *New York Times* that the assassination, indeed, was blamed on the Ustaše, an organization he described as being closely associated with IMRO.[27]

Substantive information about Pavelić and the Ustaše came from the embassy in Rome, often the source of news about Yugoslavia. The embassy noticed that the Italian police were not interested in cooperating with the French authorities, who quickly identified the assassin and arrested his Ustaše accomplices. As evidence of the success that Pavelić's minions had had in the United States, Croatian-Americans inclined to support Pavelić's cause raised money to finance the legal defence of the Croatian perpetrators arrested by French authorities.[28] The Italians, however, refused the French permission to speak with Pavelić or Kvaternik, both having been arrested by the Italian police in Turin. It did not take the French long to identify both men as key figures in the Ustaše movement, who had been visiting France in the weeks prior to the murder. Ambassador Breckinridge Long, who during World War II presided in an obstructionist manner over immigration and visa issues, reported that the embassy's assistant military attaché learned from his Yugoslav counterpart that the Ustaše were running camps at Fontecchio in Abruzzi, near Turin, and in Brescia.[29] Prior to the assassination, the Ustaše moved insurgents from Italy to the Austrian–Yugoslav border in hopes of infiltrating Yugoslavia on the day of the assassination.[30] The plan failed. By late October 1934, it was becoming clear to American authorities that Ante Pavelić, with the aid of Kvaternik, was the ringleader of the Ustaše.[31]

On the morning of 26 October 1934, the Yugoslav ambassador called on Ambassador Long, at his request, to discuss the assassination, terrorism and the Ustaše. Underscoring the dangerous nature of the Ustaše, the Yugoslav ambassador confirmed that Pavelić led this terrorist organization.[32] Long was surprised to hear that Ustaše operatives were to be found in many parts of Europe and even as far afield as the United States. Long asked him for names and addresses, but having none with him the ambassador explained that those would be provided to Washington via the Yugoslav delegation.[33] Long ended his report noting that Yugoslavia counted 'on the cooperation of the United States insofar as there are in the United States nuclei of this band, which are all operating under the direction and control of Pavelich'.[34] This meeting provided the first indication that Croatian-Americans may have had some involvement in the assassination or perhaps were supporting this newly-discovered terrorist cell. This was the beginning of a problem with which the United States would grapple for several years.

Later, Washington learned that Italy, obviously under pressure from the French and hoping to contain bad publicity, had quickly closed the Ustaše camps and forced the organization underground. This was a bone tossed to the French, because Rome had no intention of extraditing anyone for the crime for fear of being implicated in the plot. American officials in Rome and Belgrade gave very few details about Pavelić or the Ustaše.[35] American interest was more focused on how the assassination affected Franco–Italian relations than its impact on Yugoslav politics. Primarily, their concern was centred on Italy's unwillingness to cooperate with France.

What the State Department failed to fully recognize was that neither Italy nor France wanted the criminal investigation to bear fruit. There was significant concern throughout Europe that the assassinations could lead to a war fuelled by Yugoslav demands for justice. France, Britain and Italy worked closely to avoid a 1914-like crisis by shifting blame for the assassination from Rome to Budapest. Hungary's role in offering safe haven to the Ustaše, even though it had closed Ustaše training camps in April 1934, became the focus of diplomats.[36] Of course, Hungary was implicated by allowing terrorists to train in their country, but Rome, with deeper pockets, was much more seriously involved. For the security of Europe, however, Italy had to be distanced from responsibility for the assassinations.[37]

Meanwhile, French authorities had arrested Mio Krali, Ivan Rajić and Zvonimer Pospisil for their role in planning and assisting in the assassination. All three men were guilty of involving themselves with

Pavelić and Kvaternik in the schemes to kill the King, whether in Marseilles or, if that had failed, in Paris. Some Croatian-Americans, in particular the Croatian National Committee, an organization influenced by the Croatian Home Defenders, responded to the arrests by raising funds to defend the accused.[38] Substantial amounts of money were sent to Georges Desbons, a well-known defence attorney in Paris. Between February 1935 and February 1936, the Croatian National Committee, seemingly under the directions of Ante Došen, sent at least $4,500 to help Desbons in their defence.[39] Their assistance did not rest there, for the committee delivered funds totalling $750 directly to the accused.[40] It is unclear how this money was collected, but it demonstrates that Pavelić's sympathizers had more financial means than one would have believed, especially during the Depression. The money may have helped these men avoid the guillotine, because after the conclusion of two trials, all were sentenced to life in prison.

To the surprise of very few, the French government issued an extradition request to Italy in November 1934.[41] Since Mussolini and Foreign Minister Ciano were implicated in the assassination attempt, French authorities knew that Mussolini would not relinquish Pavelić or Kvaternik. Few observers believed that Italy would do more than superficially entertain the notion. Like other diplomats in Europe, American representatives, such as Breckinridge Long, were not optimistic that Pavelić or other conspirators would be brought to justice. If extradition occurred, an international scandal would be in the making with Mussolini at the centre. His ambitions in Abyssinia and in the Balkans would have been compromised vis-à-vis the League of Nations if Mussolini admitted any responsibility for the crime. Ambassador Long was able to convince Wallace Murray at the State Department that the Italians had been intimately involved in funding the assassins, harbouring the Ustaše and helping fund their operations. Murray was intrigued enough to request more detailed information about the Ustaše as well as Italian and Hungarian involvement in funding and protecting them.[42] Charles Wilson, the head of the American delegation in Belgrade and a keen observer of Yugoslav politics, confirmed that Ustaše camps existed in

Italy with the full knowledge of the Italian government, pointing out that newspapers in Belgrade had even printed pictures of the alleged camps.[43] Wilson, who served as Envoy Extraordinary and Minister Plenipotentiary from August 1933 to July 1937, kept a close and insightful watch on the ramifications of Aleksandar's assassination. He reported that training for the assassination had been undertaken in Hungary with the full knowledge of the Hungarian government. Although it was surprising that Italy and Hungary were deeply implicated in aiding and abetting the assassination, Wilson concluded that both states maintained a 'heavy responsibility' for the crime.[44] To no one's surprise, on 23 November, Italy officially refused to extradite Pavelić and Kvaternik, who had been arrested in Turin, to France.[45] Pavelić and Kvaternik did not face a trial, albeit in absentia, until 1936, when they were convicted of assassinating the King and Louis Barthou during the same trial where their colleagues were sentenced to life in prison. None of this mattered much to Pavelić or Kvaternik, because both continued to live under the protection of Mussolini.

In May 1936, Washington was alarmed to learn that the Italians planned to release Pavelić and Kvaternik. This information, which originated from the Yugoslav ambassador to Italy, made a significant impression on the State Department, at least temporarily. Charles Wilson, America's man in Belgrade, reported that the release of Pavelić was considered an affront to Yugoslav–Italian relations and would lead to Italian-backed terrorist activity in Yugoslavia.[46] The release so concerned Belgrade that Konstantin Fotić, the Yugoslav minister to the United States and a Serbian nationalist, called on the State Department on 18 May. He explained that Pavelić's freedom 'creates a very serious situation. It furthermore confirms the belief of my people that the actual hand behind the assassination of our King was Mussolini's.'[47] At this point, the United States had substantial information indicating that Pavelić was a dangerous man, whether he was independent or working with Mussolini. Pavelić's freedom, albeit heavily monitored by Mussolini's regime, was sure to remind everyone of the animosity between Italy and Yugoslavia.

The release, however, failed to permanently poison relations between Italy and Yugoslavia as Fotić predicted. In March 1937, the two countries signed the Italian–Yugoslav Friendship Treaty, which recognized the Italian–Yugoslav border and served to ease tensions between the two states. One clause of the treaty provided for the disbanding of all Ustaše camps in Italy and the removal of Italian support for their cause. Key Ustaše operatives were to be interned, while Italy was to allow for the repatriation of some Croatians. Over the next few years, Yugoslavia repatriated 220 Croatians, most associated with the Ustaše.[48] Italy, however, reneged on Pavelić's repatriation, instead placing him in a villa in Sienna, believing that he might be useful in the future.

Although they had failed to initiate a revolution in Croatia, Pavelić and his Ustaše followers had made their mark as a dangerous terrorist movement willing to go to any lengths to destroy Yugoslavia and create an independent Croatia. As years passed and he became more isolated in Italy, Pavelić needed the financial and public support of sympathetic Croatians abroad, no matter how small the contributions may have been. To the Ustaše in Europe, their supporters in the United States were a lifeline who could cultivate favour from the Croatian-American community, secure funding and bring national attention to the issue of Croatian independence.

CHAPTER 2

INVESTIGATING DOMOBRANS

Soon after news of the assassinations spread, American authorities became aware that some Croatian elements within the United States not only supported Pavelić, but might also have been involved in the planning or funding of the assassination. The State Department learned that radical Croatians were pleased with the King's death, believing that Aleksandar's assassination was the first major step towards Croatian independence. Washington, however, had a great deal to learn about Ustaše operations in the United States. After 1934, the State Department, the FBI, the Post Office and other government agencies realized that Ustaše within the country, closely tied to Ustaše operatives in Europe, held the potential to damage diplomatic relations between the United States and Yugoslavia. With significant numbers of Croatian-Americans and Serbian-Americans living in major industrial cities and a constant series of complaints from the Yugoslav Embassy, authorities in Washington had little choice but to take a closer look at Ante Pavelić and the Ustaše.

On 15 October 1934, the State Department received a letter from Serge de Tucich warning that Ustaše figures were active within the United States. Wallace Murray did not ignore the letter, because de Tucich was a well-known playwright and a prominent newspaper reporter for Yugoslav papers. He reaffirmed to Murray that Ante Pavelić was the leader of the Ustaše and responsible for planning the Marseilles murders.[1] Making it clear that the United States needed to be aware of radical Croatians organizing within the United States, the letter asserted that Dr Branimir Jelić, one of Pavelić's closest associates, had come to the United States from South America a few months earlier, seeking to organize Ustaše groups in America.[2] De Tucich, a Croatian, questioned whether Jelić should be allowed to remain in the United States because he was busily, 'haranguing Croat immigrants in the spirit of [...] terroristic philosophy'.[3] Although Murray seems to have been unaware of Jelić's arrival, the Yugoslav Consul General in New York, Radoye Yankovitch, had, as early as 7 September 1934, alerted Immigration and Naturalization at Ellis Island of the threat Jelić posed to good relations between the United States and Yugoslavia.[4] Jelić's groups were to be called Domobrans (defenders) to avoid a direct link with the Ustaše, known already as a violent terrorist organization. *Nezavisna Hrvatska Država (Independent State of Croatia)*, a newspaper published in Pittsburgh, Pennsylvania and founded by Jelić, was the American mouthpiece for the Ustaše, de Tucich rightly noted.[5] The paper, which shared its name with one started by Pavelić in Berlin in 1933, began publication in June 1934, one month after Jelić came to the United States.[6] Under his direction the paper, to no great surprise, voiced full support for Pavelić and his actions. De Tucich stressed that the newspaper was damaging Croatian interests and did nothing but spread the most unsavoury type of propaganda.[7] To underscore his charges, de Tucich provided translations of particularly inflammatory rhetoric that emphasized violence and nationalism.

Much of the information provided by de Tucich was correct and had even been printed in the *Youngstown* (Ohio) *Vindicator* a few days earlier. Since Youngstown possessed a large population of both Croatians and Serbs, the assassination had struck the city's South Slav population like a lightning bolt. By coincidence, Dr Branimir Jelić was in Youngstown when the assassination occurred. Carrying a Hungarian passport – additional proof of how Hungary sheltered Ustaše operatives – Jelić had arrived in the United States on 31 May 1934 on the fast and luxurious SS *Europa*.[8] While in Youngstown, Jelić wasted no time showing his colours when asked about Aleksandar's death. 'It was not a murder. It was the carrying out of a sentence of death imposed by the Croatian people on Alexander the tyrant,' declared Jelić.[9] Trying to rally his followers towards revolution, he remarked that, 'the Croatian people are glad. They are calling me to ask for instruction – to ask what they should do – to ask if they should raise funds immediately. The Croatian people have been delivered from their oppressor.'[10]

Jelić's inflammatory words, designed to rally Croatian-Americans to the Ustaše cause, were delivered at the culmination of a cross-country tour he had conducted the previous month. Unknown to American authorities at the time, Jelić, directed by Pavelić, had travelled to Kansas City and Los Angeles establishing Domobran chapters in both cities.[11] One of the alleged purposes of the chapters was to raise funds for the continued publication of the Ustaše's voice in America, *Nezavisna Hrvatska Dražava*. Jelić was an experienced campaigner for Pavelić's cause, having spent time in Buenos Aires, Montevideo, and other South American cities effectively organizing the Croatian population in support of Pavelić.[12] It is doubtful that large sums of money were raised, in part because many Croatians laboured in heavy industry for moderate pay. The chapters contributed small amounts that helped the paper continue its work. Some of the money raised, however, may have been used to fund Ustaše operations in Europe.

With information accumulating from several sources, the State Department had plenty of reasons to be concerned about Ustaše infiltration into the United States. By early November 1934, the Yugoslav delegation in Washington provided more evidence when it alerted Cordell Hull and the State Department to its concerns about Croatian extremists within the United States, naming Ante Došen, Ante Valenta, and Zvonko Budak as leaders, while urging Washington to prohibit gatherings designed to attack the interests of Yugoslavia, a country friendly with the United States.[13] Such sentiments were reinforced by the Yugoslav consul general in New York, who charged that Jelić was Pavelić's chosen liaison organizing Croatian-Americans to respond to their homeland in a time of great need.[14] He even suggested that Americans were being recruited and sent to Hungary to be trained as terrorists.[15]

Although this was doubtful, the information does illustrate Yugoslavia's deep concern about the potential for Americans to assist Pavelić's forces. Understandably, Yugoslavia desired that the United States immediately curtail the activities of any Ustaše or their supporters within America on the grounds that the United States and Yugoslavia were on good terms and the actions of these elements only served to foment tension.

In the previous few decades, Yugoslavs, both Croatian and Serb, had been part of the great exodus of East Europeans leaving their homelands to create new lives in the United States. Those who immigrated to America brought with them all of the ethnic and political issues which were destabilizing Yugoslavia. Since most Yugoslavs settled in the same regions, usually industrialized areas of states such as Pennsylvania, Illinois and Ohio, there were plenty of opportunities for unrest. When other nationalities like Macedonians were tossed into the equation, disturbances were even more likely.

Croatians had come to the United States in far greater numbers than Serbs. According to the 1920 census, if language is used to establish identity, there were 140,559 Croatians and 52,208 Serbians living in the United States.[16] These Croatians, whether they outwardly stated it or not, were usually supporters of the Croatian Peasant Party. As previously discussed, Maček's party was considered the voice for Croatian rights within Yugoslavia. It would be a mistake to say that all Croatian-Americans were opposed to Yugoslavism, because many wanted to retain the kingdom but with greater autonomy for Croatia. Some Croatians harboured dreams of independence, but in reality, there seemed a far greater likelihood of gaining increased autonomy rather than complete independence. Those in the mainstream opposed using force to gain a separate Croatia; a violent civil war was in the interest of no Yugoslav. Regardless of the more moderate positions held by most Croatian-Americans, the Ustaše saw these new immigrants as a potentially rich source of financial and political assistance for their cause.

The Hrvatsko Kolo (Croatian Circle), a fraternal organization founded in New York in 1928 but inspired by Croatian-Americans in Youngstown, Ohio, offered Pavelić compelling evidence that

Croatian-Americans would support him and the Ustaše. Originally, the Croatian Circle was comprised of 14 branches in the Eastern United States. One of the founding members of the New York branch was Ante Došen, a key soldier in Pavelić's cause, who was operating in the United States under Pavelić's direction.[17] The Circle was chiefly a fraternal gathering, but some of its members were keen to open the door to more than simply encouraging the maintenance of Croatian culture, duties the Croatian Fraternal Union fulfilled, and offering support to politicians like Vladko Maček. While in exile from Yugoslavia in 1929, Pavelić appealed for financial assistance from the Croatian Circle. Sympathetic to his cause, the Circle had raised $1,714 by the time the Great Depression forced them to end the fund-raising campaign in April 1930.[18]

As the 1930s progressed, the Croatian Circle became more openly political, urging national self-determination for Croatia and issuing manifestos, including requests for the League of Nations to hold a plebiscite and recognize Croatia's right to national self-determination. In October 1933, the Croatian National Council of North America, of which the Croatian Circle was a part, drafted a lengthy manifesto for the League of Nations. The Reverend Ivan Stipanović presented the document to President Roosevelt at a White House meeting on 30 October 1933. The manifesto outlined the long history of Croatia's suffering and concluded that independence from Yugoslavia was the only answer.[19] Some Circle members, however, believed that independence was proceeding far too slowly and too cautiously and thus chose, with the persuasion of Branimir Jelić, to form Hrvatski Domobran units, which closely adhered to Ante Pavelić and the Ustaše.[20] Pavelić and his allies had discovered how to tap into the American market.

Pavelić's and the Ustaše's growing momentum in the United States was demonstrated in part by a resolution passed by the All Croat Congress held in Youngstown, Ohio on 29 November 1934. After professing allegiance to the United States, the congress decreed that Ante Pavelić, Mile Budak and Branimir Jelić were the recognized voices for Croatian independence. Always touting the mirage of widespread Croatian support for Pavelić, *Croatiapress*, the English-language sister paper of *Nezavisna Hrvatska Država*, reported that 'the people with glee and joy manifested their approval of the appointment of Dr Ante Pavelich'.[21]

This resolution was not the only decision made in Youngstown that day. The All Croat Congress, also known as the Croatian National Conference, unanimously approved a manifesto and directed it to President Roosevelt under the auspices of the Croatian National Representation for Independence of Croatia. The manifesto was a strong plea for Croatian independence filled with typical Domobran rhetoric based on kernels of truth and a selective use of history. Signed by Ante Došen as general secretary, the document called the 'request for the surrender of Dr Ante Pavelić as a violation of the most elementary right and defence which, according to international customs, are enjoyed by political émigrés in all civilized countries of the world'.[22] Although the manifesto called on the American government to stridently embrace Croatian independence, the State Department contended that the League of Nations was the proper forum for requests of this nature.[23]

As Ustaše activities and Croatian nationalist movements within the United States gained greater significance, Washington became more concerned over their impact on American–Yugoslav relations and preserving tranquillity between Croatian-Americans and Serbian-Americans. On 22 November 1934, the Yugoslav chargé warned Secretary of State Cordell Hull that several Ustaše figures were actively working to recruit Croatian-Americans.[24] Branimir Jelić, Ante Valenta (the leading Ustaše representative in Argentina), Zvonko Budak and Ante Došen were named as key figures in this operation. The Yugoslav chargé wanted American authorities to prevent the above-named individuals from holding meetings in Campbell and Youngstown, Ohio, both cities home to large Croatian communities. He argued that these meetings were designed to subvert the Yugoslav government which, he stressed, maintained friendly relations with the United States.[25]

Of this group, Došen, as editor and publisher of *Nezavisna Hrvatska Država*, which consistently produced anti-Yugoslav, anti-Serbian and pro-Pavelić articles, was destined to receive the greatest amount of attention. Formerly an Austro-Hungarian officer captured by the Russians in 1915, Došen immigrated to the United States in 1924 and became a devoted Ustaše follower in the early 1930s.[26] Došen's keenness for Croatian independence was most likely influenced by his father Marko, a Pavelić intimate who, in the 1930s, lived as an exile in Hungary. He was very close to his father and financially supported him throughout the late 1930s. During World War II, Marko's allegiance to Pavelić was rewarded when he was selected as Doglavnik (deputy commander) in Pavelić's government.[27]

Some FBI informants, however, questioned Došen's commitment to the Ustaše cause, believing that he was far more interested in gaining wealth and prestige than furthering Ustaše efforts in the United States.[28] Contrary to the FBI's information, Došen's diaries, if they are to be believed, paint a picture of a dedicated soldier in the cause for Croatian independence. Regardless, FBI reports, corroborated in extracts from Došen's diaries, named Došen as Pavelić's point man in the United States. He spent the second half of the 1930s in regular contact with Pavelić and other important Ustaše operatives such as Andrija Artuković and Mladen Lorković.[29]

The State Department took these warnings seriously and began investigating Croatian fraternal associations and the activities of various Croatians residing within the United States. The Post Office was one of the first government branches involved, because the State Department knew that inflammatory newspapers were being sent through the mail. It appeared that if the Yugoslav government's allegations were true, then postal codes could be used to muzzle the dissemination of the most damning anti-Yugoslav material. Since *Nezavisna Hrvatska Država* was the most provocative publication by the judgement of Yugoslav officials and State Department authorities, there was reason to scrutinize it.

Postmaster John T. Farrell of Youngstown, Ohio, was asked to investigate Croatian meetings in the Youngstown area. One meeting in Campbell, Ohio, drew the Post Office's attention because it featured several speakers with extremist opinions, such as Zvonko Budak, nephew of Mile Budak, a famous Croatian author and Ustaše stalwart, and Ante Došen. Hoping to establish a 'national movement', this gathering was designed to create a groundswell of enthusiasm in anticipation of another larger meeting, which would include Croatians and Macedonians, scheduled for Youngstown's Ukrainian Hall on 29 November 1934.[30] IMRO and Ustaše cooperation in Europe had affected Croatian and Macedonian communities within the United States, who both recoiled from Yugoslav political ambitions. The ultimate goal of these meetings was to 'strengthen the new organization, known as the Hervatski [sic] Doboron [sic], meaning, "Croatian Homeland Defenders"'.[31]

In general, the speeches that were delivered in Campbell were dangerously nationalistic and provocative. They heaped great accolades on Aleksandar's assassin, calling him 'an honorable man'.[32] Ante Pavelić was hailed as a hero who had suffered mightily for his support of Croatian independence. The speakers described Aleksandar as responsible for Pavelić's flight from Yugoslavia – without a doubt true – and his alleged anguished life in exile. No mention was made of Italian or Hungarian assistance or Pavelić's rather comfortable life under Mussolini's protection. All of the speeches encouraged using peaceful means to change Yugoslavia, a policy endorsed by most of the audience, but they did not renounce violence, stressing that other means of opposition would be necessary if peaceful methods did not bring Croatian independence.[33]

Although no threats were made against American or Yugoslav authorities, the speakers did encourage the establishment of Blue Shirts, a sure sign of fascist tendencies in the era of black shirts and brown shirts, designed to raise awareness for Croatian independence. The Blue Shirts were to use, 'peaceful means of securing Croatian rights in the homeland, and if unsuccessful, to take revolutionary means'.[34] The speakers wanted to draw attention to the plight of Croatians, but appeared to have realized that it would take time to build American support for Croatian independence, especially if violent actions were needed to achieve this goal.

In light of the above information, the Youngstown Police Department, in cooperation with Postmaster John J. Farrell, at the request of the New York City Police Department sent Croatian-American policemen to monitor the 29 November meeting of the National Croatian Congress, a gathering of both Croatians and Macedonians, held at Ukrainian Hall in Youngstown. Featuring Frank Budak, Zvonko Budak, Ante Valenta and prominent members from IMRO, the congress enjoyed a large turnout with almost 1,200 in attendance. Croatian speakers called for Croatian independence through peaceful means but were willing to resort to force if all other avenues were blocked.[35] The congress passed a resolution that was sent to the League of Nations and major countries around the world demanding the establishment of a free and independent Croatia and Macedonia via an internationally-monitored plebiscite.[36] The manifesto was worded in a threatening manner, saying that unless something was done, 'the Croats in self-defense may cause a new world catastrophe'.[37] This was a not too subtle reference to the Balkan role in starting World War I. While the majority in attendance was uninterested in a violent independence movement, a 'considerable' amount of money was raised to develop and finance a Croatian independence campaign in the United States.[38] It is likely that much of the money collected was channelled to the Ustaše and used to finance terrorist activities in Yugoslavia, defend Ustaše in criminal proceedings, or spent to maintain Ustaše training facilities. How many of the people in attendance knew that there was the potential for their funds to be used for terrorist operations is open to question. Like the citizens of their homeland, the great majority of Croatian-Americans had nothing but distaste for any use of violence.

This Thanksgiving meeting of the Croatian National Congress also produced a letter to the French government that demanded that Paris withdraw its extradition request for Pavelić and Eugen Kvaternik. The congress argued that the men had not committed any crime and that France had no right to ask for the extradition of foreign nationals.[39] Such an argument was difficult to defend considering that the assassination had taken place on French soil and that there was a clear connection to the IMRO and the Ustaše. This letter, signed by Ante Došen and others, avoided the facts of the assassination as they had been established. There was more than a trifling of evidence that linked Pavelić and Kvaternik directly to the deaths of Aleksandar and Barthou. The letter was little more than propaganda. Croatian extremists also utilized the airwaves through WKBN radio in Youngstown. The station broadcast speeches from Ante Valenta and Frank Budak, both of whom praised Pavelić and voiced the Ustaše line in carefully crafted language. Budak was not the best choice as a speaker. Called by some a racketeer, he operated the Poland Country Club in Youngstown, a well-known spot for gambling.[40] Valenta, who had recently come to the United States after spreading Ustaše ideology to Croatians in Argentina, remarked that:

lately there arose a special hunt on a fearless man, the leader of our independence movement, Dr Ante Pavelić, a man whose only fault is his love for the Croatian people, for his fatherland, who is ready to suffer, to sacrifice all for the realization of our supreme ideal of all Croatians, and that is liberty and independence.[41]

Next, Valenta appealed to American sentiments by making Washington's leadership for independence and Lincoln's appeals for the abolition of slavery analogous to the struggle for Croatian independence; this was a theme often utilized by Ustaše supporters in the United States.[42] Praise for the Poglavnik went even deeper. 'Before the whole world we will bring out our unlimited devotion for Dr Ante Pavelić, who with his work fulfils the wish of the Croatian people.'[43] Valenta, pulling no punches, demanded freedom for the man who planned Aleksandar's assassination. These statements were irrefutable proof that the Ustaše had effectively planted its message among Croatian-Americans. Not only was their message conveyed through the printed word, but they were contacting Croatian-Americans through the airwaves as well. Ustaše leaders were doing whatever was necessary to generate dollars and followers in America, especially considering that the movement had temporarily stalled in Europe after the assassination.

Meanwhile, American authorities were surprised to learn that the Hungarian minister to the League of Nations, Tibor Eckhardt, had publicly proclaimed that Aleksandar's regicide was planned in, of all places, Youngstown, Ohio.[44] Eckhardt made this bold statement in retaliation for Yugoslav assertions that Hungary had harboured the fugitives who later successfully carried out the assassination. Before and after the assassination, Hungary was accused of providing the Ustaše with a safe haven in the hope that one day they would destabilize Yugoslavia, and Budapest would regain territories it lost in World War I. Eckhardt was quoted as proclaiming 'that last summer in Youngstown, Ohio, a big Croat meeting, attended by several thousand, was held at which a death sentence upon the King was announced and cheered'.[45] The Hungarian ambassador to the United States expressed surprise at Eckhardt's statement, delicately noting that he was a fine fellow but a bit too young and perhaps high-strung for his position.[46] In other words, these were the statements of youthful indulgence, nothing of real importance. Actually, Eckhardt was a seasoned 46-year-old diplomat.[47] Wallace Murray reminded the secretary of state that, in an earlier conversation, he had informed him that the State Department, through Special Agent R.C. Bannerman, had taken a close look at Croatian meetings in New York and in Ohio and had found no evidence of any criminal activity, although he admitted that some of the Croat groups were 'violently opposed to the present regime in Yugoslavia'.[48] Regardless of the veracity of Eckhardt's accusations, his words were a signal for the State Department to step up their investigations of Croatian-American groups and Croatians in the country who espoused pro-Ustaše ideas.

The State Department had already learned through Special Agent Bannerman that the assassination plot had not originated in Youngstown, but that it enjoyed support from some in the area. Bannerman explained that on 4 August, Youngstown had celebrated Croatian Day at Idora Park with an address by guest speaker Dr Branimir Jelić. Earlier, Yugoslavia had warned the State Department of Jelić's potential association with Pavelić and the Ustaše. Jelić had recently arrived in the United States, on 31 May 1934, after spending about a year speaking and organizing Ustaše support in Argentina. Cleverly couching his words in front of the 5,000–6,000 attendees, Jelić did not directly predict the assassination or speak of a plot, but instead delivered more ambiguous statements such as, 'tyrants do not die a natural death'.[49] All of his comments were anti-Yugoslav and directed specifically against Aleksandar. His clever phrasing, however, gave him room to convey his point without allowing the United States government an opportunity to arrest or deport him.

Unused to being the centre of discussion at the League of Nations, Youngstown was abuzz. On the front page of the *Youngstown Telegram* the headline read 'Deny Charge that Plot to Kill Jugoslav King was Known Here'.[50] Although refuting that any plot was hatched in Youngstown, Joseph Kraja remarked that money was sent 'to finance political exiles in Europe outside Jugsoslavia'.[51] This was another indication as to how some Croatian-Americans continued to underwrite Ustaše operatives in Europe.

Jelić's strong and aggressive opinions disgusted some notable Croatian-Americans, such as Joseph Kraja of the Croatian Circle and Youngstown's St Peter and Paul Church's Reverend John A. Stipanović, who favoured peaceful means of obtaining independence and who remained firmly behind Maček and the Peasant Party.[52] Postmaster John Farrell, who filed the report on the gathering, believed that Joseph Kraja's *Hrvatski List* ran articles rejecting Jelić's radical opinions and seeming willingness to resort to violence.[53] Kraja's ire may have had less to do with Jelić's allegedly objectionable comments and a great deal more to do with having to share the stage with a new, more aggressive movement seeking Croatian independence. Much to his disappointment, Jelić was unable to garner the support he had hoped for – raising only a small amount of money – and ultimately left the United States on 20 October 1934 aboard the SS *Bremen* destined for Germany and eventually a reunion with his Ustaše mates. Encouraged by opposition to Jelić, by the middle of December 1934 Wallace Murray had concluded that 'there is little need for worry about the doings of these Croatian Americans in Ohio and elsewhere'.[54] The United States, he believed, was not the fertile soil that Jelić or Pavelić had hoped.

The Ustaše was not, however, abandoning its efforts in the United States. Ante Valenta, Zvonko Budak and Ante Došen took up the baton passed to them by Jelić. In particular, Došen assumed the lead as Jelić's handpicked chief of the Domobrans in the United States.[55] As mentioned earlier, the Ustaše in the United States avoided using the term Ustaše, which was potentially politically volatile. Belgrade again warned the State Department that these figures not only had ties to the Ustaše movement but also were actively organizing Croatian-Americans against the Yugoslav government.[56] Belgrade's pleas for Washington to halt meetings organized by these Croatian extremists as well as demands for the extradition of Jelić, Budak, Došen and Valenta could not be satisfied under American law or by an extradition treaty between Serbia and the United States originally signed in 1901.[57]

Free to organize and meet, the Domobrans, having to some degree developed out of the Croatian Circle, began to gain more adherents, especially in large cities such as New York and Pittsburgh, and gradually forged a split between Croatian-Americans who favoured Maček or some form of Yugoslavism and those who wished for an independent Croatia. The Domobrans deserved attention because the members were fervent supporters of Croatian independence and were not afraid to negotiate with American Nazis to further their cause.[58] The most devoted followers took great pleasure attending Domobran gatherings dressed in blue fascist-style uniforms, complete with leather belts, military-style hats, and the checkerboard of Croatia, the šahovnica. The uniforms alone, so very similar to the style seen on the streets of Berlin and Rome, were enough to trigger suspicion about the Ustaše's ultimate goals for Croatia. At their peak, there were about 20 Domobran branches in the United States.[59]

Helping fuel the Domobran organization was Pavelić's mouth-piece, *Nezavisna Hrvatska Država*, which attracted a rather large audience, and *Croatiapress*. First published in San Francisco in 1934, the English-language publication, *Croatiapress*, was a notable addition to pro-Ustaše publishing, providing a constant flow of pro-Pavelić news. Unfortunately, only a limited number of *Nezavisna Hrvatska Država* issues survive, but issues of *Croatiapress* from the

1930s give us insight into the Domobrans and their relationship with the Ustaše in Europe.[60] Alex Dragnich, in a 1944 report written for the Department of Justice, bluntly explained that 'it is fairly evident from an examination of the various issues that *Croatiapress* was basically a propaganda sheet, seeking to influence the English reading public in favor of Pavelich's movement'.[61] In Dragnich's estimation, information for *Croatiapress* came directly from Pavelić's inner circle, most likely Ivan Perčević, one of Pavelić's closest allies and a co-conspirator in the assassination of King Aleksandar and Louis Barthou. 'Perčević apparently spent most of his time in Austria (Vienna) and Germany, from where he dispatched frequent directions to the leaders of the Croatian Home Defenders in the United States.'[62] Much of the evidence for this opinion was based on a cache of letters between Perčević and Došen discovered in World War II during an FBI investigation. They gave unmistakable evidence that instructions for articles in *Croatiapress* were being sent directly from Pavelić's inner circle in Europe.[63]

In most of the issues, Pavelić took centre stage and from 1936 forward he only appeared pictured in military uniform. The new editor, Luka Grbić, who moved the paper to Pittsburgh in 1936, consistently published articles that were highly nationalistic in character, which implied that all Croatians were fully behind Pavelić. *Croatiapress*'s messages were simple and often repeated. The newspaper emphasized Ante Pavelić's leadership and devotion to Croatia, always reinforcing his importance to the movement. In addition, the paper depicted an international Ustaše organization daily gaining supporters ready to follow Pavelić in the battle for Croatian independence. The paper was very clear about the Domobran, explaining that it was 'a nationalistic organization', designed 'to free Croatia of this Serbian barbarism, and suppress Communistic propaganda'.[64] Under direction from Ustaše in Europe, *Croatiapress* printed articles that moved well beyond peaceful change. Typical of this was an article that declared that:

> the Domobran Ustasha organization under the direction of Ante Pavelich, and his patriots and soldiers will not stop, but

will continue and develop into further bitter and uncompromising struggles which will break the last tie that binds the Croatian territory to the enemy, just as with violence they overthrew the tyrannic dictatorship.[65]

Croatiapress was gleefully anti-Serb and even attempted to smear the royal family with implausible stories. For example, in one issue Crown Prince Petar was alleged to have viciously assaulted children. 'Peter [sic] beats them until they bleed, kicks them with his feet, spits at them and acts sadistically. He also beats the servants and even his brothers when they approach him.'[66]

In the light of these events and publications, in December 1934 the State Department urged an investigation of the key Ustaše in the United States, focusing on their entry into the country, seeking to discover some illegality. The State Department rapidly grew frustrated with its inability to uncover information which would warrant the deportation of the leading Domobrans.[67] This irritation was even more pronounced because Yugoslav authorities made frequent protests about Ustaše organizers within the United States. What particularly galled the Yugoslav government, aside from *Nezavisna Hrvatska Država* and *Croatiapress*, were the meetings held by known Ustaše. Secretary of State Cordell Hull informed Belgrade that the United States was following the situation, but had no power to prevent meetings simply on grounds of suspicion. These meetings, and statements arising therefrom, many of which were distasteful and dangerous, were protected by the first amendment. This was a point that the Yugoslav representatives in Washington never fully appreciated throughout the 1930s.

Soon after the Youngstown meeting, the United States found itself dealing with the arrival of Archbishop Ivan Šarić of Sarajevo, another faithful and rabid Ustaše disciple. In December 1934, the State Department was informed by Charles Wilson in Belgrade that Šarić had arrived in the United States from Buenos Aires, where he, as others before him, had been helping swell Ustaše numbers. Wilson made it clear that Šarić was associated with a 'terrorist organization' in Yugoslavia.[68] It was rumoured that Šarić intended to meet with President Roosevelt, an event that never materialized because everyone in the State Department wisely agreed that any meeting was highly undesirable and should not take place.[69] The Archbishop's appearance in the United States had great significance. A prelate of his importance generated excitement among Catholic Croatians, who rarely enjoyed the opportunity to interact with such a high-ranking church official from the homeland. He was a devoted supporter of Pavelić and the Ustaše and was travelling to Argentina and the United States with the intention of establishing stronger Ustaše representation in both countries. While preaching in Youngstown and other American cities, Šarić was careful to avoid discussing Balkan politics publicly. Instead, he preferred to speak about giving last rites to Archduke Franz Ferdinand and the Archduchess in 1914.[70] The Archbishop's innocuous words could not hide that he was a dangerous character who championed the Ustaše and would later write poetry celebrating the achievements of Ante Pavelić. Šarić died in 1960 in Spain, where he had fled fearing arrest and prosecution for war crimes he committed while defending and encouraging the NDH's policies.

As evidence demonstrating the danger of Ustaše actions mounted, the State Department grew increasingly frustrated with its inability to prevent Croatian exploits it deemed damaging to American–Yugoslav relations. For most of 1935, disputes raged between the Department of Justice, the Federal Communications Commission (FCC) and the Post Office about who had jurisdiction in the case. All of these branches monitored the activities of Došen and his associates; however, there was no coordinated activity. Fortunately for the government agencies in this quagmire, by the end of 1935 the situation warranted less concern than in the previous year. Valenta had left the United States in May 1935, sailing on the SS *Western World* for Argentina. Although he claimed to be a student, Zvonko Budak's whereabouts were unknown. Only Došen, the most important of the three, remained in the government's crosshairs, but he had become a naturalized citizen in Hibbings, Minnesota. Though all supported the cause of Croatian independence, the State

Department's concern began to shift toward Pittsburgh, Pennsylvania and Ante Došen's newspaper.

Došen was the obvious target for American attention, because of his tireless efforts to spread Ustaše views within the United States as well as in Europe. Although the FBI and the State Department had their suspicions about him, they were unaware of the scale of Došen's contacts with Ustaše operatives in Europe and South America. His diary indicates that he was in regular communication with Ustaše, be they in Italy, Germany, Austria or Hungary, exchanging news, providing financial support and offering advice. For example, in March 1937, Došen received a letter from Pavelić and immediately sent a reply the following day by way of Germany.[71] He communicated often with Branimir Jelić, the most important of the conduits between Croatians in America and Europe, and his lieutenants, as well as Ante Pavelić, Andrija Artuković, Mladen Lorković and others.[72] Artuković and Lorković were both destined to hold high-ranking positions in Pavelić's wartime government: Artuković as minister of the interior and Lorković as foreign minister and later minister of the interior. Many of the messages were appeals for money or an exchange of news. Unfortunately, Došen's diaries, which only cover from 1937 to 1941, give us just the slightest indication of what was said in these letters and phone calls.

Došen was even involved in providing pamphlets and newspapers for distribution in Europe. In January 1937, he received a proclamation from Pavelić which he printed in the thousands and sent to Europe with the intent of infiltrating Yugoslavia.[73] Three months later, Došen printed and then mailed to Europe 2,000 copies of a Pavelić speech.[74] On several other occasions, Došen shipped copies of the *Nezavisna Hrvatska Država* and almanacs to Europe for distribution. All of this underscores the important role that Domobrans played in keeping the Ustaše movement alive while it languished in Europe.

Pro-Ustaše newspaper articles complemented by radio addresses made by Došen continued spreading dangerous propaganda. On radio in Chicago, Došen threatened that Prince Paul would meet Aleksandar's fate if he hindered the formation of an independent

Croatian state. Again, the Post Office and the FCC were alerted to these statements and asked to investigate.[75] Though the comments were provocative, the Department of Justice argued that they did not warrant legal action. The Yugoslav Legation in Washington was dumbfounded, but continued to bombard the State Department with articles and editorials, from the above sources, which praised the Ustaše while condemning in the most derogatory fashion the royal family.[76]

This scenario was repeated several times in the late 1930s. At its peak, even Secretary of State Cordell Hull joined the fray, arguing that action needed to be taken against Došen and the *Nezavisna Hrvatska Država*. Hull, reiterating the State Department's position, maintained that since the paper was publishing indecent articles that damaged the good relationship between Yugoslavia and the United States, the editors needed to be punished. These highly nationalistic articles were:

definitely harmful to the relations of the United States with foreign governments. A failure to comprehend their true purport and to take all proper steps to protect this Government from a possible charge of responsibility for some possible future political crime because of failure to enforce the applicable laws of the United States would [...] be seriously prejudicial to the interests of the United States.[77]

Hull got results from his protests. The Post Office judged that the paper's articles had violated American law under Section 598 of the Postal Code. In late February, the Post Office and the Justice Department began proceedings to indict Došen.

In a surprising twist, the district attorney in Pittsburgh decided, in May, not to indict Došen, because he reasoned that the case was too politically volatile. He believed that there was little chance of a conviction, because the case centred on interpretations of quotes. Trying to placate the State Department, the district attorney stated that he would arrest Došen and move the case forward if the State Department was determined to do so. The Department of Justice, however, suggested that a new tack, an investigation of the possible illegal entry of Došen into the United States, was the best option. It appeared that there was a realistic chance to deport Došen and avoid a trial which had little chance of success.[78] This would not be the case because Došen, an ethnic Yugoslav born in Hungary, had full right to register with the United States government as a political refugee if officials attempted to deport him. Being accustomed to political manoeuvring, this was what Došen did in the summer of 1936.[79]

The State Department, now having followed Došen into the Iron Range of Minnesota, pursued the only strategy available to it. It informed the Labor Department that Došen was not a man of 'good moral character' and thus was not a candidate for political refugee status. Wallace Murray argued that the United States had to 'see that alien agitators, such as Došen, are not permitted with impunity to use this country as a haven from which to preach their terroristic doctrines, and thus do immeasurable harm to our relations with friendly foreign nations'.[80] Reinforcing Murray's judgement, Cordell Hull, in a letter to Secretary of Labor Frances Perkins, concluded that Došen should be denied political refugee status because he had, among other things, 'advocated the assassination of high Yugoslav officials', and would do great damage to American–Yugoslav relations if he were allowed to continue his attacks against Belgrade from the security of American soil.[81]

Although these were valid arguments for expelling Došen from the United States, the case languished in this position for a solid year. Even with the Yugoslav Legation keeping pressure on the State Department, nothing was accomplished. The attorney general in Pittsburgh, whose cooperation was needed in the attack on Došen, chose not to indict the editor believing that, 'if a prosecution were instituted and proved unsuccessful more harm would ensue than if no prosecution were instituted'.[82] He feared that any prosecution would pit Pittsburgh's large Serbian and Croatian communities against one another.[83] He had little appreciation of the tensions, domestically and internationally, caused by the continued publication of *Nezavisna Hrvatska Država*. Attempting to clear his desk of the issue, the attorney general, reverting to former ineffective policies, urged that

Došen's entry into the country be challenged and his freedom to distribute his newspaper through the postal service be denied.[84] The State Department had been down that road before. The Došen case was caught in a bureaucratic maze with no branch of the government, other than the State Department, eager to halt Došen's activities.

With dogged determination, neither Cordell Hull nor Wallace Murray abandoned their attempts to prove the dire need to remove Došen from the United States. Little changed, however, other than the surfacing of new allegations of both the printed and spoken variety. Došen and his associates continued to mount attacks against the Yugoslav royal family and the Yugoslav government in general. Although the Ustaše cells were small, they made a great deal of noise. Rumours abounded that they were not only raising money for the Ustaše but were involved in counterfeiting American currency for use in financing Ustaše operations.[85] These suspicions could never be proved; therefore the United States government found itself in the awkward position of battling the First Amendment.

Outrageous statements continued to mount, culminating in Došen's remarks in the *New York Post* of 6 December 1938 in which he threatened that Croats would use any means necessary 'to get rid of our enemies in Yugoslavia'.[86] Došen was speaking in response to unsubstantiated reports that a group of Croatian terrorists had set sail from New York with the intention of killing the Regent, Prince Paul. In addition, on 11 December Došen publicly stated that the 'Croatian people will remove every one that stands in the way and I believe there will be no peace until Croatia becomes free'.[87] These remarks were cleverly worded, but seen in the context of the continued attacks on the Yugoslav government which appeared in the *Nezavisna Hrvatska Država*, they sounded highly volatile. They certainly seemed that way to Cordell Hull, who urged that all interested departments, the FCC, the Post Office, State and Labour, hold a conference to move against Došen.[88] Hull's exhortations were fruitless. Došen and his cohorts remained an irritant.

In 1938 and 1939, Došen, in a well-established pattern, was accused by the FCC and the State Department of making incendiary statements against the Yugoslav government via radio broadcasts he purchased on WWSW in Pittsburgh. Došen insisted that complaints about his broadcasts originated with the Yugoslav Embassy in Washington.[89] He was right that the embassy, in general, was the main entity complaining about his publications and broadcasts. Though criticism abounded, American authorities, as usual, were incapable of prosecuting Došen or any other Domobrans. After several years of investigation, conducted in fits and starts, the State Department had made little headway against Došen, his paper or the Ustaše, save pressuring a radio station to suspend Croatian radio addresses.[90] *Nezavisna Hrvatska Država* and *Croatiapress* were recognized as official organs of Pavelić's movement, and were indeed attempting to organize support for the Ustaše within the United States.[91] Belgrade deemed all of these actions as hostile to the continuance of good Yugoslav–American relations; however, any violations, regardless of the fiery if not libellous nature, were, at best, minor under United States Code.

The ambitions of *Nezavisna Hrvatska Država* and *Croatiapress* were enhanced in the late 1930s by the publication of the *Croatian Almanac*, also known as the *Godišnjak*. These yearly almanacs were published by Ivan Krešić, who had begun publishing a Croatian Almanac in the United States in 1924. The almanacs were widely distributed amongst Croatian-Americans, and were loaded with nationalistic appeals to support Pavelić and the Domobrans. Their pages were littered with patriotic American images juxtaposed with photographs of Pavelić and his followers both in America and abroad. In particular, each issue made a point of exalting President Roosevelt by describing him as the protector of free Croatian-Americans. Many pictures featured middle-aged men and women, who obviously joined Domobran groups as a social outlet, oblivious to the shady terrorist side of the movement. Most of the articles were relatively tame by Ustaše standards, usually portraying Croatians as victims, sometimes justifiably so, of heinous Serbian acts, such as murder, sanctioned by the Yugoslav government, all the while offering emotion-laden appeals to Croatian-Americans to support the only hope for Croatia: Ante Pavelić. Some of the articles made direct appeals to nationalism and family. Rudolf Erić, a prominent

Domobran, for example, urged Croatian-Americans to honour the suffering their grandparents endured by 'washing away the shame with blood'.[92] All of Pavelić's key aids and front men were featured in articles, including the likes of Dr Branimir Jelić and Mile Budak. The 1940 edition was most notable because it included a direct appeal from Ante Pavelić. His article titled 'Liberation' was a restrained and tactful request for Croatians in South and North America to support the Domobran movement. Pavelić discussed the American Revolution, noting how a small number of American rebels were able to win pitched battles against British troops and ultimately liberate the 13 colonies. He compared how his own movement was much like that of the colonial Americans and other successful independence movements such as the ones in South America.[93] To Pavelić, Ustaše victory was very close at hand. By painting the Ustaše as the moral and spiritual equals of George Washington and the Continental Congress, he was making a valiant attempt to draw Croatian-Americans to his cause.

Publications kept Domobran interest simmering, but they were no substitute for visits from Pavelić's associates. Ustaše supporters in the United States received a welcome boost of energy with the return of the very popular Dr Jelić on 2 February 1939. Although Jelić contended that his reason for entering the United States was to visit the Mayo Clinic, he was detained at Ellis Island and not allowed onto the mainland while immigration authorities questioned the legitimacy of his claims. Under this intense questioning, Jelić, desperately seeking entry into the country, stated that he was not 'a representative or organizer of Ante Pavelić'.[94] This was an outrageous lie. The American government had numerous documents that pointed to Jelić's association with Pavelić and his attempts to organize pro-Pavelić supporters within the country. In addition, the Yugoslav government had sent several memos to the United States underscoring Jelić's associations.

Jelić admitted that he had attempted to enter the United States under the assumed name of Andrija Artuković, a well-known Pavelić ally. With a strong case against him, Jelić was prevented from entering the United States.[95] After a hunger strike and an appeal, a higher court ruled that Jelić deserved a new hearing to evaluate his status. At the new hearing, Ante Došen defended Jelić and announced that the two of them were working for an independent Croatia, never indicating the methods through which independence was to be obtained.[96] Even with evidence that brought suspicion upon Jelić, he was eventually allowed to enter the country after a significant amount of legal wrangling.[97]

Upon learning of Jelić's entry into the country, the State Department requested that the FBI place him under surveillance. Perhaps aware of Jelić's association with high-ranking Nazis, FBI agents closely tracked Jelić as he travelled around the country from Pittsburgh to Youngstown to Akron and many other cities, often making speeches. According to at least one FBI informant, Jelić's tour was being financed by Berlin. This source noted that the Nazis saw in Jelić, Pavelić and the Ustaše an opportunity to exploit the Croatian–Serbian rift in the same way that they did the ethnic antagonisms between Czechs and Slovaks.[98] Perhaps there was some truth to this rumour, but Hitler's eye was far removed from Yugoslavia in 1939, and even domestic contacts were minimal at best. FBI agents learned that Jelić spent most of his time in Pittsburgh and Youngstown, often visiting the publishing office of *Nezavisna Hrvatska Država*. Usually, he was in the company of well-known Domobran figures such as Luka Grbić, the new editor of *Nezavisna Hrvatska Država*.[99] A native of Dalmatia, Grbić had come to the United States in 1923 and had become an American citizen eight years later. Since Jelić principally spent his time in Pennsylvania and Ohio, he was seen frequently with Grbić, Rudolph Erić and Frank Budak. Throughout his stay in America, Jelić was very careful to avoid committing any acts that were remotely controversial or illegal, as he was aware that FBI agents were following his every move. He even made a trip to the Mayo Clinic, which he had maintained was the real purpose of his coming to America.

Although Jelić met with many prominent Croatian-Americans and was seen with well-known Domobrans, Ante Došen, who had spoken in favour of Jelić's release from Ellis Island, was surprisingly and notably scarce. In January 1939, Došen had become persona non grata, having been removed from his editorial position with *Nezavisna Hrvatska Država* for allegedly pilfering funds from the newspaper. For reasons not fully clear, the Domobran leadership had turned against Došen. In particular, Frank Budak, an early Domobran and noted casino boss and racketeer, actively worked to vilify Došen and remove him from any position within the organization.[100] These tensions, not new among Domobran leaders, appear to have had more to do with personality clashes and egos than political or policy positions. To make matters worse, WWSW in Pittsburgh had suspended his broadcasts in March 1939, most likely due to government pressure.[101] Došen did not disappear, however, for he continued his campaign to create and secure an independent Croatia. He moved to New York and continued to actively support Pavelić and the Ustaše cause, dying in 1977.

Jelić's second and less successful junket ended with his departure on 26 September 1939 aboard the luxurious SS *Conte di Savoia*. Sailing for Genoa under the assumed name of Dr Felix Drazowic, one of his many aliases, Jelić never made port in Italy. Royal Navy vessels stopped the Italian liner near Gibraltar, removed Jelić from the ship and interned him in Britain for the duration of the war.[102] As they did with Aleksandar's assassins, the Domobrans raised money to support Jelić's defence, although far smaller funds were in the offing. Jelić's defence lawyer, Alberto Isola, received a mere few hundred dollars while Jelić himself collected only small sums.[103] Jelić's internment, which lasted for the duration of the war, was a blessing in disguise, because he emerged from World War II as the only key Ustaše figure free of association with concentration camps and ethnic cleansing. This allowed him significant freedom of movement that other Ustaše officials could not enjoy.

On the surface, it appeared that Pavelić and the Ustaše gained very little from their efforts in the United States. With their numbers by the late 1930s having dwindled to little more than a couple of hundred in Europe, any successes in America were critical to the survival of the organization. For much of the decade, Pavelić was more popular in the United States and Argentina than anywhere in Europe, but his message never struck a chord with any but the fringe elements in the Croatian-American communities.[104] Most Croatian-Americans were members of the working class, usually employed in heavy industry, who had little time or money to devote to Jelić, Došen and the Ustaše. Pavelić received some financial support from Croatian-Americans, even sending Stanislav Borić to the United States in 1940 for that purpose, but he never gained a powerful footing among Croatian-Americans.[105] Many Croatian-Americans had become so Americanized that violence of any sort no longer held the same appeal as it once had when they had a limited political voice in Yugoslavia or the Habsburg Empire. These hard-working immigrants did not wish to jeopardize the opportunities before them in America. *Nezavisna Hrvatska Država* and *Croatiapress* continued publication, but they remained on the outside, exercising limited influence in Croatian communities. They were, however, sufficiently influential to continue to draw attention from the State Department and the FBI.

The 1930s had been tumultuous for Pavelić and the Ustaše. Their successful assassination of King Aleksandar had failed to bring them the support they desperately wanted; however, it put the United States on notice that European affairs, no matter how distant, affected the United States. Washington had been forced to take a careful look at Croatian-Americans and what they discovered was a little disturbing: there existed a small number of Ustaše supporters who could potentially damage relations between Yugoslavia and the United States or aid in the destruction of the Yugoslav state. The leader of this cell, Ante Pavelić, although far from American shores, was becoming noticeable.

CHAPTER 3

UNLIKELY VICTORY

On 9 April 1941, the United States Embassy in Berlin notified the State Department that German media outlets were reporting that a strong movement was afoot to establish an Independent State of Croatia under the leadership of Ante Pavelić.[1] To no great surprise, German reports treated the invasion of Yugoslavia as a liberation mandated by the Croatian people both within Yugoslavia and abroad. These propaganda-laced reports showed a heroic Germany altruistically fulfilling the long-held ambition of all Croatians, an independent state free of Serb oppression. This news, like the invasion of Yugoslavia three days earlier, was a defeat for American policy makers who had tried to persuade Yugoslavia into resolutely defending itself against Germany. American interest in Yugoslavia, however, came much too late and was far too hesitant to have any appreciable influence on Yugoslav decision making. Even if Washington had recognized the significance of Yugoslavia earlier, it is extremely doubtful whether America could have significantly influenced a situation dominated by the twin ogres of Germany and Italy. Great Britain was far more interested in Balkan affairs and could do little to stymie Axis ambitions.

What was most remarkable about the sudden creation of the Independent State of Croatia was the meteoric rise of Ante Pavelić, an almost forgotten figure to much of the world. A betting man never would have wagered that Pavelić would be the first or, for that matter, only leader of the NDH. Since Aleksandar's assassination, Pavelić had resided on the fringes of society, always seeking a groundswell of support from Croatians, but only finding limited backing. The Peasant Party continued to hold the hearts and minds of most Croatians, as it had done since the days of the Radić brothers. Pavelić and the Ustaše were doomed to a subordinate status had not events, most of them beyond their control, catapulted them to success. Pavelić emerged in April 1941 as the leader of an independent Croatia, fulfilling his life's ambition. How did Pavelić achieve such sudden success? What were the reactions of the State Department and Croatian-Americans? The new Croatia was more of a nightmare than the great state for which many Croatians had hoped. Pavelić had to chart a dangerous course between Berlin and Rome, both in a position to crush him. Across the Atlantic, the United States was watching most of these events, never fully realizing that Pavelić was a man who deserved closer scrutiny.

A delicate but losing game

Since that fateful day on the streets of Marseilles, Pavelić had been held on ice in Italy presiding over a stalled movement. He was nothing more than a tool for Mussolini, who refused to discard him, believing that the Ustaše strongman might be a useful Italian pawn at some point in the future. On 25 March 1937, Yugoslavia and Italy signed a treaty that established a new and better relationship between the states, but caused Pavelić's hopes for jump-starting his movement to diminish. The treaty reflected a new Italian strategy that recognized Yugoslavia's borders and prohibited all Ustaše operations within Italy. Wanting to generate better relations with Yugoslavia while he considered his other diplomatic options, Mussolini, abiding by the treaty, deported many Ustaše but kept Pavelić in the wings out of the public eye.[2] The treaty with Italy complemented Yugoslavia's increasingly close relationship with Germany; a relationship that Belgrade hoped would forestall any acts of German aggression. Yugoslav politicians favoured improving relations with Italy and Germany, the two strongest states in the region, especially in the light of French diplomatic failures and internal ethnic fragmentation. By the late 1930s, Yugoslavia had aligned itself with the fascists while trying to maintain its independence, especially in the economic sphere where Germany was its most important trading partner. In essence, Prime Minister Milan Stojandinović, an admirer of Mussolini and a fellow well liked by Ciano, hoped that his support of fascists, although not complete, would weaken German and Italian backing of separatists like the Ustaše, who demanded the destruction of Yugoslavia. He believed that there would be no reason for Hitler to destroy a compliant Belgrade.

As Hitler marched from success to success, but especially after the Munich Crisis of 1938, the Yugoslav government grew more concerned about its place within the Führer's plans. Belgrade understood how Hitler manipulated ethnic division to destroy his opposition, with the Czechoslovakian crisis serving as a potent example of what could happen in Yugoslavia. Like Czechoslovakia, Yugoslavia was torn by ethnic division that potentially offered Hitler the opportunity to dissolve the country and create puppet regimes, if he so desired. According to American officials in Yugoslavia, extreme nationalist Croatians did not see the similarity between Yugoslavia and Czechoslovakia; they compared themselves to the Sudeten Germans and viewed the Serbs as synonymous with the Czechs.[3] Thus while the Czech crisis fuelled more calls for an independent Croatia, those holding such opinions remained a minority. After seeing Czechoslovakia's collapse, Vladko Maček and other moderate politicians, along with the Belgrade government, grew eager to reach some type of agreement that would preserve Yugoslav unity and satisfy Croatian demands for autonomy, while forging a barrier to further German and Italian desires. There was considerable concern that Hitler would drive for the Adriatic, exploiting ethnic division along the way and consequently destroying Yugoslavia.[4] Mistrust between Serb and Croat was so deep that some in Belgrade had the notion that Maček wanted to approach Hitler about a Czechoslovakian solution for Croatia. Maček, however, was no lover of the

Nazis and was eager to do whatever was necessary, including playing ball with Belgrade, to prevent a German invasion.

Seeking to quell unrest between Serbians and Croatians and therefore strengthen Yugoslavia, the Sporazum (agreement) of 20 August 1939 was signed. Although signed in the shadow of the Polish Corridor crisis and the Nazi–Soviet Pact, the Sporazum provided for an autonomous Croatia within Yugoslavia. Under the agreement, Zagreb controlled its internal affairs through a *sabor* (assembly) and a *ban* (governor), while Belgrade remained paramount in foreign policy, defence and the like. The Sporazum, however, did little to solve the ethnic problems. Muslims and Serbs who now found themselves under a Croatian government feared for their rights, believing that Belgrade had abandoned them. Likewise, Pavelić and the Ustaše opposed the Sporazum, calling it another attempt by Serbs to dominate Croatians. They argued that the accord did not go far enough, because it excluded Bosnia-Herzegovina from Croatian control and allowed for too much authority from Belgrade. Pavelić insisted that no agreement was possible and that the only solution was independence. His views were little more than sour grapes, because the agreement was certainly a step in the direction desired by the majority of Croatians. Although the Sporazum was a noble attempt to unify Yugoslavia, it was too little too late. The result was a more deeply divided Yugoslavia.

Even with the Sporazum in place, violence and unrest, conducted by Pavelić's agents, continued unabated in Zagreb and in other parts of Croatia. America's Consul in Zagreb, James J. Meily, sympathetic to Croatian interests and fairly well connected in the Croatian capital, especially close to Maček, noted that Croatian extremists had little trouble attracting considerable attention.[5] For example, on 27 February 1940, riots, which included some gunfire, erupted in Zagreb as a consequence of Masses held in honour of Ante Starčević's death 44 years earlier. Meily reported that riot leaders were 'Frankists' who chanted 'Down with the bloody dynasty, down with Maček, long live Pavelić'.[6] The riots were very sharp and involved skirmishes between Pavelić supporters and Peasant Party members. Meily, who spoke with his Croatian contacts in German due to a mutual fluency in the language, correctly judged that the Sporazum had done nothing but deepen the animosity between followers of Pavelić and Maček, to say nothing of their relationship with the Serbians.

Ambassador Arthur Bliss Lane, a seasoned diplomat with some experience in East European affairs, having earlier served as second secretary in Warsaw from 1919 to 1920 and Envoy in Estonia, Latvia and Lithuania from 1936 to 1937, was so disturbed by the riots and gunfire that he sent a detailed report of the political situation in Croatia to the State Department, trying mightily to alert Washington to the significance of Yugoslav politics.[7] Even though Washington received a very fair and somewhat lengthy analysis of Pavelić and the Frankist (generally synonymous with the Ustaše in American dispatches) movement, the New York native's words failed to generate much interest within the State Department. Although noting that Pavelić was in Italy, Lane gave the Ustaše boss too much credit for leading the 'Frankist' cells in Croatia.[8] Actually, Pavelić had significant communication problems with his followers in Yugoslavia, often unaware of their actions until he read about them in newspapers. Lane understood that the Ustaše were united on little more than their uncompromising position vis-à-vis Belgrade and enjoyed financial support from both Italy and Germany. In concluding his memo, he correctly judged that Pavelić and the Ustaše remained on the fringes, far behind Maček, who enjoyed support from the vast majority of Croatians. The tone of the report signalled that even though Croatia was suffering from domestic violence, Pavelić was not a huge threat, as long as the Croatian Peasant Party remained the dominant political force.[9] But American authorities had only a basic knowledge of the Ustaše, Pavelić and their operations. For example, they had no firm information on how large Pavelić's support was. They had been given estimates from various sources that ranged from a mere 300 followers to 25 per cent of the population.[10]

Although there was no immediate threat of Pavelić gaining power in the autumn of 1940, his supporters had caused enough problems to be considered a danger to Yugoslav stability. This danger grew in seriousness when, for the first time, the Catholic Church's involvement crept into American understanding of the complexity of Croatian politics. In a memorandum to the State Department, Lane warned that:

> the Government (Yugoslavia) is [...] disturbed because of the support of the Frankists not only by the Italian Government but by the Holy See as well. This move may react dangerously on the Catholic Church as it will encourage subversive elements in Dalmatia where Communism is already a danger.[11]

There is no solid evidence that Pavelić or the Ustaše at that time were operating with Vatican favour, but their ranks did include some Catholic priests and some of the Church's religious goals were reflected in Ustaše ideology. Nevertheless, Lane had discovered that Catholic involvement with Pavelić and his followers was a serious problem that had the potential to plague the Church. The Church's desire to defend and spread Catholicism in Yugoslavia at the expense of other faiths was a tempting opportunity that was hard to ignore. For most of World War II and the immediate post-war period, Pavelić would use his Catholic supporters to carry out his policies, and ultimately he would call on his friends in the Church to save his life.

For the remainder of 1940 and into early 1941, the Belgrade government tried to convince Lane that Ustaše activity was exaggerated and a distant threat to Yugoslavia. They were doing everything possible to allay any fears of ethnic division, hoping to demonstrate that a united Yugoslavia stood against a potential German or Italian invasion. Belgrade's assurances were hard to believe, because the Ustaše continued their policy of harassment, bombings and the like, while Yugoslav authorities tried to strike back using informants, arrests and torture. Ustaše operations were daring and well organized, to say the least. They almost assassinated Vladimir Maček in November 1940, detonating a bomb in his backyard.[12] Although the Yugoslavian police increased their efforts, and often enjoyed detailed intelligence of Ustaše operations, Pavelić's troops persevered.

World War II begins

With Hitler enjoying astonishing success in the first two years of World War II, Yugoslavia found itself fearing for its very existence, hoping to placate the Germans and Italians while preserving its independence from domestic enemies as well. Dragiša Cvetković's government, formed in February 1939, was impressed by German battlefield victories, especially its lightening-quick defeat of France in 1940. After the ill-fated Italian invasion of Greece that began on 28 October 1940, it grew more difficult for Belgrade to follow a separate course from the Axis. Greek resistance was so successful that, by the end of the year, Italian forces were driven out of Greece. Mussolini's army was left waging a defensive campaign desperately defending its positions in Albania. Not too eager to deal with Balkan affairs, Hitler nevertheless had to conquer Greece to bale out the lacklustre Italian troops from their debacle and protect, as Churchill referred to it, the soft underbelly. London was thrilled with the Greek victories, and consequently deployed British troops in Greece to strengthen Athens. Hitler could not allow Greece to become a British redoubt that could potentially destroy German supply lines to North Africa as well as form a base for British actions in the Balkans. Most importantly, Germany needed to secure its southern flank when Operation Barbarrossa, the invasion of the Soviet Union, began. All of these factors combined to draw Hitler's attention to Yugoslavia and Greece.

Finally, and much too late, Washington became interested in helping Yugoslavia and other Balkan states resist German advances. The State Department had been apathetically monitoring Yugoslav affairs in the 1930s, so it took presidential action to increase American involvement. Appreciating the threat of German expansion, President Roosevelt determined that he needed detailed information about the political and military situation in Europe from a man he could trust. One of Roosevelt's closest associates, William 'Wild Bill' Donovan was the perfect choice for a lengthy fact-finding mission to Great Britain, the Balkans, much of the Mediterranean region and ports beyond. As a Congressional Medal of Honor winner in World War I who had excelled in law and government service, Colonel Donovan had the pedigree that would impress Balkan leaders. Donovan's journey was strongly opposed by the State Department, which was determined to limit American involvement in the Balkans and often Europe in general. Hull did not like Roosevelt's practice of using hand-picked men for such missions and therefore avoiding traditional State Department channels. On 22 January 1941, Donovan visited Yugoslavia on orders from Roosevelt under the aegis of Secretary of the Navy Frank Knox. Donovan hoped not only to understand the lay of the land but also to pursue remote hopes of developing some type of Balkan front that would include Yugoslavia in an association with Turkey and Bulgaria.[13] Although few believed the cover story, the public was informed that the *Chicago Daily News* had drafted Donovan for the purpose of exploring and reporting on Balkan and Mediterranean affairs. Churchill was thrilled with the mission, in part because Donovan was an Anglophile, but also because he believed that it was another step towards drawing the United States more deeply into Balkan and European affairs in general. Donovan tried to convince Prince Paul that Washington was willing to aid Yugoslavia, if it rebuffed German offers to join the fascists and opposed German aggression.[14] After meeting with the principal Yugoslav leadership, Donovan left Yugoslavia not persuaded of the Prince's backbone, but impressed by Yugoslavia's pro-Western air force general, Dušan Simović.[15] Donovan's mission failed to create a Balkan front – a naive ambition to say the least – in part because no matter how badly the United States wished to form a Balkan bulwark against Germany, Washington had no carrot with which to strengthen Yugoslav resolve. The United States could not promise much military support. Although Lend-Lease had been proposed by President Roosevelt on 6 January 1941 and enacted two months later, it was unclear how the new legislation would function if applied to Yugoslavia or any other Balkan state. How much equipment could the United States send to Yugoslavia and how soon could it arrive? If the Germans invaded, it would be months before Yugoslavia received any appreciable aid from the United States. Although it possessed the largest armed forces in the Balkans,

Belgrade did not have a military with the training, equipment or morale necessary to resist Germany's fighting might. Thus, the United States could only offer hollow promises of moral support amid requests for Yugoslavia to fight aggression. To any realist in Yugoslavia, sympathetic words were no substitute for weapons.

Donovan's visit energized Lane, who had spent much time with Roosevelt's representative discussing the complexities of Yugoslavia. He decided to pursue a stronger and bolder American approach, manoeuvring to keep Yugoslavia from becoming a fascist pawn, regardless of the ultra-conservative State Department policy. At odds with the State Department over policy, the White House somewhat inadvertently offered moral support to Lane's activities with several statements from President Roosevelt informing the Yugoslav government that countries that fought aggression would be not only honoured and supported but also restored at the conclusion of the war.[16] Promises like these, however, rang on deaf ears. Increasingly fearful of Nazi dominion, Prince Paul, speaking to Ambassador Lane, commented that 'even if the United States helped him, Yugoslavia would be finished before our assistance arrived and the country would be destroyed in the meantime'.[17] Throughout early 1941, Lane, with unwavering determination, tried to convince his friend Prince Paul to stand firm against the Germans, who were pressuring Yugoslavia to join the Tripartite Pact. Finally, with support from the State Department having been garnered only on the insistence of the White House, Lane's activist policy had the entire government behind it. On 21 March, the State Department through Lane wanted Belgrade to know that the United States 'is prepared to offer all facilities under the Lend-Lease Bill', as long as Yugoslavia retained its independence.[18] These promises were offered much too late and were far too little to halt the country's steady drift towards the Axis.

The State Department's words sounded hollow, even to Lane, who was frustrated by his superiors' long-standing inattention to Yugoslav and Balkan affairs. For much of early 1941, Lane, an ardent opponent of Hitler and fascism, was baffled by Washington's lack of interest in Yugoslavia and the failure of the State Department to develop a consistent and appropriate policy designed to shore up pro-Western factions and stymie German ambition. Lane was perplexed as to why Secretary of State Hull could not see the importance of hindering German aggression through a more directly active American policy in the Balkans. Simply put, the State Department was not interested in an area it considered a British realm, especially one distant from American interests. Unfortunately, Yugoslavia failed to resonate in Washington until it was too late. The yeoman work performed by Lane was for naught.

Regardless of American policy decisions in 1940 and 1941, there was no way for Yugoslavia's weak military, filled with ethnic tension, to withstand a German invasion long enough for Lend-Lease to help them.[19] Believing that a German attack was inevitable and exhausted by American and British pressure to hold firm against Nazi aggression, Prince Paul expressed his frustration to Ambassador Lane saying, 'you big nations are hard, you talk of our honor but you are far away'.[20] After Bulgaria joined the Nazi camp on 1 March 1941, putting an end to any hope of a Balkan bulwark, it was apparent to Lane that Yugoslavia was going to sign the Tripartite Pact, regardless of the negative criticism from Western nations. The Prince believed that, with a bit of luck, his signature would preserve some degree of independence and avoid bloodshed. Yugoslavia negotiated clauses that stipulated only political affiliation and did not mandate military ties, a point without validity in Berlin. Regardless of this, any support for the Tripartite Pact was, in American opinion, a sell-out, no matter that the agreement was political and not military. As Germany gained influence in Bulgaria and pressure over the Italian debacle in Greece mounted, geographically placing Yugoslavia in an untenable position, Cvetković and Prince Paul joined the fascists by signing the Tripartite Pact on 25 March 1941 in Vienna. As Prince Paul had numerous British friends, including King George VI, and had even attended Oxford, casting his lot with the Nazis was a painful choice. President Roosevelt immediately showed his displeasure by ordering that all Yugoslav assets in the United States be frozen. The regent had done what he believed was right for Yugoslavia.[21]

Fateful days

With Yugoslavia's signature, Hitler had seemingly had won the day. His southern border, vulnerable to British attack, was secure, allowing plans for Operation Barbarossa to continue. The Yugoslav government, however, had signed its own death warrant as Yugoslavs erupted in protest against the Tripartite Pact. After their signatures had dried in Vienna, Cvetković's government lasted for only two more tumultuous days, both full of demonstrations against Germany and demands for the government's resignation. Some members of the Yugoslav military, who favoured the Western Allies, could not stomach joining the Tripartite Pact, which they believed spelled the end of Yugoslavia and placed them squarely in the camp of their long-term enemies. Memories of World War I had faded little in the previous 20 years. With the British urging a coup d'état, the military overthrew the government and established a new regime under General Dušan Simović in the name of 18-year-old King Petar II. Simović assumed the prime ministership. In a lightening stroke, fascism was rejected, the regency had ended and young Petar was king.

Washington was jubilant over this change of affairs and ordered Lane, with great haste, to express to the Simović government America's approval of the coup. Lane was directed to proclaim, perhaps with too much hyperbole, that 'this event constitutes a matter for self-congratulation for every liberty-loving man and woman'.[22] Washington wanted the new government to know that in accordance with the provisions of the Lend-Lease Bill, the President, in the interest of the 'national defense of the United States, is enabled to provide assistance to Yugoslavia, like all other nations which are seeking to maintain their independence and integrity and to repel aggression'.[23] Obviously, Roosevelt wished to continue the policy of promising military equipment to Yugoslavia, if they continued to stand against Germany. As this same policy had failed with Prince Paul, why would it succeed now?

By all accounts, Hitler was furious at the coup, which he interpreted as an assault against German honour. He demanded that

Yugoslavia be crushed. The Führer was certain that Yugoslavia would easily collapse under German military might, judging that the Croatians would side with Berlin against Belgrade. Hitler was correct in his estimation. The former German Ambassador to Rome Ulrich von Hassell commented during his visit to Zagreb in March 1941 that, 'Freundt (German Consul in Agram) and all Croats with whom I spoke emphasized the great differences between Croatia and Serbia. In Croatia there is no opposition whatever to Germany (with a few exceptions); on the contrary, a desire to co-operate.'[24]

Hoping to gain a bit of insurance, Germany immediately began negotiations with Croatian leaders in Zagreb promising an independent Croatia if, by chance, Yugoslavia found itself in a war with Germany. Berlin badly wanted Vladko Maček to take the reigns of a new Croatian state, believing that he would give it legitimacy that it would otherwise lack. To no great surprise, Maček rebuffed all German attempts to win his support for an independent Croatia under his tutelage, preferring to remain loyal to Yugoslavia as well as his strongly-held pacifist and anti-fascist beliefs.[25]

Back from exile

With this disappointing reality, Dr Edmund Veesenmayer, Germany's special representative in Zagreb, turned to more radical sectors of the Croatian political landscape. It did not take long before Veesenmayer was working closely with Slavko Kvaternik, one of Pavelić's key allies in the Ustaše and the leader of the movement within Croatia. Since he had served as a staff officer in the Austro-Hungarian Army in World War I and even held the Iron Cross first class, Kvaternik was a logical choice for the Germans. Seeing an opportunity for Ustaše success, Kvaternik was more than willing to aid the German cause and became an eager accomplice of Veesenmayer's.[26] Ever the loyal soldier, Kvaternik maintained that Pavelić was the only and proper choice to lead Croatia, a suggestion received with great distaste by Veesenmayer, who held Pavelić in deep contempt. Judging Pavelić to be Mussolini's stooge, the Germans had little respect for him, never even entering into direct negotiations with the Ustaše leader, who remained in his Italian villa, a bystander to these momentous events.

Though not negotiating with the Germans, preparations for Pavelić's return to Croatia, fuelled by Italy's blessings, had been in the works long before Veesenmayer arrived on the scene. Even with the Friendship Treaty between Italy and Yugoslavia, Mussolini had kept Pavelić on the payroll, occasionally discussing plans for his future use. As early as January 1940, Count Galeazzo Ciano, Mussolini's foreign minister, had proposed establishing a Croatian state led by Pavelić, but under Italian suzerainty.[27] At that juncture, the time was not appropriate for Italy or the Ustaše, neither of whom possessed the wherewithal necessary to pull off such a manoeuvre. Despite this, Ciano made clear who would be in charge, telling Pavelić that any new Croatian state would fall under the sway of the Italian government. Italy had no interest in a Croatia outside of its clutches.[28]

With the collapse of Cvetković's government and with news of the impending German invasion of Yugoslavia, Mussolini quickly decided to place his man in Croatia, fearing that without Pavelić the Germans held the best cards and could deny Italy its long-held, but ethnically unjustified, claim to the Dalmatian Coast and much more. Already reeling from military setbacks in Greece and North Africa, Mussolini could not allow the Germans to trump him again and reinforce his secondary status to Hitler. Mussolini as much as told Pavelić that when the two men met on 29 March 1941. Fortunately for Pavelić, Maček refused all offers to lead the Croatian state, preferring to oppose the fascists and cast his lot with Yugoslavia. To the surprise of Berlin but few in Yugoslavia, Maček chose to join the new Simović government and place the Croatian Peasant Party squarely behind the Yugoslav state. The stage was set for Pavelić's return to Croatia.

Yugoslavia destroyed

On 6 April 1941, the German 12th Army under Field Marshal Wilhelm List and General Paul von Kleist's 1st Panzer Group rolled into Yugoslavia, striking deep into the country with extraordinary ease. The main German thrust came from Romania and Bulgaria, where the Nazis had amassed an impressive invasion force. German soldiers were supported by Italian and Hungarian troops, delivering a crippling blow against the Yugoslavs. The assault was preceded by a crushing air bombardment of Belgrade, which shattered the capital's morale and forced thousands to flee to the countryside. Possessing antiquated weapons and suffering from poor leadership and crippling ethnic division, the Yugoslav military was no match for their Axis opponents. Most disturbing for the Yugoslav military's high command was that many Croatian soldiers, especially those who held animosity towards the Yugoslav state or objected to the preponderance of Serbian officers, did little to help form a stout defence. As early as 8 April, Croatian troops at the railroad junction in Vinkovci mutinied and lowered their weapons on their former comrades. Mutinies of this type became more common as the days passed. German propaganda, especially effective with Ustaše sympathizers in the Yugoslav army, fuelled the fires that had been smouldering for years. Most often, Serbs and Slovenes were left to defend against the German juggernaut, and neither provided much resistance against the Nazi invaders. By 13 April, a shattered and demoralized Belgrade fell to the Nazis. It was followed by Yugoslavia's unconditional surrender, signed on 17 April. In this staggering victory, the Germans captured about 344,000 troops while only 151 Nazis were killed and 392 wounded.[29] Yugoslavia was finished.

As soon as the invasion began, President Roosevelt issued a statement calling the attack 'barbaric' and 'another chapter in the present planned movement of attempted world conquest and domination'.[30] The White House had seen another pin fall and was, without a doubt, frustrated at its inability to blunt German conquests. The State Department and the White House, however, had no one to blame but themselves. Inattention was the watchword as far as Yugoslavia was concerned. America's promises of support were paper thin, carrying no weight in Belgrade. The ideology of isolation combined with a smallish and ill-equipped military hurt the United States when it tried to conduct foreign policy. Yugoslav politicians knew that the United States was making empty promises and could not come to their aid in the case of a German attack. Germany appeared to be the future and was nearby. Washington had done even less to draw the American public's attention to the crisis. Meanwhile, Lane and the American delegation were taking the brunt of the German invasion, with Stukas and other German bombers filling the skies over Belgrade. The delegation was fortunate in that no member was killed in the German bombardment of the capital city. Although the American mission suffered little damage, Lane and his colleagues were unable to communicate with the outside world, since practically all modes of communication had been destroyed. Minister Lane, now virtually powerless, spent almost one and a half months isolated, unable to deliver any appreciable information to Washington. With an untenable position in Belgrade, Lane moved to Dedinje, a suburb. It was not until 16 May that he and other Americans were able to leave Yugoslavia for Budapest. Ultimately, Lane reached New York City on 6 June 1941, two months after the German invasion began.[31] Throughout his journey back to the United States, the State Department demonstrated more concern about Lane's expense account than it did about the fate of Yugoslavia.

The Independent State of Croatia

Croatians, by and large, had done little to blunt the invasion. Croatian troops had offered limited resistance, often more inclined to desert or surrender than oppose the Germans. The Nazis captured Zagreb on 10 April with surprising ease, being hailed as liberators by an enthusiastic crowd of thousands. On the same day, Kvaternik, with Veesenmayer's urging, declared the establishment of the Independent State of Croatia in the name of Ante Pavelić, now known as the Poglavnik. The new leader of the state, however, was in Italy, not Croatia, and was surprised that Croatia was now independent and under his leadership. The speed of this volte face astonished Pavelić, who had followed most of these events in newspapers. With Mussolini's support and urging, Pavelić immediately made plans to return to Zagreb. Il Duce was anxious to place Pavelić in the capital, hoping to prevent any German plans for depriving Italy of territories such as the Dalmatian Coast. By 13 April, Pavelić and a small number of Ustaše, dressed in Italian uniforms, entered Croatia. Early in the morning on 15 April, the Poglavnik arrived in Zagreb, eager to create a new Croatia.[32]

Though head of the freshly created NDH, Pavelić exercised limited authority because he had to contend with competing interests in Italy and Germany. Pavelić knew that Germany was the more powerful of the two and that he needed Hitler's support to survive. Conversely, he could not afford to offend Mussolini, the man who had given him and some of the Ustaše quarter for much of the 1930s. Since Pavelić's chief goal was to remain in power, he was quite accommodating to Rome and Berlin, expressing his fascist beliefs to anyone who would listen, and even reluctantly willing to abandon traditional Croatian lands to preserve his government. He was convinced that Croatia, and he personally, had to follow fascist policies in order to survive. While in exile, Pavelić grew more and more committed to fascist ideology, seeing in it the path to creating a unified Croatia under his authority.[33]

Determined to establish a unified and loyal state that would follow his orders and implant Ustaše ideology among the people, Pavelić announced his first government, an exclusively Ustaše line-up, on 16 April. Determined to signal the establishment of a new and uncompromising Croatia, Pavelić was eager to exclude Maček, his chief rival for power, or any of the Peasant Party leadership from his government. This was a momentous mistake, considering that cooperation with Maček's party would have endeared Pavelić to the vast majority of peasants. With German and Italian approval looming over his regime, he saw no need to share the stage with anyone. Enjoying a brief honeymoon of power, Pavelić embraced the opportunity for the Ustaše to dominate and indoctrinate Croatia in its image. In addition, he wished to exercise dictatorial power over the government, like his supporters Mussolini and Hitler.

For the remainder of the month, most of Zagreb's citizens were thrilled with the recent events, believing that the first strides towards complete independence had been achieved. Pavelić looked like the wave of the future, a man of boldness and action, while Maček resembled an anachronism. Few held the illusion that the NDH was truly independent, but the German invasion appeared a step in the right direction. In the spring of 1941, Germany looked unbeatable and the right horse to back. Some, in their enthusiasm, were temporarily blinded to the fact that Serbian authority had only been replaced by German and Italian domination. The new state had yet to even define its frontiers, an issue destined to show its weakness. Croatia was far from free and independent. On the contrary, Croatia was part of the Axis and, to most in the Western world, an enemy of freedom and democracy. Their association with fascism significantly damaged foreign sympathy for the Croatian nationalist cause. A deal had been made with the devil, and Croatia would pay mightily.

American reaction to the NDH

In the first few days of the German invasion several telegrams from various European capitals arrived in Washington announcing the creation of the NDH. For many days, there was no firm information regarding who would lead the new state, although the *New York Times* reported on 11 April that Pavelić was in charge; that scoop and others demonstrated that the *Times* was better attuned to Yugoslav news than the State Department.[34] As late as 12 April, it was unclear to the State Department whom Italy and Germany had selected to lead the puppet state. Pavelić had been in exile for so long that some believed Maček was the clear, if not only, choice. With little understanding of Yugoslav politics, the State Department never realized that Maček was adamantly opposed to the Nazis, steadfastly refusing any cooperation with them. Over the years, Lane's memos had done almost nothing to pique his superiors' interest or educate the State Department.

With Lane and the American delegation suffering under the German onslaught, most information about Croatia came from Rome and Berlin, where all news was distributed through carefully scripted reports via government mouthpieces. Nevertheless, by 15 April,

Washington, like the rest of the world, had solid information that Ante Pavelić was the new leader of an independent Croatia, a state crafted in a similar fashion to Slovakia after the German invasion of Czechoslovakia.

Towards the end of April a clear image of Pavelić had been drawn by the American press. *Time* magazine described Pavelić in this fashion:

> He was dark, treacherous Ante Pavelitch, leader of the terroristic Ustashi, a band of rapacious Croat schemers who for years have hated the Serbs, Jews and Croatia's own peasants and plotted with Italian, Hungarian and German money to split Yugoslavia and bring the Ustashi to power.[35]

An editorial in the *New York Times* depicted Pavelić as, 'an ex-assassin long in exile, now raised by the Nazi exigency to place and power'.[36] The *Washington Evening Star* called Pavelić and Kvaternik, 'sinister figures' who 'represent the most extreme section of Croat separatists, embittered by the feuds between Serbs and Croats. . .'.[37] These types of descriptions were common in the American media. All outlets, except zealous pro-Ustaše publications, portrayed Pavelić as a dangerous murderer, a fascist terrorist who was now in the employ of the Nazi regime.

Ustaše voices within the United States were jubilant at Pavelić's victory and quickly moved to increase the rhetoric in favour of the NDH to fend off those who favoured any kind of an accommodation with Serbs in Yugoslavia. The Domobran and the Croatian National Representation, a front organization for the Domobran, sent a congratulatory cablegram to Ante Pavelić with an emphatic salutation which read 'Long live the President of the Independent State of Croatia!'[38] Although clearly enthusiastic, the statement pleaded for a fully unified Croatia that included 'all the Croatian ethnic and historical provinces'.[39] Even at this early stage, there was great concern that Dalmatia was a casualty of Croatian independence. Luka Grbić's *Nezavisna Hrvatska Država* increased its attacks on Serbs, celebrated Ante Pavelić's leadership, condemned communism and defended the NDH's early decrees. Reflecting the opinions of Pavelić sympathizers within the United States, Grbić admitted that the NDH was not the type of state desired by Croatian-Americans – it was a monarchy and not a republic – but justified its existence as a step in the right direction by providing Croatians with their long-sought independence.[40] The cost of establishing the NDH under the auspices of the Axis powers, even the loss of Dalmatia to the Italians, was deemed acceptable at the moment because statehood had been reached. A new bastion of defence against communism and the nefarious Serbs had been created, Grbić trumpeted.[41]

Losing face

The exuberance of power was short-lived for Pavelić, because the Italians, before the Poglavnik could establish residence in Zagreb, demanded compensation. For most of April and into early May, Pavelić was forced to negotiate away most of Dalmatia and other territories that were ethnically and historically Croatian. Germany showed little interest in the Italian–Croatian negotiations, being primarily concerned with Croatia's natural resources, especially bauxite. As long as Croatian raw materials flowed unabated into the Third Reich, Germany was indifferent to Croatian politics and little interested in competing with Italy for Croatian territory. Hitler gave Rome a free hand to annex whatever territory it saw fit. By the Rome Agreements of 17 May, concluded by Italy and Croatia, the NDH, territorially speaking, was emasculated, when Dalmatia, except for the extreme southernmost areas, was annexed by Italy. This alone was a tremendous blow to the NDH and severely damaged its position with the public. Even on the sliver of Dalmatia that remained in NDH hands, it was prohibited from establishing military posts.[42] The Croatian public was astonished by this devastating loss and humiliation, because to many Croatians Dalmatia was Croatia. Pavelić's regime, therefore, began life with a deep wound that never healed, even after Mussolini's government fell and Dalmatia returned to Croatian control. Pavelić's weakness was even more apparent when he was forced to accept the Duke of Spoleto, Mussolini's choice, as the new king of Croatia. Since Mussolini was making a strong play to render Croatia an Italian puppet, the playboy duke was the perfect choice. Here was a man with no interest in Croatia, who would follow Rome's leadership without any reservations, as long as he was promised the good life.

It was all made official on a soggy 17 May 1941, when Pavelić relinquished Croatia's rights to Dalmatia and offered the 'vacant' Croatian crown to the Duke of Spoleto. Trying to put a positive face on the entire event, Pavelić had travelled to Rome with a large entourage, doing his best to appear Mussolini's equal.[43] Wearing his customary military uniform with jackboots, Pavelić and his delegation travelled by carriage from the train station to the Quirinal Palace where King Victor Emmanuel presented the crown to the duke. The duke was to take the name Tomislav II, a title he thought to be uproariously humorous. No one was very excited about the crowning when, later, Pavelić met with Mussolini and Ciano to sign the Rome Agreements.[44] Appropriately, it rained the entire day.

The pageantry failed to convince anyone that Croatia was an independent state negotiating on equal terms with its peers. Herbert Matthews of the *New York Times*, later famous for his 1957 interview with Fidel Castro, fully understood Croatia's position with the Axis states. Reporting from Rome, the seasoned reporter reasoned that the NDH was 'fully dependent upon Italy and presumably Germany, for protection, self-defense and, indeed, for its very existence'.[45] The *Times* had a better and deeper understanding of Croatian affairs than the State Department, which did little more than express its great displeasure at the carving up of Yugoslavia.

The State Department's interest, however, was piqued by Pavelić's meeting with the Pope. Pavelić's audience with Pius XII surprised Vatican observers, many fearful that it was tantamount to recognition of an independent Croatia and thus sanctioning German and Italian actions in Yugoslavia. Ambassador William Phillips in Rome met with Father Giovanni Montini, the Secretary of State in the Vatican, to learn the official line regarding Pavelić's 18 May visit with the Pontiff. In a surprising justification for meeting with a convicted murderer, 'Montini explained that the Pope as head of the church could not refuse to receive catholics when requested'.[46] Montini, who later became Pope Paul VI, was careful to note that Pavelić was met as a 'private individual' and not as head of the NDH.[47] The reception therefore did not signal official recognition of the NDH. In other words, the Vatican was not recognizing the NDH nor dealing with Pavelić as a world leader, but rather as an individual Catholic.

It was and remains bothersome that Pius XII granted an audience with Pavelić, a well-known terrorist and assassin with death penalties hanging over his head. British Foreign Secretary Anthony Eden, when hearing of the audience, complained to Monsignor Godfrey, the Apostolic Delegate, 'I am much disturbed by this reception, and cannot accept the Vatican's description of M. Pavelitch as a statesman. In my view, he is a regicide. It is incredible that His Holiness should receive such a man.'[48] When Sir D'Arcy Osborne, the British Ambassador to the Vatican, protested the visit, the Pope informed him that Pavelić was a 'much maligned man' who was not responsible for King Aleksandar's death in 1934.[49] Obviously, Pius had information that differed from that which a French court had used to convict Pavelić. The British response differs dramatically from the American reaction, which showed little more than perplexed interest in the event.

Pavelić placed most of his hopes for salvaging this embarrassing and at times humiliating journey to Italy on his audience with Pope Pius XII. Although not receiving recognition was a terrific blow to his personal reputation and his state's legitimacy, he hoped that Croatians would interpret the meeting as a papal endorsement of Croatia's new regime and its policies. This is what made Pius's meeting so outrageous. If the Pontiff had chosen not to meet with Pavelić the NDH would have suffered a severe setback to its efforts to attract all Catholic Croatians to its cause. Several weeks prior to 18 May, Pavelić's regime had begun slaughtering the Ustaše's enemies and passing laws that deprived Serbs and Jews of their rights. Barely in office a month, Pavelić had initiated one of the great slaughters of World War II. Yet the Pope had met willingly with him.

Pavelić's chance

History is littered with strange and unlikely events and Pavelić's emergence from death sentences and exile to Poglavnik of the NDH is one of them. His actions in the 1930s and the realities of great power politics had combined in his favour. He must have believed that God had brought him to this point and thus sanctioned his plans for Croatia. Perhaps that was Pavelić's justification for his remarkable emergence to power.

American reaction to Pavelić's victory, except in newspapers, had been little more than a ripple. Most people in the United States, including some in the State Department, did not know who Ante Pavelić was and cared little about anything that happened in this seemingly distant state. The State Department and Roosevelt were angered and disappointed over the loss of Yugoslavia to the Axis powers and grew more anxious over Yugoslav events as they learned that the country was to be torn apart. As the United States increasingly became involved in World War II, interest in Croatia was driven by concern over how Croatian-Americans and Serbian-Americans would react to the new order. Would Serbian-American steel workers and Croatian-American steel workers battle each other in American plants? Would American industry suffer from ethnic unrest imported from overseas? As we have seen, throughout the interwar period the United States was 'a day late and a dollar short' when dealing with the Balkans. With little direct national interest and a strong sense of isolation, Washington was not eager to involve itself too deeply in Yugoslav affairs.

In spring 1941, it appeared that Ante Pavelić had won his long battle to reign over a Croatian state. His dogged determination to create an independent Croatia had reached fruition. With the imperium in his grasp, he could dictate the future of his satellite state so long as he chose not to fall foul of his fascist patrons. The newly-minted Poglavnik elevated Ustaše ideology to state policy and began a reign of terror that made his earlier terrorist exploits of the 1930s seem like child's play.

CHAPTER 4

CARNAGE

For much of World War II, a substantial amount of the State Department's information about Croatia originated in Ankara and Istanbul. Neutral Turkey, situated at an important crossroads for Germany, Britain, the United States and the Soviet Union, was an excellent location for mischief and fact finding. All belligerents found it a convenient playground for cloak and dagger operations as well as a more innocuous centre for information gathering. On 6 May 1941, a disturbing telegram, which foreshadowed future events, arrived in the State Department from the American Embassy in Ankara. Rushed to Washington, the telegram contained information gained from Yugoslav contacts. The alarming message read: 'according to dependable information partizans [sic] of Pavelić (in some cases in conjunction with Magyars) are massacring Serbs in Croatia the Voyvodina and Bosnia. There is need of urgent intervention by the Vatican at Zagreb and Budapest.'[1] The intervention so desperately sought never materialized. No one came to the aid of Serbians, Jews or Roma, all of whom suffered mightily under Ante Pavelić's reign. This telegram was the first report received in Washington that spoke of the slaughter that eventually reached catastrophic proportions. By the end of the war, Pavelić and the Ustaše had murdered between 330,000 and 390,000 Serbians, many having been tortured and executed in the most despicable manner.[2]

Pavelić's genocide began with the goal of destroying the Serbian presence in Croatia but quickly spread to eliminate other peoples deemed undesirable. Serbs, who comprised about 30 per cent of Croatia's population, were not the only enemies. Jews, Roma and Croatians sympathetic to Yugoslavism were also rounded up and executed, often in Croatian- or Nazi-operated concentration camps. Pavelić and the NDH, like their Nazi masters, operated a number of concentration camps.

The Balkans has seen more than its share of bloodbaths but little compares to the Ustaše's murderous frenzy that led to the torture and slaughter of tens of thousands. Due to Ustaše ideology, the greatest attention was directed towards the Serbians. It was not enough to simply kill or convert Serbians. Orthodox cathedrals had to be razed, the Serbian faith had to be eradicated and Croatia made pure. Pavelić's state glorified the killings and made only meagre attempts to keep them a secret. The NDH's campaign against the Serbians was, in part, a religious crusade, not unlike the Crusades of the medieval period. By associating nationality with religious identity, the Ustaše manipulated its Catholic identity to secure its political goals. To the Ustaše, Serbians were not merely a different nationality; they threatened the existence of Catholicism and therefore were both religious and national enemies. These two factors combined to generate a massacre of proportions rarely seen.

Mirroring the effects of Hitler's racial policies in Poland and Russia, Pavelić's campaign led many Serbs and Jews to join Tito's Partisans, wagering that it was better to die fighting in the resistance ranks than be led peacefully to the slaughter. The NDH's murderous policy may have saved the Partisans in the first year of the war by providing them with a constant supply of soldiers when they desperately needed them. Pavelić's ethnic agenda aided the enemies whom he sought to destroy and helped eliminate support for his state, ultimately bringing him to ruin.[3]

Where was the United States in all of this? Although US policy makers learned of NDH massacres at an early date, the evidence of the slaughter did not move them to denounce Pavelić strongly and publicly. Roosevelt and the State Department made only a few comments about the atrocities. Even with hard evidence in front of them, officials in Washington chose to remain aloof, and thus missed an opportunity to draw considerable attention to the heinous policies of one of Nazi Germany's satellites. The State Department and the White House made some efforts to enlist pro-Allied Croatians and thus bolster Tito's ranks. Washington's chief interest was trying to contain and manipulate information from the former Yugoslavia in hopes of limiting ethnic tension between Serbian-Americans and Croatian-Americans. The American government was concerned that the crisis in Croatia might foster inter-ethnic violence in the United States that would weaken the domestic war effort, especially in heavy industry where Yugoslavian immigrants tended to work.

Genocide

On 27 April 1941, a mere 17 days after the NDH was established, the Ustaše began its assault on Serbs, executing at least 180 Serbs, all civilians, in Gudovac in the district of Bjelovar.[4] By the end of the summer, the Ustaše had exterminated, exiled or terrorized most of Croatia's Serbian population in a killing frenzy that shocked even the Germans with its viciousness, and sowed the seeds of the NDH's eventual defeat.

Upon gaining power, Pavelić's initial step was to protect the NDH by eliminating all who spoke out against it, while marginalizing all non-Croatians by repudiating their citizenship. Similar to the way in which Jews were treated in the Third Reich, Orthodox citizens were required to wear blue armbands with the letter P, for Pravoslavac (Orthodox). Meanwhile, the Cyrillic alphabet was prohibited on 25 April 1941, an act designed to destroy Serbian identity and transform those Serbs deemed most pliable into Croatians. All schools operated by the Orthodox Church were closed. Serbs were prohibited from Croatian businesses and denied access to public events, such as film showings and musical concerts. Over time, Serbian private property was confiscated, much of it going directly to the NDH's leadership.[5]

The Ustaše's position on citizenship, made clear with the Law Concerning Nationality, provided the legal foundation for ending the non-Croatian presence in the NDH. Decreed by Pavelić on 30 April 1941, the law stated that 'a citizen is a national of Aryan origin who has proven by his conduct that he did not engage in activities against the liberation efforts of the Croatian people and who is ready and willing to serve faithfully the Croatian nation and the Independent State of Croatia'.[6] This sweeping edict effectively reduced all Serbs, Jews, Roma and any Croatians who had opposed independence or the NDH to the status of aliens residing within Croatia. The law fitted perfectly with the Ustaše's position that Croatia should only be ruled and inhabited by 'pure' Croatians, those who supported the NDH.

The edict was bolstered by the broad Law on the Protection of the People and the State issued by Pavelić on 17 April. Pavelić decreed that:

> whoever in any way does or has done harm to the honor and vital interests of the Croatian nation or who endangers in any way the existence of the Independent State of Croatia or its government authorities, shall be considered guilty of high treason, even if his act was but a mere attempt.[7]

Acts of treason were punishable by death. It was even retroactive and could be used against those who opposed the Ustaše before they came to power. Those who were found guilty of violating the law by hastily organized 'People's Courts' were summarily executed.[8] In practical terms, this law's oppressive power granted the Ustaše the right to murder whomever they pleased.

Pavelić was eager to settle old scores and cleanse his state of all Serbs, but he was also a cagey politician who understood that he had to serve his fascist masters to remain in power. The Poglavnik was aware that he had not been the Nazi's first choice to reign over the NDH, and therefore had to endear himself to Adolf Hitler if he wished to remain in power. Pavelić's demonization of Serbs and Jews preyed on Hitler's weakness, racial hatred, and thus was the perfect tactic for strengthening and preserving his position. Meeting with

Joachim von Ribbentrop on the German Foreign Minister's Austrian estate at Fuschl, Pavelić pursued this tactic, ingratiating himself with the foreign minister by promising to deal resolutely both with the Serbians and Jews.[9] He repeated these sentiments to Hitler when they first met on 6 June 1941. Taking the bait, Hitler urged Pavelić to handle the allegedly subversive Serbs by driving them out of the NDH. Knowing that his vicious assault on the Serbian presence in Croatia was moving forward, Pavelić confidently promised the Führer that the Serbians were being and would continue to be properly punished.[10] The Poglavnik's track record of ethnic hatred must have impressed and pleased Hitler. Likewise, Pavelić's equally heinous policy towards the Jews was calculated to curry Nazi favour. It is more than ironic that Pavelić's own wife was half-Jewish, thus showing that he would do anything to maintain his power and implement his ideology.

The NDH wasted little time unleashing its brutality on the Jews. As they did with the Serbs, the NDH rounded up Jews beginning in May of 1941. Jews were stripped of their citizenship and property, forced to wear a yellow arm band with the letter Z (Zidov), forbidden to marry gentiles and removed from all government positions. Before the end of the year, they were well on their way to extermination. The Jewish community in Sarajevo, which totalled about 10,000, was an early and easy target. By the end of 1942, Sarajevo's Jews and most other Jews were either confined to concentration camps or had been executed. Most of Zagreb's Jews, about 10,000, avoided the death camps until 1944.[11] The Ustaše enjoyed great success in abolishing the Jewish presence in Croatia by killing all but a few thousand of them, confiscating all of their private property and destroying almost all of the synagogues in the country, including the Zagreb Synagogue. Hitler and his henchmen were more than satisfied with their understudy's treatment of Croatian Jews.

This kind of success could only be achieved with the active support of many Croatians and the ambivalence of others. Since Yugoslavia was not a hotbed of anti-Semitism in the inter-war years, there were few Jews of national distinction in Yugoslavia and Josip Frank, a Jew, was part of the Ustaše's ideological family tree, what could explain this genocide? The annihilation of Croatia's Jews must be seen in the context of anti-Serbian hatred and Nazi authority in the Balkans. The anti-Serbian campaign was so ferocious that almost anyone deemed non-Croatian was a target. The Ustaše wanted only a racially pure Croatian stock to occupy its lands. Likewise, attacks on the small Jewish and Roma population also served to satisfy the Nazis and solidify the NDH's relationship with the Third Reich. Pavelić understood that if he hoped to remain in power and preserve at least a semblance of independence, Hitler had to approve of NDH policies. This could best be achieved by satisfying Hitler's anti-Semitic bloodlust.[12]

Having enacted a series of laws designed to remove Serbs, Jews and Roma from Croatian society, the government of the NDH was now ready to finalize its campaign to complete the purification of its state. They created the Državno Ravnateljstvo (State Directorate for Renewal), which established camps designed to assemble Serbs for resettlement. Serbs, usually the wealthiest first, were forcibly expelled from their homes and their property confiscated. They were often assembled at key staging areas and transported to Serbia for repatriation with only what they could carry and a paltry amount of money. Other Serbs, sensing the impending Croatian hammer, fled to Serbia seeking some kind of relief. Perhaps more than 100,000 Serbs were forcibly expelled from the NDH.[13]

It did not take long before concentration camps, rife with poor sanitation and notorious for brutal treatment, became a permanent stain on the NDH. To the casual observer they did not look much like camps; instead, they resembled cattle pens. There were few barracks and those that existed offered poor sanctuary from the elements. Serbs were tossed into barbed wire enclosures and forced to live in deplorable conditions. The NDH government had no desire to resettle anyone. Their ambition was to kill. The Serbs who did not die from exposure or malnutrition were executed by other means, such as axe blows and shooting. The open air camps merely aided the execution process.

The most infamous of all 26 camps was Jasenovac, where thousands of men, women and children were butchered with bullets, axes, hammers and any other instrument available.[14] The Ustaše guards were creative in their ability to devise means of execution, using revolvers, hoes, iron bars, whips, suffocation and other methods.[15] Built in a low-lying flood plain, Jasenovac was established in August 1941, and quickly grew into the third largest concentration camp in Europe. Actually, it was a series of five camps located along the Sava River south of Zagreb. Jasenovac was the Croatian Auschwitz. Torture and execution were daily occurrences for Jews and Serbs alike. Guards needed only the flimsiest of excuses to shoot prisoners. The chief execution site, albeit one of many, was at Gradina, where thousands were killed by Ustaše guards. Like German-operated camps, Jasenovac would discriminate upon arrival between useful prisoners and those deemed suitable only for execution. Those without the skills required were summarily killed shortly after arrival in the camp while those who were allowed to live endured a slow death from strenuous labour, malnutrition, physical abuse and unsanitary living conditions. Anyone who was hardy and skilful enough to survive longer than three months was summarily executed in accordance with camp rules.[16]

A typical holding camp was Jadovno. Zvi Loker writes:

> It was an open air camp surrounded by a barbed-wire fence, whose only two huts were for administrators and guards. During July 1941, the prisoners were pressed into difficult forced labor and suffered severe starvation. Nearly all of them were murdered by beatings, stabbings with knives or swords, or shooting by early August. While many were still alive, they were thrown into a deep pit known as 'Golubnjač', or 'Dove's Nest', since only birds could get out. In this way the camp was liquidated during the first week of August 1941. The total number of victims is unknown, but estimates range from 3,500 to 10,000. Most of the victims were Orthodox Christian Serbs, including priests. Hundreds of Jews were among the murdered at Jadovno, including [...] two hundred members of Zionist youth movements from Zagreb.[17]

Pavelić's camps were very effective. According to captured German documents, the Nazi government estimated that by December 1943, the Ustaše had killed 120,000 people in Jasenovac and another 80,000 at Alt-Gradiska.[18] Of course, these statistics do not include the mass killings that took place in villages throughout the NDH.

During the summer of 1941, Pavelić, with his henchmen, unleashed a reign of terror. A murderous frenzy possessed the Ustaše, who embraced the goal, according to Minister of Education and Doglavnik (Deputy Commander) Mile Budak, in his infamous statement, to 'convert a third, expel a third and kill a third' of the Serbs.[19] Budak, a well-known novelist and journalist and outspoken Ustaše supporter from Pavelić's early days in exile, publicly outlined this policy in Gospić on 22 June. By following Budak's plan, Serbian culture would be eliminated from Croatia, either by extermination, exile or assimilation.

And so began a killing spree designed to rid Croatia of its perceived enemies. Describing the horror, the late Irish historian Jonathan Steinberg wrote:

> Serbian and Jewish men, women and children were literally hacked to death. Whole villages were razed to the ground and the people driven into barns to which the Ustasi set fire. There is in the Italian Foreign Ministry archive a collection of photographs of the butcher knives, hooks and axes used to chop up Serbian victims. There are photographs of Serb women with breasts hacked off by pocket knives, men with eyes gouged out, emasculated and mutilated.[20]

Serb men, women, and children were pushed from cliffs, plunging to their deaths. Whole villages of Serbs were annihilated. The Ustaše revelled in the bloodlust, employing various acts of torture such as skinning and burning victims alive. Sexual mutilation was widespread and was embraced by the especially wicked. Some Serbs were hacked to pieces, with their noses, ears and tongues cut off. These techniques were often meted out to Orthodox priests, the Ustaše's most hated enemy. There was little effort to bury the dead, unless the victims had previously dug their own graves at gunpoint. Often, Ustaše victims were left to rot in the open or sometimes were tossed into the Sava River. Such unspeakable acts were commonplace.[21]

In Glina, for example, about 600 Serb men, women, and children were shot, stabbed and beaten to death in their Orthodox church, which subsequently was burned. The murders continued unabated throughout the summer of 1941. Konstantin Fotić, Yugoslavia's minister to Washington, wrote that:

> Thousands of corpses were dumped into the Sava River, which flows into the Danube at Belgrade, with the inscription "Visa for Serbia" on tags around their necks. The river [. . .] became so contaminated by these corpses that access to its beaches was prohibited by the German occupiers during the whole summer of 1941.[22]

A particularly poignant account of Ustaše crimes can be found in State Department files. In a 1946 letter, Stoyan Pribichevich described the bestial acts that were perpetrated by the Ustaše and their Nazi comrades against his Serbian family.

> I had, besides my forcibly Catholicized aunt Katitsa Basta, a father-in-law killed by hammer and thrown under the ice of the Danube at Novi Sad; one brother-in-law [. . .] riddled by the Ustashi bullets and his face criss-crossed by the Ustashi knives; one cousin killed by the Germans in Serbia; another tortured by Gestapo in Belgrade; still another tortured by Gestapo in the formerly British-owned Trepcha mines in Serbia; yet another killed in 1941 by the Ustashis under Stepinats, his heart dug out with knives; again another beaten to death in a corn field. All of these relatives of mine, except one (the cousin massacred in the corn field) were Serbs. All without exception were non-Communists, and four of them were forcibly converted to Catholicism or massacred under Archbishop Stepinats.[23]

Unfortunately, similar experiences were all too common for Serbs throughout the NDH.

A Serbian official reported in August 1941 to Karl L. Rankin, the former American consul in Belgrade, that in the district of Gatzko, 'murders were committed in the most atrocious manner. Hardly anyone was killed by bullets. Most often, the Ustasi used big hammers with which they crushed in the skulls of the victims. They cut off the arms or legs of many of them, put out their eyes and threw them still alive into the cave.'[24] In other cases, 'the Ustasi placed their victims in single file, one behind the other, so as to be able to kill as many as possible with a single bullet [...]. In certain localities, the Ustasi used hand-grenades which they hurled at Serbs gathered in groups. Upon arrival at Gatzko, the Ustasi stated that their motto was: "The last Croatian cartridge for the last Serb".'[25]

It was not enough simply to kill Serbs. Pavelić wished to destroy any trace of their existence in Croatia. To erase Serbian cultural and ethnic identity, some Serbian boys were marched into concentration camps in Ustaše uniforms, a terrible practice considering how the Ustaše guards were dealing with their fathers and mothers. Orthodox churches, some dating to the 1200s and 1300s, were destroyed, razed or denigrated by converting them into barns, stables and the like. The more than 800 Orthodox churches and religious sites in the NDH provided plenty of targets for the Ustaše. For example, the fabulous Orthodox cathedral in Banja Luka was razed as the local Catholic bishop watched. In its place was constructed Ante Pavelić square.[26] For good measure, Banja Luka's Serbs were annihilated in anticipation of turning the city into the NDH's future capital. The Ustaše took particular glee in forcing Orthodox Serbs to destroy their own churches. The fate of Nova Gradiška's St Elijah church is a good example. 'It was a single-nave Baroque church with a tall belfry and iconostasis holding more than fifty icons. It was destroyed by order of the Ustasha [...] and captured Serbs were forced upon threat of death, to participate in the destruction of their own church.'[27] In addition, Pavelić's gangs attacked Serbian historical memory by destroying Serbian books, manuscripts, icons and art.[28] Such losses meant the destruction of part of Serbia's historical legacy.

Religious conversion policies were conducted with zeal that can only be achieved when national identity is meshed with religion. Pro-Ustaše Catholic priests oversaw thousands of forced conversions, making Serbs choose between their religious faith or their lives. Stella Alexander believed that the Ustaše succeeded in forcibly converting between 200,000 and 300,000 Serbs from Orthodoxy to Catholicism between May 1941 and late 1942.[29] Although admitting that records are spotty and many are missing, Mark Biondich, in a careful study of forced conversion, has concluded that there is evidence of 97,447–99,333 forced conversions.[30] The actual number is probably unobtainable. The Catholic Church's policy that conversion be without pressure on the subject was tossed aside. The Ustaše's conversion policy had one interesting caveat. 'The laws of the NDH expressly refused conversion to anyone with a secondary education, teachers, merchants, rich artisans and peasants, and above all Orthodox priests.'[31] Only illiterate peasants were deemed suitable for conversion, as they, it was assumed, were pliable fools without a deep sense of Serb identity or Orthodox allegiance. This policy meant that Serbians with the likelihood of rebelling against the Ustaše, the intelligentsia, religious figures and anyone with an education were to be either exiled or exterminated. Conversion was not an option for them.

Some Catholic priests ventured far beyond merely converting Orthodox Serbs and became gleeful murderers. Notable examples include Father Dragutin Kamber and Father Miroslav Filipović, who sent hundreds of Serbs to their deaths.[32] The Franciscan Order was well represented in Croatia and included numerous members who fervently believed that God demanded Orthodoxy be crushed and Rome recognized by all. Soon after the war ended, Siegfried Kasche, Germany's chief diplomatic representative in Croatia, admitted that 'massacres of Serbs in BOSNIA and HERZEGOVINA were frequently initiated and led by Franciscan monks'.[33] Some Catholic priests and bishops supported Pavelić's murderous policies, believing that the massacres were part of God's plan to strengthen the Catholic Church. One of the most notorious examples was Archbishop Ivan Šarić of Sarajevo, who idolized the Poglavnik, writing poems about him and praising him to his dying day.[34] As mentioned earlier, Šarić was a long-time Pavelić minion, having recruited Ustaše in both South America and the United States in the 1930s. As Srdja Trifković writes: 'Šarić ridiculed those who did not have the stomach for total genocide, declaring it "stupid and unworthy of Christ's disciples to think that the struggle against evil could be waged in a noble way and with gloves on."'[35] Some priests became more than active participants in the killings, believing that the establishment of the NDH was a sign from God given exactly 1,300 years after Croatia became a Christian state. Regardless of the dubious validity of this claim, the genocide took on zealotry, matched only by the most maniacal SS men in the Third Reich.

The Ustaše drew much of their fanaticism from their leader's example. The Poglavnik was a practising and devoted Catholic who identified Catholicism as an integral part of being Croatian, thus Orthodoxy was an insidious enemy that always threatened Croatia. Even while presiding over this genocide, Pavelić worshipped on a regular basis, taking Mass in his palace's chapel and confessing his sins. These practices made Pavelić a different kind of fascist from most of his brethren.[36] His religious faith, however, grounded in nationalism, gave added support to the zealotry for eliminating all Serbs from Croatia. Without the Serbs, Ustaše ideology could not exist. Pavelić was a faithful worshipper whose brand of faith was deeply distorted.

The man who held the power to counter or at least diminish the Ustaše's activities was the newly-minted Archbishop Alojzije Stepinac.[37] As leader of the Catholic Church in Croatia, Stepinac never publicly denounced the massacres or used his powerful influence to have them halted. Perhaps taking his lead from Pope Pius XII, who also was publicly silent throughout the Serbian holocaust, Stepinac chose to make a handful of protests directly to Pavelić, urging him to act against assaults on Serbs and Jews. The archbishop was not an active participant in the murders; however, he knew that the Ustaše were slaughtering Serbs and Jews in the thousands.[38] Soon after the genocide began, Stepinac began to have pangs of guilt. Relations between Stepinac and Pavelić soured quickly and grew more strained after the summer of 1941. For all of the Archbishop's hand wringing, however, he continued to be a tacit participant in the NDH. He repeatedly appeared in public with the Poglavnik and issued Te Deum's on the anniversary of the NDH's creation.[39] His failure to publicly denounce the Ustaše's atrocities in the name of the NDH was tantamount to accepting Pavelić's policies. It was difficult for average Croatian Catholics to oppose Pavelić and the Ustaše if the Catholic Church did not take the lead and denounce the Poglavnik. This was akin to the reaction of German Catholics and Protestants to Nazi atrocities.

Even German officials in Croatia were shocked by the Ustaše's behaviour. General Edmund von Glaise-Horstenau, Germany's military representative to the NDH and a prominent Austrian Nazi in the 1930s, argued that 'the Croat revolution by far the bloodiest and most awful among all I have seen first hand or from afar in Europe since 1917' was feeding the Partisan movement by driving Serbs into the opposition and thus forcing Germany to station large numbers of troops in Croatia and the rest of the former Yugoslavia.[40] Glaise-Horstenau, an Austrian who was very familiar with the ethnic issues in the former Yugoslavia, was unable to stop Pavelić's genocidal policies partly because they appealed to the Nazi brass and partly because they were supported by Siegfried Kasche. Kasche was a passionate Nazi of the old guard appointed by Ribbentrop to Zagreb as German minister plenipotentiary. A native of Mecklenburg, Kasche had no experience in Balkan affairs and only a meagre appreciation of the complexities of Yugoslav society and politics.[41] From their first meeting, Kasche disliked everything about Glaise-Horstenau, from his social class to his traditional political beliefs. Kasche stalwartly defended Pavelić to Berlin, all the time trying to establish Croatia as a redoubt of Nazism. His greatest goal was to reduce Italian and German military influence, thereby exalting Nazi ideology in Croatia. Kasche therefore had no qualms about Pavelić's racial policies, often celebrating them to Berlin. With Kasche on his side, Pavelić had a powerful ally.

Since World War II, controversy has surrounded the Ustaše atrocities. Various authors with political agendas have tried mightily to decrease the severity of this holocaust or have attempted to find some justification for it. Perhaps most notable was former Croatian President Franjo Tudjman's claims that the death toll under Pavelić's watch had been greatly exaggerated. For years, there have been battles over the number of victims. All of these arguments cloud the basic fact that the Ustaše slaughtered tens of thousands of innocent Serbian, Jewish and Roma men, women and children. Furthermore, thousands of Orthodox Serbs were forced to convert to Catholicism at gunpoint. The Ustaše went so far as to attempt to destroy the Serbian and Jewish historical legacy. There is a mountain of evidence, both written and photographic, that proves the scope of Ustaše activities.

The United States loses a listening post

Since the German invasion of Yugoslavia had forced Minister Arthur Bliss Lane and the American delegation to leave Belgrade, the Zagreb consulate was America's only representation in Croatia and, for that matter, Yugoslavia. Despite this, Consul John J. Meily's outpost was not destined to last for long. The Ustaše had no interest in offending their fascist masters by keeping a potential security risk open and running. Croatian authorities were suspicious of the close ties that had existed between the British and American consulates prior to the German invasion and seized this opportunity to prove their metal. In June 1941, Meily, a diplomat sympathetic to Croatian interests, was summoned to the Croatian Foreign Ministry and ordered to close the consulate. According to NDH Minister Ivo Omrčanin, Meily was much disturbed about closing the consulate, because he 'expected President Roosevelt to recognize Croatia de jure and not only de facto as it had since April 10'.[42] Omrčanin's opinions, coloured by his well-known pro-Ustaše writings as well as his close relationship with Reverend Krunoslav Draganović and the Ratline, cannot be confirmed in United States documents. The State Department did not offer any resistance, because Washington did not wish to operate a consulate in a county it did not recognize and, most likely, was planning to close it voluntarily. Maintaining the consulate could be construed as tacit recognition of the Croatian state, something

Washington wished to avoid. In late August and early September, Croatian authorities, with the help of the Italian press, accused Consul Meily of spying on behalf of the British. Their evidence, based on a few seized American documents, did little more than prove that Meily had worked closely with the British, certainly no surprise in the days of Lend-Lease. Croatian accusations of espionage were far from valid. This weak attempt to embarrass Washington and ingratiate the NDH with the rest of the Axis never materialized.[43]

With no diplomatic ties to Croatia, information about the Pavelić regime was gained from various other sources. With Turkey's juxtaposition to the Balkans, physically and historically, and its neutrality, Ankara and Istanbul became natural centres for information. The country was teeming with ex-patriots, including a large number of businessmen, and served as a clearing house for news and rumour. Neutral Switzerland was another place where, on occasion, information on Croatia arrived, especially at Allan Dulles' desk. Later in the war, Office of Strategic Services (OSS) operatives provided additional information on conditions within the NDH. All of these outlets proved to be remarkably reliable and detailed in their newsgathering and analysis of Pavelić's Croatia. Though rarely closely involved in Croatian affairs, Washington had channels for regular and often reliable information.

Washington learns of the massacres

It did not take long for Washington to learn the full scope of the atrocities being committed in Pavelić's new state. In one of Lane's last telegrams from Belgrade, he reported that 'Serbs and Jews in Zagreb have been ordered to leave portion of city north of Illice Street. All Serbs expelled from government position in Croatia.'[44] Sent via Budapest, this message was an indication that Pavelić was following a pattern established by his fascist masters in Germany. In June 1941, a Standard Oil Company employee who had recently left Zagreb offered more evidence of persecutions conducted by the Pavelić regime when he reported to the American delegation in Geneva that 'a reign of terror' had descended on Serbs and Jews.[45] Although he did not mention deaths or executions, he explained that theft and looting were widespread. It was becoming clear that a very dangerous situation was developing in Croatia.

On 14 August 1941, a letter, accompanied by pictures reached the State Department with detailed information about mass executions. Though the number of victims was in dispute and considered to be a bit 'fantastic', it was clear 'that many thousands of Serbian civilians had (have) lost their lives, at the hands of the Ustaše'.[46] The information presented to the State Department came from an unnamed Serbian government official, and was therefore potentially easy to refute as being a source of exaggeration and propaganda. The anonymous Serbian official wrote that 'we (Serbians) are confronted with a comprehensive policy aiming at the extermination of the Serbian race in the regions in question, which would be preceded by the destruction of the Serbs from an economic standpoint'.[47] The author detailed a series of incidents in which the Ustaše had executed Serbians, starting with the first attacks that took place at the end of April in and around Bjelovar. Some victims were slaughtered, not by gunshot, but in an almost animal-like fashion with hammers and knives; bodies being hacked into pieces. Execution by a bullet may have been a welcome relief. The author purported that others were killed by hand grenades. Special attention, the writer noted, was given to the persecution and execution of Orthodox priests and former Yugoslav politicians. This highly detailed document included names of prominent individuals who had been executed by the Ustaše. He even wrote about the establishment of a concentration camp in Koprivnica.[48] Rankin thought that the information was of great value and suggested that 'more publicity regarding atrocities which the Germans are permitting, and which are possible only because of the German conquest and dismemberment of Yugoslavia, would be helpful to the Serbian and Allied cause'.[49] Rankin's advice was not accepted at the State Department.

This report came on the heels of a missive from King Petar, then in exile, which also addressed the horrors taking place in Croatia. President Roosevelt, obviously shocked by news of the massacres, asked Cordell Hull whether Petar's letter should be made public. Unfortunately, Hull recommended that it be kept private and that the White House inform the young King that the President had given the letter his full attention.[50] This silence did nothing to draw notice to the tragedy taking place in Croatia. If anything, the lack of a strong official statement from the White House meant that zealots for Croatian independence within the United States could insist that the executions and massacres were nothing but Serbian and Jewish propaganda. Doubtless, domestic peace between Croatian-Americans and Serbian-Americans played a major role in the government's decision.

Even with the above information in hand, Cordell Hull and the State Department refused to appreciate the scope of what was happening. Only once did the State Department inquire about the Ustaše's policy towards Serbs. On 29 September 1941, Hull asked the American Embassy in Rome to investigate reports of 'mass deportations of Serbs from Croatia'.[51] There is no record of a response from Rome, but Hull's lone question in response to the letters and reports already received by the State Department and those that would pour into Washington later, signified lack of interest as well as scepticism in Washington.

Some of the blame for America's slow response rests on the shoulders of the Yugoslav government in exile. Wracked by dissension between Croat and Serb members, it failed to spread the word of Pavelić's murderous spree. Too often Croatian and Serbian politicians only emphasized their nationality and jockeyed for position so as to gain the best deal possible for their particular nationality at the war's conclusion. The atrocities committed by the Ustaše became a political football. Many Croatians in the government were unwilling to proclaim the truth about Pavelić's regime mainly because they were so desirous of an independent Croatia that they chose to ignore the deaths. Croatians in the exiled Yugoslav government believed that recognizing the Ustaše's crimes in the NDH would place Croatian interests in an unfavourable light at war's end. Serbians, demanding that the horrors be proclaimed from the highest mountain, often incorrectly castigated all Croatians as murderers. Since Yugoslavism was a rare bird, most attempts to draft statements damning the Ustaše's actions were sabotaged.[52]

Regardless of the exiled government's problems, by early 1942, there were too many reports detailing atrocities to doubt that murders on an astonishingly large scale were taking place. Accounts from various sources – all repeating the same major themes, some with more detail than others – were hard to ignore. For example, an account from an unnamed 'neutral businessman' who left Croatia in September 1941 stated that the Ustaše had run roughshod over the country, terrorizing and murdering Serbs. This businessman, a resident of Croatia, noted that some sources claimed that 250,000 Serbs had been slaughtered, a figure exaggerated at this point in the war. 'These mass killings took place mostly in the country, where Ustasi armed bands went from village to village and deliberately tried to exterminate every Serb.'[53] In major cities, Serbs had 'almost disappeared' having been forced into concentration camps, ghettoized or deported. The same treatment had been dispensed to the NDH's Jews. 'They have been murdered and beaten, sent to concentration camps, herded into railway trucks by the hundred and allowed to die en route from starvation and exposure.'[54]

Even with the wealth of information at hand, President Roosevelt's attention was focused far from the Ustaše's actions and policies. When King Petar visited the United States in the summer of 1942, he delivered to Roosevelt another account of some of the atrocities committed in the NDH. According to Ambassador Konstantin Fotitch, the Yugoslav government in exile representative in the United States, the President was 'shocked at the details of Ustashi massacres'.[55] Croatian activities, however, were so far from Roosevelt's mind that Fotitch had to remind him that the NDH was at war with the United States. At that moment 'the President raised his hands in surprise and said that he had almost forgotten about that'.[56] Speaking more directly about war crimes, Roosevelt told King Petar that he would make sure that the Ustaše realized that they would have to pay for their crimes at the end of the war, something that would happen only in rare cases. More pointedly Roosevelt explained that 'he would try especially to impress "this man

Pavelich"'.[57] Fotitch responded to Roosevelt explaining that the United States could say little that would affect Pavelić.

One State Department official was deeply concerned with the Ustaše's atrocities. Roosevelt's minister to the Yugoslav government in exile, A.J. Drexel Biddle Jr, a close friend of the President's, was fed a diet of reports from the royalist Četnik leader Draža Mihailović, who was waging a halting guerrilla campaign against the Nazis. These reports were of varying accuracy and quality, because the exiled government and Mihailović wanted Washington to believe that they were the only legitimate force waging war against the Germans. Biddle was told by the government in exile that the Ustaše had killed about 600,000 Serbian men, women and children as of September 1942, an exaggerated figure designed to garner American attention. Another 300,000 had been forced out of their homes. Regardless of the numerical inaccuracy, exterminations were taking a crushing toll, especially in the ethnically-diverse Bosnia.[58]

Although the State Department had a significant quantity of information that pointed to mass slaughter in Croatia, the government offered few comments about it. The White House and the State Department were concerned about domestic unrest between Serbian-Americans and Croatian-Americans as a by-product of Pavelić's actions in Croatia and decided on a strategy of silence as the best course. In that way, Roosevelt could avoid offending either nationality while charging the Office of War Information, the government body responsible for monitoring America's various nationalities, with keeping Croatian-Americans and Serbian-Americans united in their opposition to Nazi Germany.

The genocidal actions in the NDH were not taking place in a vacuum. The United States government learned in October 1941 that the Nazis were attempting to exterminate the Jewish population of Poland.[59] This information was followed by Thomas Mann's BBC reports that echoed the same sentiments.[60] Nevertheless, obstinacy reigned in Washington. As Henry Feingold explained it, 'the Administration was reluctant to accept the reports of murder centres and discounted the idea of an organized attempt to liquidate the Jews'.[61] The fact that all of these early reports of Nazi atrocities elicited a slow response from Washington provides context for understanding why American authorities dawdled when confronted with equally horrific reports coming from Croatia. Of course, Pavelić and the Ustaše were principally targeting Serbs – a people most Americans knew nothing about – and most intelligence out of Croatia emphasized this. Nevertheless, there were reports of atrocities against Jews and even mentions of concentration camps. As has been shown by other authors, the State Department – and in particular Assistant Secretary of State Breckinridge Long – was far from sympathetic to the plight of Jews or East European peoples. There was a traditional and strong undercurrent of anti-Semitism and dislike for East European immigrants in the State Department. Long's role in ignoring the Croatian issue is problematic, however, because he was no novice when it came to Yugoslav affairs. As ambassador to Rome in the late 1930s, he was versed in Pavelić and the Ustaše, occasionally sending cables on their activities to Washington. As much as any other figure in the State Department, he understood the animosity between Serb and Croat. Yet, as the point man for refugee affairs in the Roosevelt administration, he failed to use his influence at the White House and in the State Department to urge any response to the genocide taking place in Croatia.

Historians have argued that one of the reasons Long attempted to minimize the assaults on Jews was that he opposed Jewish immigration into the United States.[62] But with the Croatian atrocities, immigration was not an issue. No one was worried about a bevy of Croatian or Serbian immigrants fleeing to the United States. From his days as ambassador, Long was aware, as were others in the State Department, that pro-Ustaše forces had been active in the United States. One must conclude that Long and his colleagues simply worried little about events in Pavelić's Croatia and thus showed no compulsion to act.

The public learns of genocide

The American public, outside of Serbian-American and Croatian-American circles, did not learn of the Croatian atrocities until an item appeared on page three of the *New York Times* on 11 October 1941. This short article stated that the Ustaše had slaughtered 300,000–340,000 Serbs and pro-Yugoslav Croatians. Citing intelligence reports from agents in Croatia and Bosnia, the anonymous reporter explained that, 'nearly 5,000 Serbs were slaughtered by Croatian Ustashi in a concentration camp outside Yatovo [probably Jadovno]'.[63] The reporter described specific atrocities, some with inflated numbers, but the reports of thousands of deaths failed to register with the American public. There was little to no reaction. Where were the editorials decrying the events in the former Yugoslavia? Where was the outraged citizenry? These murders seemed distant to most Americans, especially considering that the United States was enjoying a long Indian summer outside of the war.

The distance began to close after Germany declared war on the United States. Hitler's foolish declaration of war on 11 December mandated that Pavelić follow suit. The Poglavnik declared war on the United States and the other Allies on 15 December 1941. This action had the potential to cause ethnic unrest in several American cities, for the United States was home to the largest Croatian population in the world living outside of Croatia. Declaring war on the United States also made it difficult for Pavelić to draw further financial, diplomatic or moral support from Croatian-Americans who now had to choose allegiances. Support for Croatian independence lost most of the sympathy traditionally allotted by Americans to nationalities seeking independence. Instead, Croatia was viewed as part of Hitler's Europe, having sold its soul for a patina of independence within the fascist world.

With much bigger concerns in the Pacific theatre, the United States showed little to no reaction to Pavelić's declaration. For example, it received no more than one paragraph in the *New York Times*. What damage could Croatia do to American interests? Would American forces face Croatian troops in battle? Pavelić's announcement was recognized rightly as the action of a pawn.

By early 1942, evidence of Croatian atrocities continued to mount with the publication of a report issued by the Archbishop of the

Serbian Orthodox Church which stated that more than 180,000 people had been killed by the Ustaše prior to early August.[64] This carefully crafted document, which featured many grisly details, was forwarded to the United States government where it was received as authoritative. Nevertheless, government officials and the media did little more than read the Archbishop's report.

Even at this point there were no public statements from the White House or the State Department about the executions and tortures in Croatian concentration camps or the vast number of indiscriminate murders. One of the first confirmable reports of major concentration camps came in a 9 March 1942 telegram from Bern, Switzerland, a centre for American information gathering. The *Wiener Tageblatt* had reported that Croatia had spent 120,000,000 kuna to establish 'work camps'. Jasenovac was specifically mentioned as housing 1,050 people, mostly Jews, who were well treated.[65] This veneer was easily transparent to anyone in the State Department who followed affairs in the Third Reich. Unfortunately, this news never reached the American public.

Finally, President Roosevelt realized that a public declaration was needed to define America's position regarding these and other Axis atrocities. This was true, especially given that Serbian and Croatian newspapers in the United States were reporting evidence as well as rumours of terrible events under the Pavelić regime. After receiving a letter from King Petar II of Yugoslavia that discussed atrocities being inflicted in Yugoslavia and asked that the men responsible for these crimes face justice at some later date, the President decided to make a public declaration pledging that those who had committed these atrocities would be held responsible for their actions. As A.J. Biddle Jr said, 'The President plainly wants to publish something (a response to the atrocities) – including King Peter's letter'.[66] Knowing that the State Department favoured silence on the matter, Biddle added that 'in dealing with atrocities you do not try to be courteous, or diplomatic, or nice. The subject matter requires that it be handled with punch.'[67] The State Department was wary of taking unilateral action on war criminality, preferring to make a statement in cooperation with other Allied states. Although King Petar's letter of 22 July was the second time the Yugoslav government had made a request for an American statement on Yugoslav war crimes – the first being on 13 April 1942 – the State Department suggested that the White House only produce a statement in cooperation with the other major Allies.[68] The State Department carried the day. President Roosevelt's reply to King Petar included no public declaration to collect evidence of war crimes so that war criminals could be brought to justice, as he had originally intended. Instead, Roosevelt's response included nothing more than vague promises.[69]

In a public statement, the White House pledged that those who had committed war crimes would be held responsible for their actions.

The perpetrators of these crimes against civilization can no longer be dealt with merely as units of the national guilt of the Axis powers. Guilt is personal; and the men, as individuals, who have thus violated, and who continue to violate the most elementary rules of civilization, must be held personally accountable. When the time comes – as come it will – justice must be done, and civilized law must be vindicated.[70]

These were welcome words, but the announcement did not mention Croatia or Yugoslavia by name. Instead, it was designed as a very general statement on atrocities, carefully worded so as to in no way offend any of the Allies or be a future impediment to united Allied actions against atrocities. Such a proclamation was a far cry from what King Petar had hoped.

The wording of this announcement did presage the Moscow Declaration's Statement on Atrocities agreed upon by the Big Three in October 1943. Although the document did not mention that quislings and war criminals from Nazi satellites would be punished after the war, the Allies agreed to pursue German war criminals and try them for war crimes at the end of the conflict. The omission was unfortunate and certainly disappointed Serbians and Serbian-Americans, just as the absence of any reference to Jewish deaths infuriated Jews.

America's domestic concerns

Serbian-Americans were full of rage when news of Ustaše atrocities reached the United States' shores. The *American Srbobran*, the largest and oldest Serbian paper in the United States, reported Pavelić's crimes in great detail, beginning on 4 November 1941. In light of the news from Croatia, the paper moved towards a staunchly Serbian nationalist position, attacking Pavelić's regime and Croatians in general.[71] American authorities determined that many Serbians had seized upon Pavelić's killing spree as an excuse to favour a greater Serbia at the end of the war. The strong condemnation of Pavelić and Croatians by Serbian-American fraternal organizations and news-papers could have come as no surprise considering the magnitude of the news being reported, which included word of the deaths of family members and friends at the hands of the Ustaše.[72]

Prior to the NDH's birth, there was little notable animosity between Serbian-Americans and Croatian-Americans, except between fringe elements. The Ustaše's crimes changed this. It was fortunate for American interests that the Pittsburgh paper *Nezavisna Hrvataska Država* found it increasingly difficult to follow its pro-Pavelić line as news from Yugoslavia drifted back into the United States. After Pavelić declared war on the United States, the paper, under the leadership of Luka Grbić since 1938, was forced to close down in March 1942.[73] Its cessation was beneficial to the American war effort; otherwise this fervently pro-Pavelić newspaper would have done nothing but fuel ethnic hatred. Small numbers of Croatian-Americans sympathetic to Pavelić, however, continued to spread their views. The Domobran movement had ceased to exist after 30 May 1941 because its goal of an independent Croatia had been reached.[74] But although all Domobran cells in the United States disbanded, elements devoted to Pavelić continued to function.[75] Beginning in early 1941, FBI agents monitored the Domobran and their associated organizations, concerned about fifth columnists and potential pro-Nazi influences within the remnants of the Domobran movement.[76] Although none of the key Domobrans were arrested in this early period of investigation, J. Edgar Hoover was vigilant in investigating allegedly fifth columnist elements among Croatians living in the United States.[77] According to FBI agent C.H. Carson, Hoover was 'very much interested in the background and history of a national Croatian organization then known as the "Ustashi"'.[78]

The FBI quickly concluded that Ante Došen, as the highest profile Pavelić operative in the United States, necessitated special attention. Under investigation since 1934, Došen was indicted by a federal grand jury in November 1941 on charges of perjury and 'fraudulent registration under the Alien Registration Act of 1940'.[79] The perjury charge, without a doubt a technicality designed to finally put a halt to Došen's troublemaking, resulted from a hearing in July 1941 at which Došen maintained that he had been continuously in residence within the United States since 1924.[80] He had failed to mention that he had spent several days in 1926 in Canada and had illegally re-entered the United States.[81] Došen, not meekly accepting the indictment, mounted a strong defence, with political assistance that included letters of support from both United States senators from Pennsylvania.[82] Clearly frustrated by the Došen case, an OSS agent very familiar with Pavelić sympathizers within the United States remarked that:

regardless of our constitutional rights, this man should not receive the benefits of said rights which he has flagrantly violated for years [. . .]. Even if this man is convicted on illegal entry and a technical charge of perjury, he still would not receive just punishment.[83]

Although Došen was clearly a troublemaker, with FBI informant Stanley Todd Karran alleging that he was associated with Axis agents, the United States was unable to get any charges to stick to him.[84]

By 1941, Došen had fallen out of favour with other Pavelić supporters and no longer held any significant influence among Domobrans. At least publicly, Došen seemed to moderate his views and even landed a position with the more subdued *American Slav* magazine using the alias Mr Anthony.[85] After years of investigations and legal disputes, in March 1943 Došen was convicted of violating his immigration into the United States and was sentenced to a six-month jail term.[86] This was a small consolation for the American authorities who had doggedly pursued him. He was destined never to regain a prominent position in Croatian affairs.

On 18 April 1941, the FBI ordered J.E. Thornton, special agent in the Pittsburgh office, to begin a new investigation of the Ustaše within the United States.[87] The request went beyond merely the Pittsburgh office to many other cities such as Butte, Montana, San Francisco, New York and Seattle. The charge was to determine the goals and purposes of Croatian organizations operating on American soil.[88] The timing of this request was far from coincidental, considering that Ante Pavelić had assumed control of Croatia on 10 April. The FBI was very interested in Domobrans, the Croatian Fraternal Union and Macedonian organizations. Appeals were made for FBI offices to conduct investigations of local Croatian organizations. In Tacoma, Butte, Sacramento, San Francisco and New York, FBI investigators found little need to be concerned with Croatian extremists.[89] These reports, however, did provide very useful background information concerning the history of the Ustaše and its front organizations in the United States. Although active Ustaše organizations were not found in many parts of the country, the reports indicated that the FBI needed to continue its monitoring of extremist Croatian organizations, especially regarding their potential links to the pro-Nazi movement in the United States.[90] Likewise, the FBI, through these investigations, had firmly established that Ante Došen and Frank Budak were threatening figures with the potential to damage American interests.[91]

By late 1941, the FBI was convinced that some pro-Pavelić activities in the Midwest were being led and directed by several Catholic priests. This was the case in St Louis, where Father Hugolin Feis was named by informants as 'the active leader of the Croatians who were favouring an axis victory'.[92] Feis's support of Pavelić, which was evident from the pulpit, caused attendance at his church, St Joseph's Croatian Catholic Church, to dwindle. Even though a prominent figure like Feis favoured Pavelić, there were very few

Pavelić collaborators in St Louis, probably no more than 50, according to the FBI.[93] Nevertheless, the FBI continued to monitor his activities as well as those of pro-Pavelić followers associated with him. One informant called Father Feis 'the strongest pro-Axis sympathizer' in the region.[94] In 1942, Stanley Karran judged Feis to be such a dangerous figure that he urged the FBI to arrest Feis because of his 'fascist and violently anti democratic' ideas.[95] Regardless of his sympathy for the NDH, Feis could locate only a small number of St Louis priests and church members interested in favouring any state over the United States.[96] Croatian-Americans in Missouri and Kansas saw themselves as Americans first. As in St Louis, the Croatian Catholic Church in Cleveland contained some pro-fascist elements. An FBI informant charged that Monsignor Tomislav Firis was 'definitely Pro-Fascist and in full agreement with the Pavelich Government'.[97] But like Feis, his followers were few in number.

Interested in identifying any Axis supporters or sympathizers, the Office of War Information and the FBI believed that the Croatian Catholic Union (CCU), headquartered in Gary, Indiana, had pro-Pavelić members. Articles appearing in its weekly paper *Nasa Nada* (*Our Hope*) gave the impression that the organization was at least in favour of Croat separatism and at most pro-Pavelić. The initial investigation into the CCU began on 30 July 1941 when the FBI office in Indianapolis instructed the Gary, Indiana Police Department to investigate the organization.[98] Attention swirled around Stanislav Borić, a Croatian arrival from 1939, who was alleged to have been one of the leading figures in the CCU and was involved in raising money for Ante Pavelić. One trusted source explained that Borić, a proponent of the Nazi cause, termed 'Pavelich's agent extraordinary' by a FBI informant, had been raising money in Pittsburgh during 1939 and was associated there with Branimir Jelić.[99]

As early as 1941, there was evidence that the CCU, an organization known for having a zealously Catholic base, was opposed to any criticism of Pavelić, or even Hitler, on the grounds that *Nasa Nada* was not a political newspaper. Francis X. Kolander, the paper's editor, condemned Pavelić's declaration of war against the United States and was reprimanded by George Rakić, the CCU president and one of the organization's founders. Kolander was warned not to print articles in opposition to Pavelić again.[100] In May 1942, the FBI had recognized that the CCU had 'never issued any statement condemning the present Quisling government of Dr Ante Pavelićh in Croatia'.[101] There was ample evidence from FBI informants that Stanislav Borić, now the newly-named leader of the CCU, as well as other members of the organization, were strongly pro-Pavelić.[102] According to Karran, Borić had arrived in the United States on a visa, having been selected by the Ustaše to foster the pro-Pavelić movement in the United States by organizing CCU lodges.[103] Of these lodges, the FBI and the State Department had identified St Joseph's of Congress Park, Illinois as the most dangerous. It was rumoured that members of St Joseph were in shortwave radio contact with Zagreb.[104]

It was no great surprise that the FBI became interested in removing the CCU's Board of Directors from their positions, deeming them to be dangerous Nazi sympathizers who were operating under the aegis of Ante Pavelić.[105] In the autumn of 1942, Kolander, was defeated for re-election to his post as editor in part because he had 'openly condemned [. . .] Pavelić for having declared a state of war against the United States. . .'.[106] Later, Kolander, who had a son fighting in the United States Army, produced a letter written by *Nasa Nada*'s new editor, Monsignor M.G. Domladovac, that described the sentiments of some in the Croat Catholic Union. Domladovac resolved that:

> whatever PAVELIĆ may be, he at least has freed Croatians from Serbian chain. That he is not a traitor [. . .] is seen from the fact that neither Hitler nor Mussolini believe him, because Pavelić's children and wife are as hostages in Italy so that Hitler and Mussolini have a guarantee [. . .]. Therefore: As American citizens we are bound to help our new fatherland in its war, but no one can force us to condemn anyone in the old fatherland until we know the TRUE situation in the old country.[107]

Monsignor Domladovac's comments were interesting if not a bit delusional. Despite all the evidence against Pavelić, the editor refused to condemn him and incongruously sought to support both America and Croatia in their war efforts, even though Croatia was at war with the United States.

Certainly, Kolander was not surprised by the CCU's response, because he had seen their colours a few months earlier when Borić, along with a Croatian priest, Reverend Ardas, boldly proclaimed their approval of Pavelić and Nazi policies.[108] In the process they had condemned Kolander's attempt to pass a resolution that would condemn Pavelić and the Nazis while expressing loyalty to the United States.[109]

The investigation of the CCU was merely part of a much broader investigation into pro-Ustaše activities within the United States. For much of 1941, the FBI had conducted an extensive investigation into the Ustaše movement in the United States using the assistance of many informants including Catholic priests and the Yugoslav Consul in Pittsburgh.[110] The FBI was becoming convinced that pro-Ustaše Croatian-Americans were a danger to American interests.[111] FBI agent J.E. Thornton informed the United States Attorney General's office that former Domobran elements and their front organization, the Croatian National Representation for the Independence of Croatia, as well as the newspaper *The Independent State of Croatia*, 'are engaged in activities inimical to the best interests of the United States'.[112] The Attorney General's office agreed and in February 1942, the notorious Frank Budak was issued a subpoenas *duces tecum*, along with other Croatian-Americans in Cleveland, Youngstown, Akron, Barberton, Ohio, Campbell, Ohio and Warren, Ohio. J.E. Thornton, the FBI agent in Pittsburgh in charge of investigating Croatians, justified the subpoenas by saying that these men and their associations were dangerous to the security and interests of the country.[113] In total, the FBI issued subpoenas to 22 people.[114] Most of the subpoenaed individuals provided little to no useful information; they usually pled ignorance. There were some notable exceptions, however. Frank Budak, the secretary/treasurer of the Domobrans, willingly complied with the subpoena and provided a large cache of information to the FBI.[115] In the interview, Budak confessed that the Domobrans had begun in Pittsburgh in 1934 to further Pavelić's cause for an independent Croatia. Since Croatia was now allied with the Axis states, Budak stressed that Pavelić was no longer hailed as the leader for Croatian independence.[116] This was not completely true, because Pavelić continued to enjoy a level of popularity. In total, the FBI agents were disappointed with Budak, writing with little surprise that 'he was never specific concerning various phases of the organization'.[117] Although the FBI could not charge Budak with any crime related to his Domobran activities, he was indicted on running an illegal lottery the following year.[118] By the end of the war, Budak's criminal past had caught up with him. Instead of leading a campaign for Croatian independence, he was in prison, having been convicted of income tax evasion.[119]

The FBI was using alleged violations of the Voorhis Act as justification for the subpoenas.[120] Enacted in 1940, the Voorhis Act required any agency of a foreign power as well as any subversive group seeking to overthrow the government to register with the United States government. The act was intended to weaken Communist and Nazi organizations that were funded by foreign states from operating in the United States without Washington's approval. Obviously, the Voorhis Act could be applied much farther afield than Communists and Nazis. As the United States had been at war with Croatia since late 1941, it appeared that figures like Budak and Došen and any organizations they represented were in violation. Since violations of the Voorhis Act carried no penalty and Croatian organizations were going to be problematic under the legislation, J. Edgar Hoover requested the investigation use Section VIII of the Neutrality Act of 1939 as the foundation for any future prosecutions. Summarizing the germane part of the act, Hoover explained that it 'indicates that it is unlawful to solicit or receive any contribution for or on behalf of any belligerent government, or any agent or instrumentality of any such state'.[121]

Although the subpoenas did not provide the kind of detailed information FBI agents had hoped to find, the FBI raids, at least, received extensive media attention. The media coverage alone was enough to alert Domobran followers that federal authorities were closely monitoring their activities. The nationwide scope of the raids was further indication that they were under careful observation.[122] Figures who favoured Pavelić's independent Croatia were now put on notice that their activities held the potential for arrest and prosecution. The FBI's actions indicated significant concern regarding pro-Pavelić activities in the United States. Even after these raids, Wallace Murray in the State Department remained concerned about émigré activities within the United States, remarking that 'I have the uneasy feeling that we are storing up serious trouble for ourselves in the future by permitting the propagation of bitter controversial questions among foreign residents and foreign-born American citizens in this country'.[123]

The Office of War Information and the OSS were aware of the activities of Došen and Domladovac, but their concerns went beyond these two figures. Reverend Ivan Stipanović of Youngstown, Ohio and Ivan Krešić, the editor of *Hrvatski List i Danica Hrvatska*, attracted interest because of their staunch and public support for Ante Pavelić. Stipanović served as president of the newly-formed Supreme Council of American Croats, one of the heirs to the officially dormant Domobran cells that Branimir Jelić and his followers had worked so hard to establish. The actions and beliefs of Stipanović and Domladovac were symbolic of how Pavelić's message had infiltrated Croatian Catholic leadership within the United States, particularly among Franciscans. Both men were so obsessed with establishing an independent Croatia that their vision was clouded as to the horrors being conducted in the NDH. Hatred of Serbs combined with intense nationalism and a romanticized view of Croatian history dictated their thoughts and actions.[124]

FBI informants in Cleveland indicated that by late 1942 the vast majority of Croatian-Americans were loyal to the United States and not affiliated with the weakening pro-Pavelić element.[125] Support for Pavelić, it appeared, was successfully eliminated, or at worst retained the interest of only a handful of people in Youngstown, Cleveland and Akron. More concern was directed towards the Argentine newspaper *Hrvatski Domobran*, which informant T-9 stated was 'thoroughly anti-Democratic and all news was given from a pro-Axis standpoint'.[126] The informant worried that the Domobran who were driven underground had the potential to cause unrest in the United States by fomenting division.[127]

As Croatian and Serbian rhetoric increased, Yugoslav politicians in the United States became sources for controversy. Serbian Konstantin Fotić was accused, to some degree correctly, of 'whipping up anti-Croat sentiment'.[128] Others alleged that Momčilo Ninčić, within the Yugoslav government in exile, was 'the chief instigator of this Greater Serbia campaign'.[129] The State Department and the FBI judged that such accusations could elevate Serbian and Croatian rivalry to the point of seriously damaging the American war effort.

The battles between Serbian and Croatian newspapers reached such a boiling point that Elmer Davis, the well-respected radio journalist with CBS who had been put in charge of the Office of War Information, and, held a meeting on 18 September 1942 with editors of some of the more influential papers, explaining that they had to suspend their 'quarrelling'. Davis, an excellent choice to lead the Office of War Information, and the State Department in general believed that the newspapers were creating 'a danger to the American war effort'.[130] A resolution calling for unity and declaring loyalty to the United States was drafted and signed, with more than a little intimidation, by the newspaper editors and others in attendance.[131] Fortunately, the division between Serbs and Croats never damaged the American war machine, in part because most Serbian-Americans and Croatian-Americans favoured the reestablishment of a Yugoslavia at the war's end or were largely apathetic to events in the old country. These immigrants had become Americans.

Print was not the only medium in which pro-Pavelić forces communicated their message. The NDH made regular shortwave broadcasts to the United States with the intention of drumming up support for the Ustaše. The FCC investigated Radio Rakovica's broadcasts and determined that they originated from transmitters near Rome, another indication of the NDH's weakness.[132] The name Rakovica was a reference to a short-lived rebellion in 1871 designed to forge Croatian independence from the Habsburg Empire. According to FCC Chairman James Fly, the broadcasts, thick with patriotic calls for Croatians around the globe to support Pavelić and the NDH, were created in Zagreb and delivered to Rome for transmission to North and South America.[133] The FCC reported that Zagreb radio on 13 April 1943 announced that on the second anniversary of the NDH's founding, Pavelić received, *'greetings from the Croats of both Americas'*.[134] The greeting read, in part, 'on the occasion of the second anniversary of Croatia's independence the Croats of both Americas wish to express once again their loyalty to Your Excellency and to the new Croatia'.[135] These words of support were echoed on Radio Rakovica, the NDH's Croatian-language radio network which transmitted to North America. Both South and North American Croatians declared 'unquestioned loyalty to Your Excellency and, with you, to the new Croatia'.[136] The declaration was signed by several notable figures including Ante Valenta, who was continuing his efforts to build Domobran organizations in South America.

Though small numbers of Croatian-Americans pledged allegiance to Pavelić, the vast majority remained fervently loyal to America's cause and implacable enemies of the Axis. As we have seen, Croatian-Americans were torn over favouring Yugoslavism, supporting an independent Croatia sanctioned by the United States and Western Europe, or settling for Pavelić's state. The Office of War Information worked tirelessly to convince Croatian-Americans that their first allegiance must be to the United States. As Elmer Davis noted while speaking before the Croatian Conference on 19 September 1942, 'no American citizen can have more than a secondary interest in what government is workable in the old country. One thing we can be sure of is that (the future Jugoslavia problem) will be solved there by people rather than by people in this country.'[137] The Office of War Information's chief interest was to unite Serbian-Americans and Croatian-Americans in the crusade against the Axis. As Davis emphatically explained, any dissension between them would only serve to harm the war effort.[138]

Sensing pressure from the United States government, Croatian organizations in the United States made an appeal to meet on 20–21 February 1943 at the fashionable Hotel Sherman in Chicago to proclaim just such sentiments. In their call for action, these prominent, mainstream Croatian-American organizations clearly demonstrated their support for the United States and their condemnation for Pavelić. They proclaimed that 'those who follow Pavelich are baiting Croatians against the Serb people', and maintained that Pavelić and Serbian strongman Milan Nedić were 'heirlings' of Hitler and Mussolini.[139] They even called Pavelić a bandit. Speakers were careful, however, to avoid clear mention of the Ustaše's atrocities. This was understandable, but a bit regrettable, as a forthright approach to Pavelić's crimes probably would have won them a great deal of respect from the American government and the begrudging esteem of Serbian-American groups. This meeting was followed in September 1943 by the 6th Convention of the Croatian Fraternal Union, the largest Croatian organization in America, at which Croatian representatives pledged their loyalty to the United States and their devotion to the war effort, while rejecting Pavelić and his movement.[140] It was clear that very few Croatian-Americans could abide by Pavelić's policies regardless of whether or not there was an independent Croatia. Only obsessively nationalistic and ardently anti-communist groups like the CCU were willing to support or even tolerate Pavelić's regime.

Even in the last days of the war, however, the CCU attempted to garner sympathy from the American government for the establishment of an independent Croatian state. Addressing their concerns to Secretary of State Edward Stettinius, the CCU, proclaiming a non-political membership of 10,000, strongly requested that the United States favour the creation of a Croatian homeland. Trying to handle the difficult issue of Croatia's declaration of war against the United States, the CCU proclaimed that Croatia was not an Axis member, 'by her own choice, but by the force of circumstances from which She could not escape'.[141] Continuing with this revisionist doctrine, CCU leaders argued that 'Croatia IS and HAS Been a Democratic Country ever since its people embraced Christianity and civilization more than thirteen centuries ago'.[142] They ignored the Ustaše horrors, failing to even mention them, while emphasizing Croatian suffering at the hands of the communist Partisans as well as painting Croatians as victims of oppression who sought only justice. The CCU's positions reflected an inability or unwillingness to examine Croatian issues in a sober fashion, preferring to describe Croatia as a victim whose democratic ideals had been violated by Nazi force. To no great surprise, their pleas went unheard.

In some ways, the Domobran movement and the decisions made by Croatian-Americans mirrored the actions of German-Americans when confronted by the German-American Bund. Like most German-Americans, most Croatian-Americans were proud of their ancestral traditions, but they were now devoted to their new adopted land. There was little interest in the pleadings of nationalists bent on involving Americans in affairs far beyond its shores.

Weakness everywhere

Instead of strengthening Croatia, the NDH grew steadily weaker as its murderous campaign impelled thousands of Serbs to join ranks with the Četniks or the Partisans. As early as September 1941, the State Department learned that the massacres were driving Serbians and some Croatians into the Partisans and other opposition forces. Disorder reigned in Croatia, caused by uncontrollable Ustaše bands as well as resistance forces, and Pavelić had turned to blaming all the disturbances on the communists, a convenient target.[143]

To Western observers, Pavelić appeared so very weak that his days as Poglavnik seemed numbered. Even his allies thought that he could not hold on for very long. Pavelić had never recovered from the loss of Dalmatia to Italy, which had dealt a staggering blow to his authority. The Ustaše gangs had created enemies of all the Serbs and Jews as well as many potential Croatian supporters. By not cooperating with the popular Croatian Peasant Party, Pavelić could not count on support from traditionally the most attractive sector of the political landscape. By the spring of 1942, the NDH's authority reigned over little more than the environs of Zagreb.[144] In other areas of the country, control was much more nebulous, with frequent acts of sabotage and skirmishes between the Partisans and the Ustaše. According to German and Allied reports, the Domobran, the NDH's army, was not very reliable in combat. It had few of the fanatical, nationalistic zealots in its ranks, because that type of pro-Pavelić trooper found a home in the Ustaše. After German defeats in the east mounted, Domobran soldiers became even less dependable, often expressing pro-Allied sentiments.

These serious weaknesses forced Pavelić to make several changes to his government in October 1942. No reorganization, however, was going to blunt the opposition, which drew its strength from revenge. His weakness was further illustrated when he tried to establish a Croatian Eastern Orthodox Church to take the place of the Serbian Orthodox Church that he had destroyed. Such a pathetic action held no legitimacy among the surviving Orthodox in the NDH, especially after rivers of Serbian blood had been spilt. It placated no one, and it only deepened the hatreds between Serb and Croat. Pavelić's attempts at reform were recognition that everything was far from right in the NDH, and that opposition forces were scoring successes.

Governmental modifications, which placed Pavelić in charge of the Ministry of Defense and command of the Croatian Armed Forces, occurred on the heels of a 22 September 1942 meeting between Pavelić and Adolf Hitler at Hitler's headquarters in Vinitza, Ukraine. With Soviet resistance causing strain on the German military machine, Hitler became more cognizant of the slowly bleeding wound in the Balkans. The Führer was furious over the constant unrest in Croatia and demanded that something be done so he could remove most of his troops there and dispatch them to the Eastern Front. In addition, Hitler understood that the only way to exploit Croatia's natural resources and its manpower was to push back the Partisans. To ensure his supply of bauxite and foodstuffs and sustain his flagging attack on the Soviet Union, all guerrilla activity had to cease. But Pavelić's changes did nothing to stop the bleeding.

The German High Command was frustrated at the growing success of the Partisans. Wehrmacht officers rightly believed that Ustaše atrocities led to swelling Partisan numbers and had been convinced by General Edmund von Glaise-Horstenau that Pavelić's removal would do much to deplete Partisan support. Always the survivor, Pavelić insisted that Partisan activity was declining and that the NDH was a loyal and stable ally. Impressed by Pavelić's racial attacks on Serbs, the Führer chose to stick by Pavelić. Primarily concerned that the Allies would launch an attack in the Balkans and receive support from the Partisan elements there, Hitler was persuaded to support a major German assault against Tito. Operation Weis, the largest and most intense of the many campaigns against Tito, all of which failed, began in January 1943.

Unlike Hitler, the OSS, which compiled detailed information on the Axis states, had an excellent grasp of the Poglavnik's struggles. The OSS determined that Pavelić's ethnic policies, economic difficulties and other factors were causing his state to crumble. They aptly described Croatia as, from its very beginning, 'swinging from one crisis to another', facing growing discontent day by day. Many of the NDH's problems, the OSS reported, stemmed from Pavelić's inability to bring Vladko Maček into the government, therefore excluding the popular Croatian Peasant Party and its leader from any governing role. Facing guerrilla activity in all corners of the state, Pavelić's regime appeared to be teetering on the brink of collapse, barring a stout defence by Germany.[145] This conclusion was shared by the German High Command, who began taking greater control over the NDH's military and even reduced Ustaše autonomy.[146]

Pavelić and his regime suffered another vicious blow in December 1942, when news reached Croatia of the Soviet encirclement of German forces in Stalingrad. Among the troops taking the brunt of the Soviet onslaught was the Croatian 369th Regiment. These well-trained soldiers, wearing the checkerboard of Croatia on their shoulder, sustained catastrophic losses at Stalingrad. By the time Field Marshal Paulus surrendered, the regiment was reduced to little more than a battalion. Their annihilation was due to Hitler's stubbornness, not a lack of bravery. The 369th fought valiantly to the very end. The survivors were shipped to Soviet prisoner of war camps, and few of them ever set foot on Croatian soil again. The destruction of the regiment severely damaged the Croatian public's will to fight with the Germans against communism. Some Croatians judged that, in light of the defeat at Stalingrad, Germany was destined to lose the war. Consequently, Pavelić looked like an incompetent leader who was destroying the fruit of the country.

The debacle in Stalingrad spread a sense of doom throughout Croatia, which influenced average Croatians as well as some government figures to question Pavelić's leadership. Washington received a parade of reports from Croatian sources all maintaining that the mood in the country was that Germany had lost the war.[147] There was a growing hesitancy to serve in Pavelić's government, out of fear that any close association with it would be a death warrant. It seemed that only Pavelić and Mile Budak remained convinced of an inevitable German victory. Even in the face of such disasters, Pavelić remained defiant, maintaining that he, and not his ministers, was responsible for the welfare of all Croatians and the conduct of the war.[148] Of course, Pavelić never had a problem with being bold. His real difficulty was that he had never gained an emotional attachment to his countrymen in the way that Adolf Hitler had. As Milovan Djilas explained, 'He (Pavelić) was their boss, a man who could be replaced by someone else when and if it became necessary'.[149] Regardless of Pavelić's pronouncements, rumours spread that some in the Croatian government were desirous of establishing contacts with the West, either with the Allies or the Yugoslav government in London. Possible channels for contact were via NDH ambassadors in Sofia or Bucharest or a potential representative in Istanbul.[150] Compounding the defeatism was the fear of reprisals from the Partisans once the Allies were victorious. One American source explained that 'many Croats fear that when the Axis is defeated there will be wide spread massacres of the Croatian population'.[151] Considering the severity of Ustaše atrocities, there was good reason for this fear.

On the surface, Italy's defeat in September 1943 appeared to be an opportunity for the Ustaše to restore some legitimacy to their regime. Dalmatia, which had been confiscated by Italy in the Rome Agreements of May 1941, would now, it was hoped in Zagreb, fall into the Ustaše's hands. Pavelić believed that by reclaiming these lands, Croatians would grow more satisfied with his government. The Poglavnik, however, never had the chance to exercise any authority in Dalmatia, because German officials took it for themselves. The Wehrmacht needed to secure the Adriatic coast, and Croatians were not allowed to administer the territory for fear that Pavelić's ranks would wreak the kind of unrest they had perpetrated in the NDH. The Italian withdrawal therefore did nothing to help Pavelić. By not being allowed to administer Dalmatia, Pavelić looked ever more the Nazi puppet.[152]

Attempted contact from the West

Reports of chaos in Croatia gave encouragement to William Donovan of the OSS. Donovan saw the potential to rip Croatia from the Nazis by establishing links with pro-Western forces in the NDH. After speaking with Dr Ivan Šubašić, the former Croatian ban (governor) under the pre-war Yugoslav government, now living in the United States, he decided to pitch his idea to President Roosevelt. Donovan wrote that 'the *Ban* believes that now is the propitious time to contact not only the resistance groups in that country (Croatia), but the General Staff of Croat Puppet Government army [Domobran]. . .'.[153] The ban had agreed to go first to Italy and then to Croatia, as an agent and soldier for the Allies and without 'political commitments' of any particular kind. His duties would be, 'eliciting all possible information re present conditions in Yugoslavia, in persuading the military leader of the Croatian Puppet Army to join us; and to establish liaison with Tito, with whom he hopes to work very closely'.[154] Šubašić also wished to have a meeting with Roosevelt, not in a diplomatic capacity, but to discuss his potential activities in Croatia. Donovan spoke highly of the ban, noting that he was a reasonable man not imbued with the ethnic tension found in the exiled government. The OSS chief was careful not to ask for a meeting between Šubašić and Roosevelt, but he did contend that 'the Ban can be of great value to us in paving the way for our forces'.[155]

Such a mission was precisely the type of work at which the OSS excelled. Unfortunately for Donovan, his plan, which had a high probability of success, was inevitably discovered by the State Department. Always conservative in such matters, almost obsessed with repercussions, the State Department opposed the ban's mission. Under-Secretary of State Edward Stettinius rejected any meeting between Šubašić and Roosevelt, believing that it would offend the Yugoslav government. Likewise, he had serious reservations about the mission's potential for success. Though noting that Šubašić's intent was well founded, he wrote, 'I cannot believe that he will refrain from engaging in internal Yugoslav political activities (Croat versus Serb)'.[156] His chief concern, however, was that Šubašić would be viewed by the Yugoslav government as an agent of the United States operating against the wishes of King Petar and his exiled government.[157]

Although Roosevelt chose not to meet with the *ban*, the plans for Šubašić's trip to Croatia continued to be discussed. The OSS was convinced that Šubašić could deliver Croatia to the Allied camp. But the State Department muddied the waters by suggesting that Tito and the Soviets needed to be asked their opinions about the mission. Such requests effectively ended any hopes for a mission to Croatia.

The opportunity to contact pro-Allied Croatians within Pavelić's government and without was lost. A chance to strengthen Tito and force the fascists out of Croatia was missed. An invasion held the potential to lessen Soviet advances into Eastern Europe, thereby altering the landscape of post-war Europe. Some of the blame for this bypassed opportunity must rest with the State Department, which recused itself from taking an active role in a weak and collapsing Croatia. Efforts to exploit Pavelić's prostrate state never materialized.

Roosevelt and Croatia's future

As Pavelić struggled to maintain a modicum of political legitimacy and stability, Balkan observers in the United States questioned the fate of post-war Yugoslavia. This was a very delicate issue considering the disintegrating relationship between Croatian and Serbian communities in the United States. As we have learned, President Roosevelt feared alienating either constituency, always trying to ensure that all Americans were united in their opposition to the Axis. He could not, however, divorce himself from the controversy surrounding post-war Yugoslavia. Could Croat and Serb live peacefully in a re-united Yugoslavia or was separation the only viable answer?

Roosevelt hinted at his position as early as October 1942, in a meeting with Konstantin Fotić. Sympathetic towards the Serbs and fond of their young king, Roosevelt informed the ambassador that Serbian desires were paramount, considering their commitment to the Allied cause. Roosevelt did not oppose the continuation of Yugoslavia, but he wished for South Slavs to determine their fate without it being dictated to them by Western powers.[158] These opinions were suitably vague enough in the early part of the war to allow Roosevelt to alter his views as events dictated.

The President's position had shifted somewhat by early 1943. In a meeting with Anthony Eden and Harry Hopkins, Roosevelt contended that the Croats and Serbs had virtually nothing in common, and that the concept of re-uniting them in one state was 'ridiculous'. Roosevelt believed that Serbia deserved to emerge as an independent state while Croatia would exist under a trusteeship of some sort. All of this possessed the obscurity of casual conversation. Influenced a bit by the Yugoslavian government in exile, Eden thought that Yugoslavia could exist again with Croat and Serb side by side.[159] Post-war Yugoslavian affairs were far from the President's main concern. In discussions surrounding the Moscow Declaration, which dealt with holding war criminals responsible for their crimes at the end of the war, little was said about Yugoslavia's ultimate fate. The President merely reiterated his position that 'Croatia may have to be set up separately from Serbia'.[160] Neither Britain nor the United States believed that Tito would forge a united Yugoslavia under his star power and the communist banner.

Desperate days

As the leaves turned red and gold in 1944, Mladen Lorković and Ante Vokić, two of Pavelić's key government ministers, with Pavelić's tacit approval, began looking for ways to mitigate the NDH's impending defeat. Like rats on a sinking ship, these NDH officials made efforts to contact the Western Allies in hopes of jumping from Germany's sinking ship to the safe arms of the United States or Britain. They proposed establishing an anti-communist alliance and pledged that they would fight with any forces that wished to combat communism. Such proposals were a pathetic attempt to ward off defeat and potentially the hangman's noose. These were the ideas of desperate men, because there was no possibility that the American or British governments would ally themselves with Pavelić's murderous regime, but rumours persist that there was limited contact between British forces and Croatian government representatives.

Pavelić responded to these peace efforts by having Lorković, the former interior minister and foreign minister, and Vokić, the former minister of the armed forces, tried and convicted of crimes against the state. The Poglavnik had given his approval for the Western contacts only so that he could eliminate any challenges to his authority by announcing that those involved in such communication were treasonous. Even in the Axis's death throes, Pavelić was determined to keep all political authority in his hands. In the final days prior to Germany's surrender, both men and their alleged comrades were executed. By then Pavelić reigned over little more than ashes.

By the end of 1944, Pavelić remained in power only at the behest of his Nazi masters and a devoted corps of Ustaše. The Poglavnik had murdered thousands upon thousands of Serbs and Jews in heinous fashion. His policies, declared in the name of national and religious interest as well as solidarity with the Nazis, did nothing but forever damn his regime. Those who had survived his killing spree swelled Tito's ranks. The Partisans were filled with Serbians anxious to wreak vengeance upon the NDH government. Desperately trying to cling to power, Pavelić had purged his government of all but sycophants. The long-awaited Independent State of Croatia had become a cauldron of suffering that would not cease with the end of the war. It was not independent, nor was it a state, nor did its borders enclose historical Croatia.

Pavelić's crimes had made little impact in the United States, outside of the Serbian-American and Croatian-American communities. The State Department knew that odious acts had been committed against Serbs, Jews and Gypsies, but they intentionally or unintentionally refused to recognize the scope. As the Allies inexorably marched to victory, Pavelić, again, was faced with the prospect of exile and a life on the run. As in days of old, the Poglavnik knew that he could depend on well-placed friends to save him.

SETAF 41 BONA FIDES

DYNAMO is in possession of one-half of the nine-of-diamonds playing card
which has been cut diagonally across. Agent Handler will present himself
and say to DYNAMO "VINCIT QUI SE VINCIT" (He conquers who conquers himself).
DYANMO will answer "VERBUM SAT SAPIENTI" (A word is enough for a wise man).
Agent Handler will then ask DYNAMO for his half of the bona fides which will
match with the half in possession of the Agent Handler.

FRANCO

Note: Bona fides with instructions were established on 2 September 1959 while
DYNAMO was in Verona.

334 E
339

Figure 1 Reverend Krunoslav Draganović was not only key to organizing
and operating the Ratline in the late 1940s but, as the playing card attests,
he remained an American contact for many years afterwards. Courtesy of the
National Archives.

Figure 2   Ante Pavelić speaking in Rome during his first trip to Italy after being named Poglavnik. Note the Nazi and Italian flags, the hastily assembled uniforms, as well as the Ustaše 'U' on the soldiers' caps. Courtesy of the National Archives.

Figure 3   Although the NDH's end was near, Ante Pavelić is greeting German Ambassador to Croatia Siegfried Kasche and General Edmund von Glaise-Horstenau in 1944. Courtesy of the National Archives.

Figure 4   King Aleksandar and Foreign Minister Louis Barthou pictured only moments before their assassination in Marseilles. Courtesy of the *New York Times*.

Figure 5   The funeral procession in Belgrade for King Aleksandar was sombre. The assassination failed to generate a Croatian revolution in Yugoslavia as Ante Pavelić had wished. Courtesy of the *New York Times*.

Figure 6 Wallace Murray as head of the Division of Near Eastern Affairs for the State Department during the 1930s was an early voice expressing concern about radical Croatian elements in the United States. Courtesy of the National Archives.

Figure 7 American Chargé d'Affaires John M. Cabot determined that the Yugoslav war criminal issue was an unnecessary thorn in American–Yugoslav relations. He repeatedly demanded that American authorities arrest and extradite Croatian war criminals to Yugoslavia, but his appeals were met only with intransigence. Courtesy of Harry S. Truman Library.

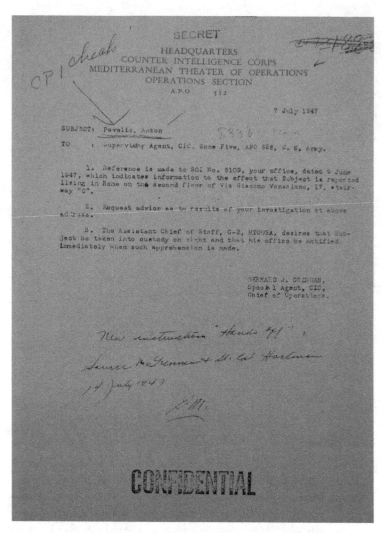

Figure 8 On 7 July 1947, an arrest order was issued to apprehend Ante Pavelić. Seven days later, it was countermanded. The United States never got closer to arresting Pavelić. Courtesy of the National Archives.

CHAPTER 5

THE ESCAPE

By late 1944, only the most fanatical Nazis believed that Germany would win the war. German forces were in wholesale retreat in the East and West. The constant defeats necessitated a withdrawal from the Balkans to shorten Germany's defensive lines in hopes of making a stand against the Allies. Allied victories on both fronts enlivened the Partisan forces in Yugoslavia; Tito's troop strength grew inexorably. Without the support of the German Army, the NDH would have quickly collapsed, because it struggled to control Zagreb and its environs, even with German assistance. Ustaše leaders and other NDH sympathizers, fearing retribution at Partisan or Red Army hands, realized that their only option was to flee the country. In the chaos of the war's last days, many NDH officials made their way across the border into Austria, hoping to blend into the masses of fleeing people seeking anonymity and safety. One of these refugees was Ante Pavelić.

The Allies had made pledges to arrest and extradite quislings and war criminals, most notably in the Moscow Declaration of 1943, but as German defeat became a reality, it was becoming clear to the United States and to Great Britain that a new war was emerging and the enemy would no longer be fascism. Allied zeal to bring criminals to justice dwindled as communism increasingly came to be seen as the great threat to the future of Europe and the world. After several diplomatic confrontations during the war between the Western half of the Big Three and the Soviet Union, it was apparent that post-war Europe was going to be a contentious place. With the Red Army firmly in control of much of Eastern Europe and conquering more territory daily, the West realized that communism would be the determining factor in almost all political and diplomatic considerations, especially as the war passed into memory. Soon after the war, strong anti-communist credentials began to overshadow a record of past atrocities. Pavelić was an unintentional beneficiary of this post-war climate. As an ardent enemy of communism and Tito's Yugoslavia, Pavelić held a trump card. As he was Croatian who had not fought directly against Western forces, he was of less interest to Great Britain and the United States.

The last days of power

In October and November 1944, German General Maximilian von Weichs led Army Groups E and F out of Greece and into Yugoslavia. Red Army successes along Germany's Eastern Front forced the retreat. Oberkommando der Wehrmacht's (OKW's) goal goal was to secure Germany's southern flank by ordering troops in the Balkans to fall back toward Hungary and Austria. There was legitimate concern that German soldiers in the Balkans would be cut off from planned Nazi resistance in Hungary and Austria. Meanwhile, Marshal F.I. Tolbukhin, in command of the Soviet Third Ukrainian Army, moved on Belgrade seeking to join with Tito's Partisans in an effort to prevent the German retreat. Belgrade was liberated by the combined action of Tolbukhin's forces and Tito's Partisans on 20 October.[1] Zagreb, however, remained under Ustaše and German control for months to come, as the Germans were determined to keep the Sarajevo–Brod rail link open. As late as January 1945, German troops proved their resolution by recapturing Travnik, a key railroad junction 55 miles northwest of Sarajevo. With the fall of Budapest and the rest of Hungary, however, Army Group E had to withdraw rapidly to Germany.

Attempting to show resilience in the face of obvious defeat, Pavelić insisted that he would continue the war. In a 3 November

1944 cabinet meeting, the United States learned from sources still unknown that there was a discussion about whether Zagreb should be defended, in light of the German retreat. Pavelić, showing defiance, insisted that 'he would defend Zagreb with Ustashi alone if necessary'.[2] After some discussion, the cabinet members agreed that Zagreb would be defended if the Partisans attacked but would be evacuated if the Red Army appeared.[3] Though Pavelić put up a resolute front, he, too, realized that he needed to make plans for his escape from Croatia.

The United States, with limited vigour, tried to keep abreast of Pavelić's movements throughout the last months of the war. Despite this, America's information about Pavelić was sporadic and sketchy at best, most of it coming via second-hand sources. On 24 February 1945, the OSS reported that Pavelić's family had left Zagreb five days earlier by plane for Germany. It was believed that they were travelling with ten boxes of 'valuables' and were accompanied by a German general and a Domhbran (Domobran).[4] This report, however, was incorrect, as Pavelić's wife and his daughters had fled Croatia for Salzburg, the home of a Croatian consulate, in November 1944.[5]

Meanwhile, Washington believed that Pavelić had the illusion that he could remain in power even in the face of complete defeat. Perhaps this was a good assessment of the situation, if one considers planned British initiatives in the Adriatic. Since early in the war, Churchill had advocated the opening of a Balkan front to strike Hitler from the south. In 1944, when Churchill still believed that such an attack was a possibility, Pavelić may have offered to switch sides and join the Allies in the hope of finding himself on the winning team when the war ended. Since the end of the war, there has been a persistent rumour that the British Army had been in contact with Pavelić's representatives with the intention of producing such a scenario. If true, this could be one reason why the British opposed Operation Anvil, the invasion of southern France, and sought an invasion in the Balkans through the Ljubljana Gap.[6] The United States believed that Pavelić was trying to ingratiate himself with Vladimir Maček, with the expectation that Maček would look kindly upon Pavelić if he became leader of Croatia after the German withdrawal.[7] Although Maček never mentions such discussions in his autobiography and there was no reason for Maček to cooperate with Pavelić, he was one of the few political figures the Poglavnik could appeal to for assistance. The Ustaše kept Maček under house arrest and never expressed serious interest in supporting his candidacy for political power in Croatia until the last days of the war.[8]

The disaster befalling their regime compelled Pavelić and his cabinet to appeal one last time to the Western Allies for leniency. Approved but not signed by Pavelić, this desperate request, dispatched to Field Marshal Harold Alexander on 4 May 1945, asked the British and American forces to occupy Croatia immediately to save it from the Partisans. It went as far as to make a case for preserving an independent Croatia at the war's end. Nothing came of this memo, which argued that Croatia deserved to be independent in part because it had only fought a defensive war. Concentration camps, mass executions and forced conversions were mentioned nowhere. A British officer offered an appropriate epitaph, writing that 'Croatia may be heard again some day, but for the present it is finished'.[9]

On the same day, Pavelić appeared in public for the last time, giving an address to the Ustaše Women's Organization. Many NDH officials, including the infamous Andrija Artuković, had long since left the dying state for Austria, Germany or Italy. The remaining members of Pavelić's government were trying to avoid capture by the Partisans or the Red Army by joining refugee columns moving in the direction of American and British forces.[10] On 6 May 1945, German General Alexander von Löhr told Pavelić that Germany was prepared to surrender. From this point on, the story of Pavelić's escape from Croatia becomes murky, with several conflicting accounts. Uncertainty about Pavelić's movements should not come as a surprise, considering the tens of thousands of people clogging roads and desperately seeking safety from American and British troops in Austria. It was a chaotic scene that contrasted sharply with the natural beauty of the region.

Siegfried Kasche, the German Minister Plenipotentiary to Croatia, offered a complete and probably trustworthy account of Pavelić's last days in Croatia. Speaking to his British captors, Kasche maintained that on 7 May, Pavelić, with an entourage of prominent Ustaše, left Zagreb headed for the Jelačić estate near Zaprešić, about 15 miles north of Zagreb. That evening, discussions took place about which potential escape routes offered the best chance of avoiding Soviet troops. On 8 May, at Rohitsch-Sauerbrunn, the group, which now included the remnants of German representation in the NDH, was informed of the planned German surrender the following day. After a rowdy session between Croatian and German officials, Pavelić decided that Croatia should surrender to the Western Allies. Kasche last saw Pavelić, escorted by his bodyguard, setting out for Klagenfurt.[11] This account differs from one given by Pavelić's son-in-law, Srećko Pšeničnik. He alleged that on the afternoon of 6 May, Pavelić, along with his son Velimir and another Ustaše officer, probably Lt Dragutin Došen, began a long journey into exile in a black Mercedes heading for Salzburg, where his wife Marija and the rest of his family were waiting.[12]

In his wake, Pavelić left a looted and shattered city descending into chaos. As the war came to its end, the OSS reported that 'the Germans and Ustashi are beginning a reign of terror in Zagreb'.[13] The Partisans entered Zagreb on 8 May 1945, eager to deliver retribution upon Croatian collaborators and all members of the Ustaše.[14] They had barely missed the Poglavnik, who was now one of several thousand refugees moving steadily north.

The escape

Confusion abounded as refugees, war criminals, quislings and ordinary soldiers fled toward Austria with the Partisans and the Red Army in hot pursuit. Many Croatians hoped to reach Graz, the home of a Croatian consulate that perhaps could offer some protection. The Ustaše and the Domobran believed that the British forces would grant them quarter, especially in the light of their mutual anti-communist beliefs. This was not to be the case, as the small British force around Bleiburg, numbering only about 150, was swamped by thousands of Croatians. Although sources are unclear as to what happened, the British appear to have forced the Croatians back to Yugoslavia, where large numbers were slaughtered by Tito's forces.

Partisan retribution was fierce and merciless after World War II, with thousands of Croatians executed, some for no other reason than being Croatian. It is unclear how many Croatians were killed at Bleiburg, because the issue has been heavily politicized by right-wing Croatians and NDH officials who survived the war and dabbled in propaganda about Bleiburg to keep their cause alive.[15] Regardless of what happened at Bleiburg, countless other Croatians reached Graz and other Austrian cities, seeking anonymity and security.[16]

In the midst of this confusion, Pavelić's escape route remains somewhat of a mystery.[17] Neither American nor British authorities knew where Pavelić or many other key Ustaše were immediately after the war. According to the British military it was a 'complete disappearance'.[18] Much later, the United States Army Counter Intelligence Corps (CIC) learned that Pavelić had left Croatia and made his way to Celovec (Klagenfurt), on the Yugoslav–Austrian border.[19] Pavelić's son-in-law, Srečko Pšeničnik, disagreed with the details of the American assessment. In an interview with the author, he said that Pavelić abandoned his car soon after leaving Croatia because his escape had been cut off by the Red Army. For ten days, Pavelić travelled on foot, ultimately reaching Salzburg, where he was reunited with his family.[20] It is certain that he spent some time in or around Salzburg. Perhaps in the safety of the Convent of St Gilgen, Pavelić found himself under American occupation forces. This mountainous area rife with forest land and difficult terrain provided an ideal hideout. Siegried Kasche, in his interrogation after being captured by the Allies, corroborated the claim that the former Poglavnik's goal was to reach St Gilgen, a small and strikingly beautiful tourist town on Lake Wolfgang, only about 18 miles from Salzburg.[21]

Though Pavelić was hiding in an American occupation zone, neither the CIC nor military intelligence showed much enthusiasm in their search for him. Thinly spread in the region, the CIC in Salzburg, Rosenheim, Bad Ischl, Traunstein, and St Gilgen possessed a total of 17 men. They were poorly staffed, so the 430th CIC, headquartered in Salzburg did nothing to pursue the Poglavnik, one of the most prominent quislings alive. Military Intelligence (G-2) noted on 5 June 1945 that Pavelić was perhaps hiding in the area controlled by the 12th and 6th Army Groups.[22] For some time, at least until the middle of November, American authorities believed, probably correctly, that the Poglavnik was in the American zone, but they did not know where he was. With several hundred thousand refugees in the American zone in Austria, Pavelić had chosen a good hiding place.[23] On 31 August, the *New York Times* reported that Washington had agreed to hand over Pavelić to Belgrade, as it was rumoured that Pavelić was in American custody in the United States zone in Austria.[24] This news report was based on information alleging that he had been captured by American forces in Austria but had not been recognized.[25] There is some evidence to support this contention. The Deputy Theater Judge Advocate's Office reported on 5 November 1945 that Pavelić 'is believed to be in custody in the United States Zone, but his exact location is unknown'.[26] A later addition to this report noted that Pavelić was held at CIE #6 in Moosburg, an internment camp commanded by the Third United States Army.[27] It is conceivable then that Pavelić spent at least a little time in American custody. This theory, and all theories regarding Pavelić's apprehension by Allied authorities, was challenged by Pšeničnik. According to Pšeničnik, who was an official in the Croatian Embassy in Rome during the war, Pavelić was never in American or British custody and successfully hid himself in Austria and later in Italy.[28]

American and British documents, however, challenge this view. By late 1945, Pavelić was reported to be in the British zone and perhaps in the custody of the British 5th Corps. The first mention of this was in a memo from the United States War Crimes Branch Liaison Office on 15 November, which reported that Pavelić was '"now detained" by British Authorities'.[29] United States records on Pavelić indicate that he had been arrested by the British at Klagenfurt, although the exact date of the capture is unknown. This was reinforced in a 19 February 1946 letter to the Yugoslav War Crimes Liaison stating that the Deputy Theatre Judge Advocate had been notified by the Director of the Central Registry of War Criminals and Security Suspects (CROWCASS) in Paris that Pavelić 'was arrested at Klagenfurt, Austria (British Zone) by the British authorities'.[30] Thus the Judge

Advocate General officials explained to the Yugoslavs that the Pavelić case was closed, as far as the American government was concerned. Either the British were keeping tight-lipped about Pavelić's whereabouts or they knew nothing about reports that placed him in their custody. The latter seems to have been the case, as the Foreign Office had no confirmation of Pavelić's arrest, something they very much wanted.[31] Circumstantially, this is supported by the fact that British military officials 'refused permission for Yugoslavs to go to the vicinity of Klagenfurt'.[32] This policy may have been in place to limit Yugoslavian territorial ambitions in the area or to prevent the Yugoslavs from interfering in the race to capture and exploit high-profile wartime fugitives. Regardless, there is circumstantial evidence that points to the Poglavnik's arrest by British military authorities unknown to the Foreign Office. It is clear, however, that American officials were convinced of British intrigue with Pavelić. In an October 1946 memo, a United States Counter Intelligence Corps officer wrote that 'there can no longer be any doubt that the British aided the escape of Dr Ante Pavelich'.[33] The British were accused of repatriating Ustaše to the Yugoslavs, 'with the exception of Pavelich himself who was taken away one night in a British jeep'.[34] The counter intelligence officer did not offer an explanation for why London sought to protect Pavelić.[35] After about two weeks, he may have negotiated his way out of British custody either by bribing his captors with plundered gold or by convincing them that he was more valuable free than in Tito's hands.[36]

By most accounts, Pavelić had not fled Croatia empty-handed. As we have seen, he had been deeply involved in siphoning money to Switzerland during the war and was smart enough to have squirrelled away a significant treasure that could be used for bribes. At least one report alleges that shortly before the end of World War II, 'Pavelić sent to Austria 12 cases of gold and jewels. This treasure, which was property of the Croatian State, was concealed in a wall near Salzburg in the US zone of Austria.'[37] It is inconceivable that a man of Pavelić's skill and experience, well acquainted with the needs of a fugitive, would have exited Croatia without a large cache of gold and jewels.[38] The Eizenstat Report, issued by the United States State Department in 1998, argued that Pavelić may have arrived in Austria with as much as $5 million to $6 million worth of gold.[39] More gold was brought to Austria and Italy to grease palms and facilitate the escapes of Ustaše officials. Ultimately, some of the looted Croatian treasury was used to finance the escape and lifestyles of former Ustaše officials in Italy and South America.

As early as October 1946, American authorities understood that Vilko Pečnikar, Pavelić's son-in-law, the former commander of police in the NDH and a highly sought war criminal, had access to large sums of gold.[40] Having experience as an early Ustaše member, organizing terrorist training facilities and having held many offices in the NDH, Pavelić placed great trust in his colleague. Pečnikar's service in Italy was complemented by Lovro Sušić in Austria and Bozidar Karan. The Yugoslav government had charged Sušić with war crimes for having served as minister of national economy and minister plenipotentiary to the German SS Prinz Eugen Division in the NDH government. According to sources friendly with American interests, all three men, war criminals against whom a *prima facie* case had been made, 'dispose of great amounts of money and they finance the whole ustashi activity'.[41] There may never be a full accounting of the money with which Pavelić and his followers fled, but rumours abounded that the Ustaše escape routes were well funded.

The Americans, like the British, were under some obligation to divulge all information about Pavelić's whereabouts, because the Yugoslav government had made a formal request for the Poglavnik's extradition on 31 October 1945. In addition, his standing as a major quisling dictated Washington's involvement. The Yugoslav extradition request issued by Lt Colonel A. Pejovic detailed the former Poglavnik's crimes, saying that he 'helped the breaking of the Yugoslav Army in April 1941. He formed the Army who fought against the Allies. He is responsible for [the] all mass murders, destroyings, incendarisms, lootings, robbings, killings of hostages and other atrocities. . . .'.[42] The request specifically mentioned precise orders issued by Pavelić which led to the formation of death camps and the execution of Serbians and other Yugoslavs. It noted that orders were issued:

for rooting out the Serbian elements in NDH territory, for organization of death camps Jasenovac, Stara Gradiska and other camps in which were killed several hundreds of thousands of Yug. Citizens, for liquidation the all soldiers YNOA (Yugoslav National Liberated Army) who come in their hands, and to the remaining military units for continuation of battle after the Germany's capitulation.[43]

Even with this information, the request did not scratch the surface regarding Pavelić's crimes.

At least publicly, the American Army remained determined to arrest all Croatian quislings and war criminals. A 16 November 1945 order from British Lieutenant General Fredrick Morgan, the Deputy Chief of Staff Supreme Headquarters Allied Expeditionary Force, stated that, 'Ustasi and leaders and officials of the former Serb and Croat Quisling regimes should be arrested. This headquarters will be informed of their arrest and arrangements will be made for them to be sent to a PW or internment camp.'[44] At this early date, relations between the United States and Yugoslavia, though strained, were not yet soured to the point where the search for war criminals and quislings was compromised.

Yugoslav–American tensions

Following his May 1945 escape from Croatia, Pavelić benefited from the tense and suspicion-laden relationship between Yugoslavia and the United States. Several events so deepened the animosity between Washington and Belgrade that neither the army nor the State Department had significant desire to pursue suspected war criminals demanded by Yugoslavia. Relations with Tito, sour even before the war had ended, grew worse after the war as Tito actively pursued his communist programme.[45] Washington officials believed that as long as Tito led Yugoslavia it would be held firmly in the Soviet sphere. Chief among Tito's goals was the nationalization of industry, which was scheduled for completion in late 1946. Although there were only a few American firms involved, Washington was angry at this turn of events. Ambassador Richard C. Patterson, a businessman, was adamantly opposed to Tito's nationalization policy. A native of Omaha, Nebraska and an executive with RKO, Patterson was a poor choice as Ambassador to Tito's government. He had been assigned in November 1944 by President Roosevelt as ambassador to the Yugoslav government in exile. This London-based government despised Tito and the communists, having thrown their support behind Draža Mihailović in the hope of restoring the monarchy to Yugoslavia at the war's end. When Tito's government was recognized, Patterson, who opposed recognition, moved to Yugoslavia. A better selection for the ambassadorship would have been George Kennan, who some believe was the second choice for the position. In Belgrade and in the United States, Patterson remained a vocal critic of the Tito government. His links to the royalist regime damaged his already limited ability to deal with the Yugoslav government. His vehemently anti-communist views were a constant impediment to bettering Yugoslav–American relations.[46]

Patterson knew that the State Department had leverage in New York City that they planned to use against Tito's nationalization policy. The United States held $46.8 million in Yugoslav gold reserves that had been transferred in 1941 to New York from the Yugoslav National Bank to prevent German capture. Tito's government made repeated demands for the gold reserves, but Washington refused to relinquish them. Post-war Yugoslavia was in desperate need of the gold, since the country's economy was in ruins. The gold was a bargaining chip that Washington hoped to use to force Belgrade into easing its nationalization policy and resisting Soviet influence.[47]

Tito's active support of the Greek communists in their civil war further hardened relations with the United States. Tito's assistance was all the more conspicuous because the Soviet Union, irritated by Tito's aggressive actions, kept out of Greece, refusing to send weapons or money. As the United States became drawn into this imbroglio, especially after Britain chose to end its involvement, Washington grew to resent Tito more than ever.

Frustrated by American and British intransigence and fully aware that the United States was not following through with its wartime pledges to turn over war criminals and quislings, Belgrade petitioned the United Nations for relief. This turn of events was embarrassing to the Americans and further heightened tensions. On 20 August 1947, the Belgrade government asked the United Nations to include the following on its agenda: 'Recommendations to be made to ensure the surrender of war criminals, traitors and quislings of the States where their crimes were committed.'[48] This agenda item was discussed in the Legal Committee meeting where the Yugoslav representative emphasized that in February 1946 the United Nations passed legislation urging its members to 'take all necessary measures for the arrest and surrender of war criminals....'.[49] The Yugoslavs argued that this resolution, the Moscow Declaration, and the Agreement of the Council of Foreign Ministers were being violated. The latter was a pledge to extradite war criminals from displaced person camps to the country where their crimes were committed. The Yugoslav government proposed a new resolution that recommended immediate action on behalf of member states.

Naturally, the Soviet endorsement of the Yugoslav resolution, combined with a stinging indictment of the inadequate screening procedures in displaced persons camps, produced a stout defence from the West. The State Department responded by drafting a comprehensive internal document that explained the history of the war criminal issue in general and as regards Yugoslavia and provided a series of recommendations for American strategy at the United Nations General Assembly meeting. As it had done on numerous occasions, the State Department emphasized the need for a *prima facie* case to be in place prior to the arrest of any war criminal or quisling.[50] It was also suggested that American officials go on the offensive, questioning the respect for human rights in Yugoslavia as spelled out in Article 55 of the United Nations Charter, and stating that the Yugoslav government had failed to provide legitimate evidence against many of the individuals requested for extradition.[51] It must be remembered that this document was constructed with an undercurrent of profound disagreement with Yugoslavia and its allies regarding war criminal issues and there was no mutually acceptable definition of quislings and traitors. As the

State Department explained, the war criminal, traitor and quisling question had been discussed:

> in the UNRRA, in the Allied Control Council in Berlin, and at the Council of Foreign Ministers in Moscow. The argument has always been heated; accusations made as to the harboring of war criminals, quislings, and traitors have been steadfastly and vigorously denied by the United States as by the United Kingdom.[52]

The Yugoslav issue, in particular the Pavelić case, was a source of profound animosity between Yugoslavia and the West, helping forge intense suspicion that only deepened the newly-emerging Cold War.

The United States and the United Kingdom doggedly denied all the charges made by the Yugoslavs and the Soviets. They reiterated the somewhat disingenuous argument that those extradited should have their guilt established *prima facie*, and said they would not relinquish political exiles. The United States was using the *prima facie* argument to cover, when it was necessary, its intention to combat communism by protecting those persons it found potentially useful, regardless of their wartime track record. Pavelić, Andrija Artuković and others against whom a *prima facie* case was made were not urgently pursued, as their crimes dictated they should be. Rightly, Yugoslavia insisted that by requiring a *prima facie* case, the United States and Britain were assuming the right to establish the guilt or innocence of alleged criminals and quislings, disallowing the country in which the atrocities were committed from acting as judge and jury.

Yugoslavia's appeal to the United Nations stirred Washington officials to assemble a vigorous defence of their policies. In a thorough and detailed document, the United States Mission to the United Nations justified American policy towards suspected Yugoslav war criminals and quislings, reiterated the need to make a *prima facie* case and also argued that the Yugoslav government had failed to provide detailed and thorough information on numerous figures requested for extradition. Yugoslavia was labelled as a country where human rights, guaranteed by the United Nations Charter, were ignored thus allowing for innocent figures to be charged and convicted of crimes without any establishment of guilt.[53] For example, Belgrade had convicted Konstantin Fotić, the pro-Serbian Yugoslav Ambassador to the United States, in absentia to ten years of forced labour. Although an enemy of Tito's government, Fotić was in no way a war criminal. Such decisions, rooted in settling old scores, damaged Yugoslavia's legitimate claim for the arrest and extradition of well-known Ustaše members like Pavelić.

Yugoslavia lost its bid to increase the pressure on the West after lengthy debates showed that it could not muster more than a handful of votes. Ultimately, the United Nations passed a resolution reaffirming its 13 February 1946 resolution. Drafted to support the American and British position, it called for countries requesting alleged criminals to support their claim 'with sufficient evidence to establish that a reasonable prima facie case exists as to identity and guilt. . .'.[54] With this resolution, number 170, Yugoslavia suffered a significant blow to its quest to extradite and try NDH officials as well as embarrass American policy makers. Particularly damaging was that the resolution allowed Washington and London to determine whether sufficient evidence was in place to extradite an individual. This stripped Yugoslavia of the right to determine the guilt or innocence of individuals it sought for war crimes. This tame resolution confirmed that some major criminals would never be returned to Yugoslavia. The alibi of political refugee had won the day.

In addition to these tensions, 1946 brought two major trials that did nothing to improve relations between Washington and Belgrade. On 13 March 1946, Aleksandar Ranković, Tito's head of security and long-time comrade, announced that Draža Mihailović, the Četnik commander and alleged collaborator, had been captured. Though this was a great success for Tito, the West, in an almost unanimous voice, came to Mihailović's defence. When news of the capture and impending trial became known, 'a veritable storm arose in the United States and a lesser one in Great Britain'.[55] Thousands of letters and telegrams supporting Mihailović, the majority from American veteran groups, bombarded the State Department. Petitions signed by thousands of Americans demanded that

Washington intervene to save Mihailović. No issue in Yugoslav history had attracted this type of attention and emotion from the American public. American officials argued that Mihailović had fought for the Allies against the Germans, an argument inherently weak considering that Washington and London had determined in 1944, largely from the reports and advice of Fitzroy MacLean, Churchill's hand-picked liaison to Tito's forces, that Mihailović was not actively resisting the Nazis. Evidence was produced that hundreds of American flyers shot down over Yugoslavia owed their lives to the Četniks. This was true, but it did not change the basic issue. Mihailović did not aggressively fight the Nazis, because he saw the war in Yugoslavia as a civil war between the communists and the royalists. His chief goal was to destroy the Partisans first, not the Nazis. Petitions were signed throughout the United States and an organization called the Committee for a Fair Trial for Draža Mihailović, which included significant American intellectuals and politicians, was formed to demand that Mihailović be tried before an international tribunal.[56] Belgrade was not about to allow an international trial for a man who allegedly collaborated with the Germans and fought battles against Partisan forces. Mihailović's trial ended in his conviction and subsequent execution on 17 July 1946.[57] The sentence only increased the strain on American–Yugoslav relations and forever tainted Belgrade in the eyes of many Americans.

On the heels of Mihailović's execution came the trial of the highly controversial Archbishop Alojzije Stepinac. During the war, Stepinac had served as the leading Catholic official in Pavelić's Croatia. His involvement with the NDH regime and failure to publicly renounce its practices made him an enemy to the new communist government. Tito's government could marshal strong evidence against Stepinac, a figure in some ways similar to Pope Pius XII, his superior. But Stepinac had numerous supporters, primarily in Italy and the United States, who believed that he had done his best to preserve Catholicism in a difficult situation. He was portrayed as a great defender of Christianity against the aggressive forces of atheism that masqueraded as communism.[58] When he was brought to trial in September 1946, Stepinac said little in his own defence, instead maintaining that his conscience was clear. Even with the notable defence efforts of his attorney, Ivo Politeo, the archbishop was convicted and sentenced to 16 years in prison.[59] Although the Stepinac trial was only part of a 16-person trial that included important Ustaše officials, his conviction put a serious strain on Yugoslav relations with the United States almost leading to a severing of diplomatic relations. Well into 1947, the State Department continued to receive letters from Catholics throughout the United States decrying the Stepinac verdict and demanding redress.

Another source of tension between the two countries was the downing of American planes by Yugoslav aircraft in 1946. Yugoslav fighters shot down two American C-47s, one on 9 August and the other on 19 August. In the second episode, five American fliers were killed. Both incidents drew significant media attention. Furthermore, Yugoslav authorities prevented American officials from visiting with the captured Americans. Secretary of State James 'Jimmy' Byrnes issued an ultimatum to Belgrade demanding satisfaction from the Yugoslavs or the United States would resort to alternative means of obtaining justice. The captured fliers were returned and restitution made to the families of the dead. The United States denied that the planes were in any way violating Yugoslav air space or doing anything untoward.[60] Despite this, Washington may not have been entirely truthful about these planes and their missions. John Cabot, the American chargé to Yugoslavia, revealed in an address delivered to the National War College in October 1947 that 'even with regard to the shooting down of the American planes I was told on good American authority that our men had made reconnaissance flights over Yugoslav territory and had even flown over it just to bait the Yugoslavs...'.[61]

With these and other vexing issues driving a deep wedge between Yugoslavia and the United States, the pursuit of war criminals and quislings became a political football. Tito and his government, distrusted and despised by the United States and viewed by some as conduits for world atheism, would be stymied in their pursuit of

Pavelić. Regardless of the magnitude of his crimes, the United States doggedly refused to commit itself to locating, arresting and extraditing Pavelić or many of his close associates. There was little Belgrade could do to change the scenario.

Neglect and obstruction

With a *prima facie* case established against the Poglavnik, rumours swirled about Pavelić's whereabouts. The pursuit increased as Yugoslav authorities made repeated demands for the Allies to find, arrest and extradite him to Yugoslavia. These demands were usually directed towards the British government; however, the Pavelić case became a sore spot in American–Yugoslav relations because the United States consistently answered Yugoslav requests for Pavelić by explaining that they had no idea where he was hiding. This was true in part, but the records show that Washington had no desire to look very hard or share information with Belgrade about Pavelić or others.

As we have seen, American officials were fully aware of atrocities that had been committed by the Pavelić regime; however, they showed little interest in tracking Pavelić or arresting him once the war had ended. There is no better proof of American disregard than a comment written on a G-2 report dealing with war criminals in Croatia. The memo, which originated in Madrid, cited numerous examples of atrocities perpetrated in Croatia by figures such as Eugen Kvaternik and Andrija Artuković. The following conclusions were given.

This file has been sent to the Mediterranean Theater of Operations... and has been administratively closed by the theater and returned by it (and is consolidated herein) on the ground that the facts are insufficient to warrant prosecution. And that case is not of primary interest to the US.[62]

The last sentence, handwritten on the document, indicates that the United States Army believed that crimes in Croatia were secondary and therefore there was little need to aggressively pursue Croatian criminals and quislings. It was becoming clear that Tito was entrenched in Yugoslavia, at least for the time being, and there was little the United States could do to change that reality. The United States' paramount interest was the arrest and prosecution of German war criminals, in part because American soldiers had died in battle against soldiers of the Third Reich not the Ustaše. American troops also had discovered Nazi horrors first hand when they liberated concentration camps. As American soldiers did not occupy Croatia and therefore did not see the evidence of Ustaše atrocities, there was a more cavalier attitude towards apprehending and prosecuting Croatians responsible for tens of thousands of deaths.

Washington officials maintained that they would relinquish Pavelić and other Croatian war criminals if they were found in American or British custody. In what became standard policy, Secretary of State Byrnes explained that the United States and British government had agreed to turn over quislings and war criminals against whom the Yugoslav government had made a *prima facie* case. These figures would be extradited to Belgrade as long as they were not needed in connection with trials of other major war criminals. Byrnes noted that a *prima facie* case had been made against Pavelić and that the Poglavnik 'may' be extradited to Belgrade when he was located in American or British territory.[63] This measured statement demonstrated the State Department's unwillingness to commit itself to a policy of full extradition when it came to a communist state like Yugoslavia. With pledges like the one above, Washington, as early as October 1945, displayed reticence to comply with the extradition of Pavelić and other Yugoslav criminals. Such would be the case throughout the post-war era.

American government officials were intentionally hesitant about all Yugoslav requests for extradition, especially in 1946 and 1947 when relations between the two countries became something much less than correct. Officials feared that the Yugoslav government was making extradition requests with the intention of executing or imprisoning political enemies, not trying legitimate criminals or quislings. For example, on 14 June 1945 Dr Sloven Smodlaka, the Active Representative of Yugoslavia on the Advisory Council for Italy (ACC-Italy), requested a list of prisoners being held in Italy under suspicion of war crimes. This request was made because a large number of Yugoslavs had fled to Italy at the close of the war. Smodlaka met with British Brigadier General M.S. Lush, vice-president ACC-Italy, who explained to him that it would be much quicker if the Yugoslav government presented the Allies with a list of war criminals. The general asked his superiors whether he should provide Smodlaka with any sort of list of war criminals.[64] The suggestion of such a list was met with disapproval from Henry Hopkinson, a deputy high commissioner at ACC-Italy, who noted that, 'this is all part of the Yugoslav internal war as played in Italy. The request amounts to a demand for statistics of dissident Yugoslavs. The next step will doubtless be asking for them to be handed over to Dr Smodlaka for repatriation.'[65] Hopkinson interpreted the request, with some justification, as little different from seeking a shopping list of war criminals. This was, however, a recognition of the complexity of the Yugoslav case. The Americans faced the serious problem of determining who was a political dissident and who was a war criminal, because the newly-installed Yugoslav government had its own agenda when dealing with former NDH officials. Hopkinson explained that 'our policy has hitherto been to refuse to hand over to the Yugoslavs, person who differ politically from the existing regime'.[66] He noted that the United States should not protect legitimate war criminals, but the Yugoslav government needed to provide the Allies with a list of war criminals.[67] Hopkinson believed that the communists would seek reprisals against any of their enemies whether they were legitimate war criminals or political exiles. The actions and image of Tito's communist government therefore discouraged American officials from arresting and extraditing legitimate quislings and criminals. American authorities were already dragging their feet with those who had impeccable anti-communist credentials.

This was the opening salvo of what would become a difficult problem for the Americans that clouded their judgement concerning legitimate quislings and criminals such as Pavelić. Although not wanting to be seen as harbouring legitimate war criminals or quislings, Washington officials were fearful that the Yugoslav government would move to prosecute all Yugoslavs of an anti-communist bent. This situation became more complex as Allied authorities began returning political power to the Italian government, because Italy was a haven for Yugoslav war criminals and quislings on the run. The Truman Administration was very concerned about the chances of Italy turning communist and went to great lengths to prevent such an occurrence. The Vatican, in cooperation with the United States, tarnished all communists as enemies of Christianity, thus the Americans had little desire to bother the Vatican about a few Croatian war criminals. Belgrade, as time passed, therefore grew frustrated as it was told to deal directly with the Italian government in all cases of war criminal extradition within Italy. This was America's standard response to Yugoslav requests by the middle of 1946. But Yugoslavia had not re-established formal relations with Italy, and Italian authorities showed no interest in tracking and arresting Croatian war criminals.

As of March 1946, Rome was given full control over population movements in and out of the country. But Italy possessed virtually no immigration controls and had no system for registering refugees or aliens within its borders.[68] With such lax immigration standards, Italy had become a convenient sanctuary for war criminals on the lam. To the United States military as well as the State Department, this was not much of a concern. They had abrogated their responsibility and wartime pledges to apprehend and extradite proven war criminals and quislings and were primarily interested in restoring Italy to the family of Western nations to prevent a communist revolution.

The lack of assistance with extradition wore on the Yugoslavs, who interpreted this slothful movement as an attack upon the Tito government. On 23 July 1946, Smodlaka, always voicing his concerns about war criminals, visited Rear Admiral Ellery W. Stone, chief commissioner for the Allied Commission in Rome. He told Stone that 'in Italy there are many Jugoslav traitors whose extradition has been agreed by the Governments of the United States and the United Kingdom [...]. The extradition of Jugoslav traitors is proceeding very slowly.'[69] Smodlaka requested a meeting at Allied

Forces Headquarters (AFHQ) to discuss extradition policies. One month later, Colonel A.L. Hamblen, the assistant chief of staff at G-5, responded saying that 'since the restoration of Administration of Italy to the Italian Government the power of arrest in Italy lies with the Italian Government and that requests for arrest should therefore be made to that Government'.[70] The only exception to this policy was if the alleged criminal was in Allied custody. Smodlaka never got his audience with AFHQ and his concerns were ignored. The Italian government, which had little to no zeal for extraditing war criminals, especially those with strong anti-communist credentials, was a convenient answer for the Americans.

Even prior to Smodlaka's protests, the Foreign Office in London had voiced concerns about America's unwillingness to pursue Yugoslav war criminals. London believed that 'US authorities in Italy are not anxious to cooperate with the British military authorities in taking the measures necessary to arrest and hand over to the Yugoslav Government those traitors and collaborators whom it has been agreed to surrender to them...'.[71] The Foreign Office disagreed with American trepidation about the Yugoslav legal system, rightly contending that these criminals were so heinous that they deserved no protection under American or British law. In a minute attached to a Foreign Office document discussing American policy, British frustration was evident. 'We have made very slow progress in carrying out this obligation [to arrest criminals against whom a prima facie case had been made] partly owing to a certain amount of passive resistance by the United States military authorities in Italy.'[72] Unfortunately, the document does not name names. The Foreign Office's frustration on this issue, however, was evident throughout 1946 and 1947. In their opinion, the United States, for a variety of reasons, was uninterested in tracking down Yugoslavs, no matter how guilty of war crimes they may have been.

Smodlaka, seemingly never discouraged, continued making demands of the Americans, who became irritated with his perseverance. Pavelić was the most sought after of all Yugoslav war criminals, yet the Americans were doing little to apprehend him. Some of the problems were bureaucratic. For example, the Allied

Commission in Italy could not determine who was responsible for acting as the liaison between the Yugoslav government and the Italian government, especially on the issue of war criminals. On 3 September 1946, Brigadier General M. Carr restated the official policy regarding this issue which had been established on 22 August. He explained that Dr Smodlaka, as Yugoslav representative in Italy, had the right 'to approach the Allied Commission and to ask them to request the Italian Government to arrest Jugoslav Traitors, approved as such by the Allied Governments after AFHQ have notified this Headquarters that such Traitors are not in Allied custody'.[73] On the surface, the policy appeared set, but a lengthy debate proceeded about proper channels for Yugoslav requests. After much discussion, a new official policy was conveyed to Smodlaka which stated that 'the Jugoslav Ambassador in London was, on the 26 July 1946, informed that the Foreign Office did not consider matters affecting the surrender of Traitors and Quislings to be within your competence as a member of the Advisory Council for Italy'.[74] Not everyone was united on this policy. Some argued that diplomatic channels were necessary as they would encourage the reestablishment of relations between Yugoslavia and Italy. The Allied Commission, however, was established as the liaison through which foreign governments would handle affairs in Italy.[75] Belgrade interpreted this as, at the least, yet another attempt by the Allies to impede the arrest and extradition of war criminals hiding in Italy and, at the most, believed that the Allies were using the war criminal issue to harm Tito's government. These interpretations were on the mark.

Smodlaka did not let this issue die, and he continued to make requests through the Allied Commission for the arrest and extradition of war criminals. In a powerful letter dated 15 January 1947, addressed to Lieutenant General John Clifford Hodges Lee, the supreme Allied commander of the Mediterranean Theatre, Smodlaka described the weak attempts by the Allies to pursue Yugoslav war criminals. This letter may have been part of the impetus necessary to force the Americans to actively pursue Pavelić. Smodlaka reiterated that the Allied military authorities were pledged to 'take care of arresting and handing over to the Jugoslav authorities of Jugoslav traitors, collaborationists and war criminals living in Italy'.[76] Although the Allies had returned governmental authority to Italy, Smodlaka insisted that 'the Supreme Allied Commander is obliged by the Armistice terms to take necessary steps upon the Italian Government' to find, arrest and extradite war criminals.[77] The Yugoslav Commissioner was referring, in particular, to a clause in the peace treaty with Italy that provided that any questions about Italian war criminal apprehension powers would be submitted to the Allied ambassadors in Rome. With that said, he proceeded to relate the details concerning the escape to South America of Yugoslav war criminals in Italy aboard the SS *Andrea Gritti* which boarded passengers in Genoa and Naples on 29 and 31 December 1946, respectively. Smodlaka maintained that more than 100 Yugoslavs, 'many Jugoslav traitors and well known war criminals whose extradition was repeatedly requested by the jugoslav government', were on the ship.[78] Smodlaka accused the Vatican's Assistenza Pontifica (Pontifical Assistance), a relief and charitable operation, of providing these war criminals with visas. Actually, Pontifical Assistance, as it was more widely known, probably went far beyond simply issuing visas and helped finance the escape of Croatians suspected of war crimes. The Intergovernmental Committee on Refugees was blamed for purchasing tickets and reserving space on the ship for these figures. Smodlaka listed a number of individuals wanted for war crimes, including former Ustaše ministers, who were allowed to board the ship. Vjekoslav Vrančić, Stjepan Hefer and Ante Nikšić were some of the most notable figures Smodlaka named as being allowed to set sail for a new life in Argentina. In summary, he charged that:

> The case of the S/S 'Andrea Gritti' shows that the responsible Allied and Italian authorities do not sufficiently controle [sic] the departure of ships from Italy and that they do not take care to impede leaving Italy of Jugoslav traitors who should be arrested and handed over to the Jugoslav authorities. It is clear from this case that, further, the 'intergovernmental Committee on Refugees' and the 'Assistenza Pontifica' use money and

procure visas in order to enable Jugoslav Traitors, collaborationists and war criminals, who should be arrested and handed over to the Jugoslav authorities, to leave Italy and to go to the overseas countries, where their being found out and extradition will be even more difficult.[79]

Smodlaka even gave locations frequented by key war criminals: the Fraternity of St Hyerolimus (San Girolamo) and the Yugoslav Welfare Society. He requested that both of these organizations be prohibited from issuing any identity papers or documents.[80] Smodlaka's frustration and anger with Allied policy was evident throughout this sharply worded missive.

The letter made waves in the State Department. Homer Byington, United States deputy political adviser at Allied Force Headquarters, informed Secretary of State George C. Marshall that Smodlaka's letter was a 'lengthy and vehement complaint'.[81] His telegram to Marshall explained that the Italian authorities handled war criminal issues in Italy; however, he questioned whether this policy included quislings. If quislings were not included under Italian jurisdiction, then the door to American involvement would be widened. Overall the telegram was optimistic, noting that more screening teams would be arriving in Italy thus reducing the number of war criminals escaping from displaced persons camps. Screening teams, however, were not useful when there were hundreds of people like Pavelić not detained in any camp, on the loose in Italy. Byington forwarded a copy of Smodlaka's letter to the Italian government without any comment.[82]

Marshall replied to Byington with a direct and clear telegram. He wrote that 'AFHQ providing ITAL GOVT list YUGO quislings whose delivery to YUGOS agreed'.[83] This was an empty reassurance, because there was no chance that the Italians would search vigorously for Yugoslav quislings like Pavelić and his ministers. Continuing, Marshall explained that 'quislings should be handled similarly to war criminals in so far as consideration of requests is concerned'.[84] He said nothing about Smodlaka's allegation regarding war criminals escaping to South America and expressed no surprise that this type of escape was taking place. Responding to Byington, George

C. Marshall curtly maintained the policy that Yugoslavia should negotiate with Italy when dealing with wanted war criminals outside of territory under United States military governance.[85] Belgrade had no recourse other than to make requests through the Italian government for the pursuit and arrest of Pavelić. This policy had no hope of success, because Pavelić was being protected by Catholic contacts who reached the highest levels of the Vatican. Italian officials were little interested in confronting the Papacy with allegations of harbouring fugitives, especially when the United States, in cooperation with the Vatican, was doing its utmost to prevent communist victory in Italy.

The CIC investigation

Pavelić fled Austria for Italy in, perhaps, April 1946. His movements in this period were difficult to trace in the post-war period and remain so today. Most rumours surrounding Pavelić's journey allege that he made the trip disguised as a priest, probably under the name Gomez. In his 1948 war crimes trial, Ljubo Miloš, an officer at the infamous Jasenovac and other camps, stated in court that he travelled with Pavelić from Austria to Italy in October 1946 using false documents obtained by Father Krunoslav Draganović.[86] It is possible and likely that Pavelić crossed the border on a few occasions, especially since Miloš was able to accomplish that feat without much difficulty. Perhaps most interesting about this is that there is the potential that British officials helped Pavelić cross the border into Italy. The Austro-Italian border, though manned by Italian soldiers, could be breached if someone was being transported by Allied troops. If British soldiers escorted Pavelić to the border, Italian authorities would not have dreamed of stopping or questioning them.[87]

Pavelić made a successful escape across the Alps into Italy, where he had numerous allies from the 1930s and the war years. There was no doubt that he would find safe quarter among Ustaše sympathizers in an often-times chaotic Italy. His first stop was Florence, but he soon journeyed to Rome where there was safety provided by Catholic allies who enjoyed extra-territoriality. CIC files include an Italian document from 10 May 1946 that demonstrates how well-connected Pavelić was. The document states that Pavelić was in hiding with his secretary in a stable within Vatican City jurisdiction. The last paragraph notes that Pavelić 'maintains frequent meetings with Monsignor Montini, Secretary of State of the Holy See'.[88] If this document, probably from an Italian informant, is to be believed, Montini, the future Pope Paul VI, was holding meetings with a man responsible for the deaths of tens of thousands. There is evidence that suggests Pavelić's contacts were with some of the highest Catholic officials in Rome. Certainly, Church officials were instrumental in keeping him free from arrest and extradition to Yugoslavia and certain death. Without full access to Vatican documents, we may never know the details of these alleged meetings or the validity of many accusations. As we shall see, there is plenty of circumstantial evidence as well as a good deal of solid evidence to support the contention that Montini and others in the Vatican often met with and even actively worked to protect the Poglavnik.

According to American documents, Pavelić travelled to Rome with a member of his bodyguard, Lt Dragutin Došen. 'Both were dressed as Roman Catholic priests. They took refuge in a college there in Via Giacomo Belli, 3, [The college at this address is Collegio Pio Pontificio in Prati] which is the only college in ROME enjoying complete extra-territoriality. . .'.[89] Došen's participation in Pavelić's escape lends credence to allegations that Britain was responsible for protecting Pavelić. American military authorities believed that Došen, a notorious Ustaše accused of killing Serbs with his own hands, was a British operative who assisted Pavelić in his escape from Yugoslavia to Austria and Austria to Italy.[90] CIC Special Agent Robert Clayton Mudd learned from his informant that Pavelić had obtained a passport from the Spanish Consulate in Milan under the name of Don Pedro Gonner, and, in addition, he held a visa for either South America or perhaps Canada, although that was unlikely. In all likelihood, Pavelić had used this passport to travel unhindered from Austria into Italy. Mudd identified a trend involving Croatian war criminals in Italy. His informant had penetrated Ustaše operatives in

Italy and Yugoslavia and learned that a pipeline, Grumo–Rome–Venice–Trieste–Ljubljana–Zagreb, operated to move Croatian war criminals to safety.[91] Furthermore, he concluded that the entire operation was 'run under the cover of the Roman Catholic clergy whose priests in these monasteries are nearly all of Croat extraction'.[92] Mudd correctly judged that the centre of this operation was the College of San Girolamo degli Illirici located at Via Tomacelli, 132 in Rome.[93] This Croatian college close to the Vatican had been part of Ustaše operations before, during and after World War II. The church on this site was built in 1587, by South Slavs who fled Turkish attacks.

Even with the protection that his friends in Rome offered, Pavelić well understood that he was being hunted by Yugoslav and Soviet intelligence. A CIC memo confirmed that 'Pavelić is being frantically sought by the [OZNA] and elements of the Soviet GHEPEU'.[94] Both intelligence services were 'offering large sums' for information about Pavelić or his whereabouts. Although unable to find or arrest Pavelić, OZNA was particularly zealous in its pursuit of Pavelić and had contacts deep within the Ustaše. Seemingly all Ustaše actions in Yugoslavia in the late 1940s were quickly defeated and those who were involved arrested or killed. This was true as early as May 1945. The most celebrated example of Belgrade's knowledge of Ustaše activity involved Erik Lisak, a key leader in the Krizari (Crusaders) movement, who was placed on trial in 1946. At least in part under Pavelić's direction, the Krizari were Ustaše followers who waged a failed guerrilla campaign, with at least some American and British support, against Tito's government in the years immediately following the war. Under pressure from Soviet and Yugoslav intelligence, Pavelić returned to Austria in the summer of 1946. He spent time in the Carinzia region of Austria, which was part of the American zone of occupation. The Poglavnik was back in Rome by November 1946, again under the protection of Catholic clergy.[95]

In January 1947, Special Agents William Gowen and Lewis Caniglia, both of the United States Army's 428th CIC, and other agents began an in-depth investigation of the Pavelić case to determine his whereabouts. Orders to begin an investigation were sent to Lt Colonel Gono Morena from G-2 at Mediterranean Theater of Operations, United States Army.[96] Why this investigation was ordered is open to question. As we have seen, the Pavelić case was a growing source of friction between the Americans and the Yugoslavs. If the CIC located Pavelić, the United States would have two options. They could hand him over to Belgrade in the hope that relations between the two states would be improved by the gesture; however, perhaps Pavelić was more valuable free, albeit under American surveillance. If at all possible, Washington wanted to weaken Tito's government, incorrectly viewed by the State Department as Stalin's closest ally. The State Department may have seen Pavelić as a tool to destabilize Yugoslavia, because American authorities were well aware of the Krizari and the devotion that many Croatians had for Croatian independence. By allowing Pavelić to remain free, but under careful watch, the United States could utilize Pavelić in much the way that Mussolini had done, keeping him in the wings until he was needed. In doing so, however, the United States would be in violation of a wide range of promises to pursue and arrest quislings and war criminals.

Regardless of the reason, Gowen, armed with a great deal of background information, began the search for Ante Pavelić. According to Gowen, the Pavelić file had considerable information on the Poglavnik and his whereabouts, much of it having been assembled by British sources.[97] On 22 January 1947, Gowen reported that his contacts believed that Pavelić was in a secure compound at Lungo Tevere Aventino in Rome. The compound held five Catholic organizations within its walls: the Monastery of St Sabina of the Dominican Order, the St Alessio School for Roman Studies, the Cavaliers of the Sovereign Military Order of Malta, the Benedictine Monastery of St Anselmo and a school run by nuns. The area was reputed to be full of underground tunnels, which made it perfect for hiding. Although it was presumed to be his hideout, Pavelić had not been sighted there. Nonetheless, the fortress-like St Sabina was, according to Gowen, the most logical location for the Poglavnik, in part because it was on the Tiber and difficult to enter. One of the key elements in this early part of the investigation was that a tram line ran beneath the Aventine Hill. Gowen wrote that the tram line 'to the Circus Maximus, the Coloseum and Via Cavour is the connecting link between Pavelić and Via Cavour, 210 int. 3, which is an Ustascia base well known in Rome'.[98] He explained that the Ustaše allegedly held a meeting at a house on Via Cavour every Friday night around 9:00 pm. Gowen concluded that:

> While the informants in this case are considered reliable it is difficult to evaluate their reliability in relation to Pavelić who has been dodging around Europe as his own master for about 15 years. All the information seems plausible and paints a plausible picture when it is taken as a whole. However, it would seem that only direct action against the Via Cavour house, illegal entry into extra-territorial territory or action against such known Pavelić contacts as DRAGANOVIĆ, Krunoslav can ultimately reveal the hiding place of Pavelić and lead to his apprehension.[99]

Gowen continued his investigation of Pavelić.

Eight days later, CIC Special Agent Robert Clayton Mudd re-emphasized the need to find Pavelić and arrest him. Mudd, stationed in Naples and anxious to travel, was strongly anti-Croatian and regularly monitored the activities around San Girolamo. Noting that Pavelić was at the top of the list of quislings wanted by the Yugoslavs, Mudd declared that he was, 'expending every effort to try to trace PAVELIĆ AND HIS WIFE'.[100] Mudd recommended that the government do everything possible to find and arrest the Poglavnik. Explaining that Pavelić was a war criminal and a political criminal, he urged that:

> Every effort should be made to apprehend him and ship him back to the Jugoslav Government for trial. In so doing not only would the Yugoslav propaganda guns be silenced and the people of Jugoslavia forced to admit that their previous propaganda was all false, but also a serious threat to security would be removed and the position of the Anglo-Americans

strengthened with regard to those south Slav elements who were pro-Allied before the war.[101]

Mudd's policy recommendation was well-reasoned and should have been adopted. The arrest and extradition of Pavelić to Yugoslavia might have improved American–Yugoslav relations, although the Yugoslav regime probably would have proclaimed that the United States had been forced to arrest him because of pressure from Belgrade. Unfortunately, the United States had no intention of handing over Pavelić to the Yugoslavs. According to Gowen, in an interview given to the author, the United States would not have arrested or extradited Pavelić even if they had known his precise whereabouts.

Rumours about Ustaše activities in and around San Girolamo were widespread in the intelligence community. Mudd's report naming San Girolamo as the centre of Ustaše operations in Italy only further confirmed what was commonly known.[102] In his investigation, Mudd determined that San Girolamo was part of a line of Ustaše support that started with the Vatican and extended to San Girolamo and even Fermo, a holding camp for questionable Croatians.[103] Mudd's information was extensive and accurate, in part because he had placed, for a short while, an agent within San Girolamo's walls. This agent reported that:

> in order to enter this Monastery one must submit to a personal search for weapons and identification documents, must answer questions as to where he is from, who he is, whom he knows, what his purpose is in the visit, and how he heard about the fact that there were Croats in the Monastery. All doors from one room to another are locked and those that are not have an armed guard in front of them and a pass-word is necessary to go from one room to another. The whole area is guarded by armed Ustashi youths in civilian clothes and the Ustashi salute is exchanged continually.[104]

Mudd determined that San Girolamo and other Vatican properties were havens for the most notorious of Ustašes and listed ten well-known Ustaše who were either living within the monastery or visiting it. These included figures such as Vjekoslav Vrančić, deputy minister of foreign affairs, Dr Dragutin Toth, minister of the Croat State Treasury, and several military officers.[105] Due to the tight security and that a Vatican car with diplomatic immunity was used to transport Ustaše to San Girolamo, there was little chance that American authorities would arrest these important Ustaše officials.[106]

Meanwhile, while investigating Pavelić, Gowen obtained a copy of San Girolamo's registration file which provided the names of regular visitors and those who had a meal card or ate there. Gowen made three copies of the registration files, sending one to Mudd, one to James Angleton and one to Lt Colonel Morena. Mudd was thrilled with the list as he identified 18 Ustaše who were wanted for war crimes.[107] Unfortunately, none of these lists has survived and today San Girolamo refuses to provide access to any lists of visitors.

Criticism of American policy

Pavelić's ability to remain free surprised news outlets like *The Economist*. In a 1 February 1947 article, the editorial staff was amazed that a Nazi ally of Pavelić's magnitude was not only free but had seemingly 'disappeared'. Reporting, somewhat naively, what was becoming painfully obvious, the editorial declared that 'the Jugoslav Government believes that the British and Americans are protecting him. This is doubtless untrue, but if formal and urgent orders were given from the highest quarter to all Allied security services, it would surely be possible to find him.'[108] The editorial staff was correct in believing that Pavelić could be arrested and that his continued ability to escape apprehension was a significant stumbling block in relations with Yugoslavia, but it did not appreciate the Cold War environment that convinced British and American authorities to monitor but not arrest Pavelić.[109]

As the investigation into Pavelić's whereabouts gained momentum, Belgrade put more pressure on the State Department. On 25 February 1947 General Vladimir Velebit explained to the

American Chargé d'Affaires John M. Cabot, a long-time foreign service hand mostly experienced with Latin American affairs, that the war criminal situation needed to be addressed if relations between the two countries were to improve. Velebit, a Croatian, was a tough negotiator and had served valiantly with the Partisans since 1941. Tito trusted him implicitly. According to Cabot, Velebit 'said that the Western Allies had turned over to Norway all their Quislings, to Belgium their Degrelles, and to the other western countries all their traitors', yet they had not extradited the thousands of traitors to Yugoslavia.[110] After enduring a one-and-a-half hour speech, Cabot collected his thoughts and calmly responded that there was no doubt about the criminality of Ustaše leaders, a point on which his superiors did not fully agree, and of Serbian Milan Nedić's followers.[111] He noted, however, that the United States differed with Yugoslavia on its view of the Četniks. The State Department argued that the Četniks were political opponents rather than traitors or collaborators, except in cases where collaboration could be proved.[112] It is clear from Cabot's papers that Velebit's comments and the constant Yugoslav demands affected the newly-appointed official. Although inexperienced in the complexities of the Yugoslav situation, Cabot was a career diplomat and a man of much skill. Having graduated Harvard in 1923, Cabot had spent most of his career in Latin America before his arrival in Belgrade. Although fascinated by Balkan intrigues, he was shocked by the police state he encountered in post-war Yugoslavia. In his memoirs he remarked that 'Belgrade was depressing from the beginning. There was that constant feeling of being watched, of being closed in.'[113] The Boston native held the view that the United States had a moral obligation to negotiate in favour of its interests but in a fair and open fashion. He had replaced the ineffective and damaging Ambassador Richard Patterson, who had returned to the United States and resigned his post on 25 October 1946. Having served as ambassador to the Yugoslav government in exile, Patterson had difficulty understanding and negotiating with Tito's government. By most accounts, Patterson's tenure was a disaster for Yugoslav–American relations.[114]

Never one to mince words, Cabot, temporarily in command of the American delegation in Belgrade and determined to improve the relationship with Yugoslavia, told his superiors that the war criminal issue was extremely sensitive to the Belgrade government and a source of unnecessary tension between the two countries. With support from British Ambassador Charles Peake, Cabot urged the State Department to take 'energetic steps to see that any legitimate Yugo grievances in this matter are satisfied'.[115]

Velebit's sometimes sharp comments convinced Cabot that the quisling and war criminal issue was a legitimate grievance. He confided in his diary, 'I intend to do something about war criminals – they (the Yugoslavs) are right there'.[116] But 'doing something' about this problem was more difficult than it sounded. Cabot met with Bishop Joseph Patrick Hurley later in the evening of 25 February and 'sounded him out about war criminals'.[117] Since Hurley, an American, was the Papal representative in Yugoslavia, he was privy to much of the information regarding Catholics, guilty or innocent, trying to flee from Tito's government. The bishop had enjoyed a good relationship with Ambassador Patterson in part because both men were fervently anti-communist. In a revealing comment, Hurley told Cabot that 'it would be terrible to turn anyone over to this country. We protect our own, no matter how guilty.'[118] This stunning admission illustrates the strong position enjoyed by Pavelić and other Ustaše in hiding. If they could count on protection from the Papal representative to Yugoslavia regardless of the wartime atrocities they may have committed, Pavelić and the Ustaše could find a great deal of security and help in Rome.

Ignoring Hurley's comments, Cabot repeated some of his concerns the following day, urging the State Department to satisfy legitimate Yugoslav grievances regarding war criminals and traitors.[119] The State Department was not interested in addressing Cabot's or Velebit's concerns. Instead, it wanted to redirect the Croatian war criminal issue as they had other interests that were more important than Ante Pavelić and his cohorts.

On 11 March 1947, the State Department finally responded to Cabot's request for guidance on the war criminal issue. Dean

Acheson, the acting secretary of state, wrote that the United States and Great Britain had agreed to a policy regarding the arrest and extradition of war criminals to Belgrade. Section one of the agreement stated that 'US and UK Govts wish express to Yugo Govt their sincere determination to hand over those persons who can be found in camps in Italy under Allied control who are quislings requested by Yugos and proved members of Ustashi to whose surrender both Govts agree'.[120] This new policy, however, focused on those quislings and criminals who were being held in internment camps and not those who remained in hiding. The document reiterated that the American and British governments had no further responsibility for the arrest or extradition of Yugoslav quislings 'at large in Italy', but pledged to assist the Italian government in this endeavour.[121] In no way was Acheson offering a kernel of credence to Yugoslav complaints. Acheson even suggested that the Yugoslav government offer amnesty to all Yugoslav refugees not wanted for war crimes.[122] In a series of cables that culminated in a 28 March missive, the American Embassy in Belgrade was told that American authorities would not hand over all Ustaše to the Yugoslav government, a practice that, if carried out, would deem all of them quislings and war criminals.[123] Instead, the new policy was to tell screening teams to 'consider Ustashi on same basis as others, i.e. each case will be judged individually and on its merits'.[124] Therefore, being an Ustaše in an internment camp did not warrant extradition to Yugoslavia. In addition, the United States and Great Britain agreed that they no longer had any responsibility to arrest or extradite Yugoslav quislings who were in hiding in Italy. Now the Italian government possessed the right to arrest such figures, and London and Washington were willing to help the Italians apprehend those who had a *prima facie* case made against them.[125] This was a rather remarkable renouncement of responsibility and certainly a policy that would create more ill-will between Americans and Yugoslavs. This new policy, favoured more by the Americans than the British, was contrary to the wartime Moscow Agreement, which provided for the arrest and extradition of war criminals, and a United Nations resolution recently signed by both the United States and

Britain. The United Nations Resolution of 13 February 1946 stated that member states needed to arrest and extradite war criminals to the countries where they had committed their crimes.[126] The fact that Washington's new policy offered the Ustaše the same consideration as legitimate political exiles was appalling. These were murderous thugs by the estimation of all of the Allies. Pavelić and his followers were not simply political enemies of Yugoslavia; they were criminals who had committed dreadful acts against the Yugoslav people. This *volte-face* shows the lengths to which the United States would go to oppose Tito and communism, including ignoring mass murder.

On 9 April 1947, Cabot issued a memo to the Yugoslav government carefully detailing America's policy towards war criminals and quislings. After emphasizing American devotion to arresting and extraditing war criminals, the document proceeded to renounce any responsibility to do so. The Italian government with American and British assistance would now have all of the responsibility for the pursuit, arrest and extradition of war criminals and quislings.[127] Again, only those who had been judged to have a *prima facie* case against them would even be considered for arrest. This last statement was sure to anger Yugoslav authorities, who argued that only Yugoslavia had a right to judge those against whom a war crimes indictment had been made.

Belgrade responded to Cabot's document with a stinging attack on American policy towards quislings and war criminals. In a 13-page rebuttal, the Yugoslav government explained that the United States had essentially ignored Yugoslavia's numerous demands for the arrest and extradition of those Belgrade had deemed to be quislings and criminals.[128] Belgrade insisted that only Yugoslavia's judicial system had the right to decide the guilt or innocence of war criminals and quislings, insisting that the United States and Britain had no such authority.[129] Perhaps most galling to the Yugoslav government was the American and British renouncement of any obligation to locate and arrest quislings hiding in Italy. Belgrade was adamant that the Italian authorities not be responsible for locating and arresting quislings.[130] Indeed, Belgrade demanded that all quislings be extradited to Yugoslavia prior to the British and American withdrawal from Italy.[131] It must be remembered that Yugoslavia had no affection for or faith in Italy because Rome had occupied most of Dalmatia during the war; there were numerous Italian officials wanted by Yugoslavia for war crimes and the Trieste question was far from resolved.

Later in the month, Cabot wrote that Yugoslav officials had made repeated requests for the extradition of quislings, arguing that Yugoslavia was the only country with the right to determine the guilt or innocence of alleged collaborators. This was a thinly veiled assault on the American opinion that many Ustaše were little more than political exiles. Irritated by Anglo-American delays in working with the Italian authorities for the arrest of such figures, Yugoslav officials again emphasized that 'responsibility for such apprehension rests with Allied military authorities who should complete arrests prior to withdrawal from Italy'.[132] They knew that the Italian government would make little or no effort to find and arrest quislings. Yugoslav demands were justified, even though they were often worded in a rather sharp fashion that worked against their interests.

In early 1947, the Yugoslav press, in particular *Borba*, pursued an active campaign designed to demonize American and British policies regarding the return of war criminals and quislings, emphasizing that if the Allies wished they could arrest numerous Ustaše and extradite them to Belgrade.[133] Cabot informed the State Department that the Yugoslav, 'press continues to use [Pavelić] as a glaring example of Anglo-American failure to cooperate in the release of war criminals to Yugoslavia'.[134] Cabot suggested that the State Department take a close look at its war criminal policies to make sure that the charges levelled by the Yugoslav media could be shown to have no merit.[135] He understood, however, that if the United States agreed to return numerous war criminals requested by Belgrade then Belgrade would use this cooperation 'as evidence that we have yielded to their pressure and publicity'.[136]

Belgrade's demands produced no results in Washington. By early May, Secretary of State George C. Marshall enunciated his version of Allied policy, explaining that the Supreme Allied Command no longer had 'responsibility for apprehension and handover Yugoslav quislings [...] except those now in Allied DP and PW/SEP Camps or otherwise in military custody'.[137] Italian authorities now had the responsibility to deal with quislings and criminals at large. American Ambassador James Dunn in Rome supported Marshall's policy, explaining that in his view American military staffing in Italy was too limited to consider searching for quislings and war criminals a realistic option. Nevertheless, he admitted that the British had worked with the Italian police to arrest war criminals and quislings at large who were residing in Italy.[138] The British achievement had been performed with staffing far below American standards.

Cabot's accurate portrayal of America's policy toward quislings isolated him from the State Department. He realized that American strategy was designed not to arrest quislings but to forestall Belgrade with a display of smoke and mirrors. Cabot was very critical of a forthcoming American position, announced on 29 May 1947, which stated that 'the United States Government opposed any use by [...] (the Supreme Allied Commander) of police powers to search for alleged quislings and traitors not currently in Allied custody'.[139] This change of policy, which would only deepen enmity between Yugoslavia and America while depriving the United States of the moral high ground, led Cabot to increase his criticism of American policy. Arguing that American efforts to satisfy Yugoslav demands were slothful, Cabot stressed that the 'Yugo govt is justified in feeling that we have not scrupulously respected our commitments and that it is therefore the more incumbent upon us to bestir ourselves now'.[140] If the State Department believed it was justified in not arresting quislings on the grounds of Yugoslavia's system of justice or dislike for Yugoslav policies, a frank admission to the Yugoslav government would be favourable but embarrassing. In this fiery critique of the American position he asserted, 'I do not see what justice or wisdom there could be in sheltering notorious quislings and war criminals from their just desserts'.[141] Noting that he only supported turning over those against whom a *prima facie* case had been made, he argued that 'it appears that we could easily arrest many whose guilt is perfectly plain. I respectfully submit that it is inexcusable after these many months to reiterate our commitments and yet not only take no effective action but also to obstruct others from taking it.'[142] These, combined with earlier comments, further removed him from regular State Department channels. Information about the pursuit of quislings and war criminals was not directed to Cabot, who had irritated Washington with his bold and sometimes irreverent cables. Instead, he was forced to rely on the British Embassy and the Yugoslav press to determine whether progress was being made. Cabot saw only one alternative. If the United States was not interested in arresting quislings and wished to give that duty to Italy, then Washington was obligated to make sure that the Italians energetically pursued it.[143] Of course, the chance that Italian authorities would do that was painfully slim. The British Foreign Office, for example, was not eager to alert Rome of potential Ustaše hiding places for fear that Italian officials would notify Pavelić and he would escape overseas.[144]

It appears that some of Cabot's fears regarding American intransigence in the face of a more aggressive British policy were well-founded. Peter Solly-Flood, the second secretary at the British Embassy in Washington and a veteran of the Special Operations Executive in Yugoslavia and Poland, fleshed out British policy towards Yugoslav quislings and war criminals, explaining that since 1945, Britain had maintained that it would deliver to the Yugoslavs all those against whom a *prima facie* case was made.[145] Later, the British agreed 'to hand over all proven active members of the Ustashi'.[146] The Yugoslav government had been informed repeatedly of these policies. Although not wishing to handover any individuals but the guilty, Britain was not particularly concerned with the fairness of the Yugoslav justice system. London 'considers that sympathy is wasted upon persons who whatever their motives gave their support to the regimes of Pavelić and Ljotic'.[147] The British ambassador in Belgrade, Charles Peake, citing examples, believed that there were no grounds to maintain that Yugoslav courts would unduly harass and persecute large numbers of refugees and war criminals if repatriated.[148] Continued delay in following through on obligations only deepened the Yugoslav suspicion, according to the

British ambassador in Belgrade, that the United States and Britain hoped to use war criminals and quislings abroad to destabilize the Yugoslav government.[149]

British concerns were acknowledged but not accepted by the Acting Chief of the Division of Southern European Affairs Walworth Barbour.[150] Barbour was not a novice when dealing with Yugoslav affairs, having served in Athens and Sofia prior to America's involvement in World War II. Perhaps coloured by his experiences as second secretary to the exiled Yugoslav government in Cairo, Barbour was far from sympathetic to the demands made by Tito's government. Noting that the United States had agreed with the British position of returning all against whom a *prima facie* case was made as well as 'proved members of the Ustashi', Barbour declared that events had led to a change in American attitude.[151] The United States could therefore no longer agree to return all Ustaše to Yugoslavia because the Yugoslav judicial system was a 'perversion of justice' and violated basic protections for the innocent.[152] Furthermore, the United States was unable to say anything about quislings and criminals solely under British jurisdiction, but in the case of those under joint Allied jurisdiction, Washington demanded to examine each case and only to allow extradition to Yugoslavia with American approval.[153] At least from this dialogue, Cabot was right. American authorities were far less inclined than the British to surrender Ustaše to the Yugoslav government.

Regardless of Cabot's criticisms, policy debates and Yugoslavia's demands, Supreme Allied Command Mediterranean (SACMED) announced that because of a shortage in manpower and the re-establishment of diplomatic relations between Rome and Belgrade, the 'military should be relieved of the problem of the apprehension and handover of Yugoslav quislings, except those in military custody'.[154] Furthermore, they stretched the truth by stating that they had made every effort to arrest quislings in Italy and that such would be the case in the future.[155] Ironically, the CIC was conducting an efficient investigation of Pavelić and Ustaše activities in Italy at the same time that SACMED maintained that, because of a shortage of men, such investigations were not possible.

The United States was searching for excuses to dispense with its responsibility to arrest quislings.

Cabot was not deterred by any of this. He was intent upon improving relations with Belgrade and wished for grievances to be eliminated or ameliorated. He was not an idealist, and he understood that the Yugoslavs could be difficult to handle and at times 'tortuous'.[156] His personal diary features many complaints directed towards the arrogance and untruthfulness of Yugoslav officials. Likewise, Cabot's communications to Washington are littered with comments pertaining to the difficulties involved in dealing with the new Yugoslav government. He did, however, want the United States to act in a just and moral fashion, as a country good to its word. Cabot was reaching his breaking point by the middle of June 1947. In a blistering condemnation of American policy, he wrote that, 'We have flouted our own commitments and that by our attitude we are protecting not only quislings but also [those?] guilty of terrible crimes committed in Yugoslavia. I presume we must protect our agents even though it disgusts me to think that we may be using the same men we so strongly criticized fascists for using.'[157] After explaining that the United States had impeded British actions against war criminals and quislings, had not actively tried to arrest quislings and was not insisting that Italy seriously track them, he charged that 'we are apparently conniving with Vatican and Argentina to get guilty people to haven in latter country. I sincerely hope I am mistaken, particularly regarding latter point.'[158] Unfortunately, Cabot was right on the mark. He argued that if Yugoslavia took the quisling issue to the United Nations, the United States and the Vatican would look very bad and would lose their moral force in the world. Even if the Italians arrested quislings, Washington would be unable to use the quisling issue to improve its relations with Belgrade, because the Americans would appear weak and obstructive. Cabot was realistic though and had no problem connecting the quisling issue with other foreign policy issues in a quid pro quo fashion. The basic argument was that American action was needed on the quisling issue.[159]

By late June, Cabot's understanding of the situation was becoming mature. Sensing that the United States government was aware of

Catholic assistance to quislings and war criminals, Cabot requested from the State Department that the Vatican provide them with a list of Yugoslavs that it was protecting.[160] Having made no significant progress with the quisling issue, Cabot declared that,

> what is vital is for us to take vigorous measures to see that those Yugoslavs in Italy whose extradition has been requested and whose guilt is established beyond reasonable doubt are ferreted out and delivered to Yugoslav authorities in order to demonstrate our intention to fulfill our commitments. Many thousands having been massacred and enormous property damages having been done in Yugoslavia, it would be strange justice to condone crimes of those whose responsibility has been reasonable established merely because they may not receive a fair trial in Yugoslavia.[161]

Thinking it best not to end on too strong a note, he struck this concluding line: 'Our present record in this whole matter is a disgrace.'[162]

Cabot did not have long to continue his campaign because Cavendish Cannon, another long-time diplomat — although junior to Cabot — with significant Balkan experience was officially installed as the new American ambassador to Belgrade on 14 July 1947. Cannon agreed with Cabot's analysis of the war criminal issue and made his opinion known to the State Department. Nevertheless, with Cabot relieved of his post, the strongest voice in opposition to the United States' policy on quislings and war criminals was removed.

Pavelić and the investigation

Meanwhile, the CIC continued its search for Pavelić. In March 1947, they thought that the former Poglavnik was at the Collegio Pio Pontificio in Prati located at Via Giacomo Belli, No. 3 enjoying the protection of Vatican authorities. It was believed that his secretary and aide were there with him. The investigators obtained information that Pavelić would be leaving for Spain under a false passport, but rumours of this nature had been wafting around Rome for some time and it was difficult to determine if they were valid.[163]

At long last, the Pavelić case began drawing a lot of attention from Counter Intelligence. On 11 April 1947, Colonel Blunda, acting assistant chief of staff of G-2, Lt Colonel Tom Hartman officer in charge of G-1 MTOUSA, Mr Bernard Grennan officer in charge of CIC MTOUSA, Mrs Heda Stern, and Captain M.H. Scott from the Allied Military Government Trieste met at G-2 MTOUSA to discuss the whereabouts of the Poglavnik. By discovering the location of Pavelić's family, they hoped to ultimately locate the quisling himself. They had received information from two of the family's ex-chambermaids, who served the family in Italy before and in Croatia during the war. They told a CIC informant that 'each time the "Allied Officials" were about to capture the Pavelićs they were moved elsewhere by Allied personnel who were hiding them, and who were each time rewarded by the Pavelićs with jewelry and money amounting to great sums'.[164] Although fantastic on the surface, the evidence presented by the chambermaids supports the evidence found in American documents that Allied personnel were involved in aiding Pavelić's movements. His servants' comments provide more circumstantial proof that Pavelić was using loot obtained from the Croatian treasury – much of it having been stolen from Ustaše victims – to finance his survival and ultimate escape.

The CIC explained that their 'best and most valuable' source of information was a long-standing friend who was highly trusted by the Pavelić family. The subject, possibly the Reverend Krunoslav Draganović, had to be played properly so that he would not suspect that the CIC was on his trail. Mrs Stern, who lived in Croatia for a long time, was the contact for this unnamed source, who the CIC was certain would lead them to Pavelić's hideaway.[165] The report was an optimistic portrayal of the search for Pavelić; it seemed simply a matter of time before the former Poglavnik was captured. The CIC agents leading the investigation did not realize that their work was for naught because their superiors had no interest in capturing Pavelić.

Meanwhile, the United States military received news of an impending escape attempt by Pavelić from Rome to Spain. An unnamed

Vatican source on 3 June 1947 reported that Pavelić had obtained a passport under the name of Padre Gomez and that he was preparing to leave in the near future. The contact maintained that his flight was arranged by Jesuits in the Vatican.[166] This last bit of information is somewhat suspect and may have been produced to relieve the Franciscans, of whom Draganović was one, of responsibility. Pavelić's connections were with the Franciscans, who were a powerful force in Croatia; however, there is some corroboratory evidence to support the claims that a Jesuit helped Pavelić escape. According to information out of Buenos Aires obtained in 1951, a Jesuit named Ivan Nikolić, one of Draganović's close friends, may have been, 'instrumental in bringing Pavelić to Argentina'.[167] In support of this view, Pavelić's son-in-law, Srečko Pšeničnik, maintained that a Jesuit, although he would not provide a name, was responsible for arranging the Poglavnik's escape.

The information that Pavelić was attempting to reach Spain came at the same time that the United States handed the responsibility for pursuing war criminals to the Italian government. General John C.H. Lee, commander of the Mediterranean Theatre at AFHQ, was 'relieved of all responsibility for the apprehension and handover of Yugoslav Quislings [...] except those now in Allied Displaced Persons and Prisoner of War/Surrendered Enemy Personnel Camps or otherwise in military custody....'.[168] The memo stated that Lee should 'extend to the Italian authorities all practicable assistance consistent with your available resources in the location and apprehension of Quislings whose surrender has already been agreed'.[169] Pavelić was included in this category of quisling. This policy was tantamount to a recognition that no further searches should be made for Croatian war criminals, because Washington knew that Italian authorities would do precious little in the search for these figures. Since the police and security forces in Italy were at times staffed by former Mussolini supporters and the Ustaše continued to hold favour in the Vatican, Pavelić was in good shape.

Even with the new policy in place, an order for Pavelić's arrest was issued by Special Agent Grennan of CIC Headquarters at MTOUSA on 7 July 1947. It stated that Pavelić was reported to be living 'in

Rome on the second floor of Via Giacomo Veneziano, 17, stairway C', on a quiet, picturesque, and narrow street.[170] Furthermore, 'the Assistant Chief of Staff, G-2, MTOUSA, desires that Subject be taken into custody on sight and that his office be notified immediately when such apprehension is made'.[171] There was no mention of what would be done with Pavelić once he was in custody. There was no certainty that he would be handed over to the Yugoslavs, because the United States in the past had been hesitant to return many Ustaše to Yugoslavia. In an interview with this author, William Gowen, one of the CIC agents involved in tracking Pavelić, doubted that the United States would have extradited Pavelić even if he had been arrested, due to the deep animosity between Washington and Belgrade.

One week later, on 14 July, the arrest order was voided. A handwritten message on the order read, 'new instructions "Hands off" Source Mr Grennan and Lt Colonel Hartman'.[172] This retraction was signed with the initials GM, most likely CIC agent Gono Morena. Grennan, the chief of operations for the CIC, and Lt Colonel Hartman, of G-1 MTOUSA, had revoked the arrest order probably on orders from unknown higher ranking military officials. Why was the order rescinded only one week after it was written? Who was protecting Pavelić and why? Was the State Department involved in what had looked like an army affair? Perhaps it took over one month for the directive to defer searches for quislings to Italian authorities to reach the 428th CIC, although this seems unlikely. The CIC was actively involved in the investigation of Pavelić and other quislings in Italy. As the orders given to General Lee were germane to the CIC, a delay would have been highly unusual. The order was rescinded by a high-ranking military official perhaps under advisement from someone in the State Department.

Another factor may have played a role in the rescinding of the arrest order. Eva Peron arrived on 7 June 1947 in Madrid for an extended visit with Francisco Franco as well as a grand tour of the country. Her visit to Europe was the cause of great celebration, particularly in Spain, where her arrival was given supreme importance, demonstrated by providing her plane with an escort of 51 Spanish fighters.[173] On 25 June, she continued her journey with a visit to Italy, where she had an audience with Pope Pius XII and on a separate occasion with Father Krunoslav Draganović.[174] The only explanation for why she would meet with a rather unknown priest was to solidify the immigration of Croatians to Argentina. At the end of the war, Argentina, like other South American states, was actively pursuing the immigration of Europeans who were anti-communist and possessed professional skills. Draganović was known to have close contacts with Croatians, in and out of DP camps, who possessed the abilities desired by the Argentine government. Mrs Peron may have discussed the movement of Croatians with Draganović. It is unknown, however, whether she knew or supported the immigration of war criminals and quislings to Argentina. Certainly, Juan Peron wanted only those immigrants who would favour his government, thus finding the Ustaše a good fit. He would get skilled workers and strong anti-communists.

Another important development helped place Pavelić on the path to freedom in Argentina: the creation of the Ratline in the summer of 1947. Special Agent Paul Lyon of the 430th CIC in Salzburg recruited Father Krunoslav Draganović, 'the Good Father' as he was known to the CIC agents, as a conduit to aid the relocation of Europeans who had helped the United States, under the cover of secrecy, or could be of help to the United States in the future.[175] These figures could not immigrate by passing through public channels, since they were often wanted by various authorities. It was not unusual for one branch of the American government to be protecting war criminals while other American authorities were searching for them. Draganović's activities as head of the Ratline have been well documented; however, some information on him is necessary to get a clear picture of the Pavelić case.

Born in Brcko in 1903, the son of a professor of natural science, Draganović received a good education in Vienna, Sarajevo and Rome. In 1930, he entered the priesthood in Sarajevo and quickly rose to prominence in the Catholic hierarchy, becoming secretary of the Confraternity of San Girolamo. Draganović was a Croatian nationalist sympathetic to the Ustaše cause, which he believed was a bulwark against communism, and a fervent believer in Croatian independence. With the establishment of the NDH, Draganović became a key cog in forcing Orthodox Serbs to convert to Catholicism.[176] In 1941, Draganović was named Professor of Ecclesiastical History in the School of Theology at the University of Zagreb. Two years later, at the behest of the Archbishop of Zagreb, he moved to Italy and became a representative to the Croatian Red Cross, a position that gave him carte blanche in Rome. His wide-ranging acquaintances at the Vatican, in South America and within the Red Cross made him the natural choice for the Americans. Being fervently anti-Serb and pro-Ustaše, he was likewise well-positioned to aid Pavelić and other Ustaše.

After the fall of Croatia in May 1945, Draganović often served as Pavelić's keeper, the two having been acquainted before the war started. Draganović maintained regular communication with the former Poglavnik, meeting with him on several occasions while Pavelić was hiding in Italy. His extensive contacts penetrated all crevices of the Vatican. Draganović was simply waiting for the right opportunity to send Pavelić to the safety of South America.[177] In the final analysis, American agents characterized him as 'famous for personal ambition and for engaging in nefarious activities. He is intelligent, active and courageous.'[178]

In exchange for his services, Draganović, who had been meeting with American Army personnel as early as 1945, demanded that the United States agree to ignore the escape of Croatian war criminals to South America. As Paul Lyon, the Ratline's originator, described the arrangement between Draganović, code named Dynamo, and the United States: 'The agreement consists of simply mutual assistance, i.e., these agents assist persons of interest to Father Draganović to leave Germany, and, in turn, Father Draganović will assist these agents in obtaining the necessary visas to Argentina, South America, for persons of interest to the Command.'[179] The CIC had established a quid pro quo system. If Draganović helped the CIC get sensitive figures out of Europe, the CIC would at minimum look the other way when Draganović desired the emigration of a Croatian war criminal. The commander of the 430th CIC, James Milano, defended the Ratline, writing that 'American intelligence agencies in Austria were not in the business of catching Yugoslav war criminals. Their job was gathering current intelligence on the Soviet armies, not exacting retribution for past crimes.'[180] The CIC paid Draganović between $1,000 and $1,400 for each figure he helped reach safety, with some of the money later used to finance the escape of Croatian fugitives.[181] The Ryan Report on America's involvement with Klaus Barbie, 'the Butcher of Lyon', who was helped to the West by the Ratline, maintains that there is 'no evidence that CIC actually assisted Croatians to escape from Europe', though it offers a caveat saying, 'the possibility that the 430th CIC in Austria assisted Croatians, especially prior to 1949, cannot be conclusively ruled out'.[182] These remarks miss the point. Active CIC participation in the escape of Croatians was *not* needed by Draganović. He needed only for the United States to ignore quislings and war criminals so that their flight could move smoothly. Thus the United States was culpable for the escape of Pavelić and other Croatian criminals, because it had struck a deal with a man who was known to be working via an extensive network of agents and fellow Croatian priests to get Croatian war criminals to safety. If the United States had blown the whistle on Draganović, they would have encountered a tough time moving sensitive assets to the West. American authorities chose to deal with Draganović and take the consequential heat from the Yugoslav government.

Since Draganović was the key figure in protecting Pavelić and moving him to various safe-houses in Rome, it is possible that the order for arrest was rescinded, because Pavelić's apprehension would foul the Ratline. It is not a coincidence that Lt Colonel Hartman, as head of the CIC at MTOUSA, attached his name to the order rescinding Pavelić's arrest. The CIC believed that the Ratline was critical to waging the Cold War against the Soviet Union and ensuring American security by protecting American operatives and potential assets. United States officials could further rationalize this policy by arguing that Pavelić and the other Ustaše figures were passionate anti-communists and potentially valuable assets who might help destabilize Yugoslavia, and that if Yugoslavia collapsed, Pavelić or one of his followers would form a bulwark against communism on the Adriatic.

Even with the pursuit of Pavelić in the hands of Italian authorities, the diplomatic corps in Washington and London, apparently oblivious to the arrest order and its revocation, realized that the former Poglavnik was such a well-known figure that his arrest should take precedence over and above their official policy. In late July 1947, the Department of State notified the British government that the United States military would cooperate with the Italian authorities 'to [the] extent [sic] possible in Pavelić case'.[183] Washington believed, however, that Pavelić's apprehension would do little to help ease tensions between Yugoslavia and the United States over quislings.[184] Secretary of State Marshall hedged his bets, writing that 'such cooperation, however, is not to be considered as precedent contravening our general position that matter of alleged quislings outside Allied jurisdiction Italy is ITAL responsibility'.[185] In response, the British government noted that 'HM Government are in full agreement that this man [Pavelić] should be apprehended on the terms proposed by United States State Department'.[186] Those terms were established in the 29 July memorandum which turned over power of arrest to the Italian authorities. But British authorities ignored the new policy with regard to this case. British Political Advisor P.W. Scarlett urged that London was 'most anxious that no time should be lost in laying the plan. All details available on the British side are to be found in Rome and I am to ask that your representative should call at HM Embassy as soon as possible to concert action.'[187] To the British, Pavelić was a major quisling whose importance was so great that Italian authorities could not be trusted. Washington, however, insisted that the Italians be closely involved in Pavelić's apprehension, a tactic the British believed was unnecessary, risky and destined to fail. As the British Foreign Office explained to its Rome Embassy: 'British government thinks Pavelić's arrest would be better and more efficiently carried out by Allied forces, but the United States does not agree. They see political advantage for the Italians to gain more of the credit.'[188] Plans to arrest Pavelić were in the works, regardless of the Italian policy, and the Americans intended to arrest Pavelić as late as 9 August 1947. The British Foreign Office, in particular, was anxious to move against Pavelić as rapidly as possible for fear that delay would allow for leaks, especially considering that the Italians were involved.[189] The commander in chief of MTOUSA, Major General Lawrence C. Jaynes, recommended that Brigadier General Anderson work with the British to arrest Pavelić outside of Vatican property – no easy task – and return him to the Yugoslav authorities.[190] Such an operation could be accomplished because the Allies had detailed information about Pavelić's hideout in Rome. The problem was that he was under the protection of the Vatican at Via Giacomo Venenziano no. 17-C, thus creating a serious extra-territoriality issue. Furthermore, when he left his apartment, he travelled in a car with Vatican licence plates.[191]

Relinquishing responsibility

American interest in arresting Pavelić waned soon after it reached its peak. Neither American nor British authorities developed precise and formal plans to apprehend Pavelić. CIC agents continued their monitoring of Pavelić's and the Ustaše's activities in Rome, even discussing a potential meeting. On instructions from Gono Morena, the supervising agent of the Pavelić case, Special Agents Gowen and Caniglia gave a complete report on the Pavelić investigation on 29 August 1947. Their account was a careful and thoughtful evaluation of the Pavelić inquiry detailing the intricacies of the Poglavnik's career, evaluating the status of the CIC's search and offering suggestions on the future of the investigation. The agents explained that Pavelić was probably in Rome, but that his actual whereabouts were unknown. It was suggested that his family should be carefully monitored in the hope that they would lead investigators to him.[192] The memo stated that Pavelić was receiving support not only from the Vatican but also probably Great Britain – though they did not distinguish between the Foreign Office and military authorities – for this was the only way for the Poglavnik to remain hidden. The agents believed, but could not confirm, that British authorities had protected Pavelić in 1945 or 1946 and helped transport Croatian loot to Italy. They suggested that this money from the Croatian Treasury was being used to finance Krizari activities in Tito's Yugoslavia.[193]

These allegations have gained some support over the years, with newspaper reports stating that Great Britain and the Vatican obtained at least a portion of the Croatian Treasury and perhaps even possess it today.

Pavelić's real protector, however, was the Vatican. The Poglavnik's reputation was so well-known and his contacts so varied that Gowen and Caniglia postulated that Pavelić was 'indubitably [...] being supported and exploited by some power'.[194] His high-placed contacts within the Catholic Church such as Secretary of State Montini were fervent in their desire to save Pavelić from a Yugoslav noose. The agents theorized that 'in the eyes of the VATICAN, PAVELIĆ is a militant Catholic, a man who erred, but who erred fighting for Catholicism'.[195] Thus the Vatican saw Pavelić as a warrior against communism; he had made mistakes but had fought the good fight. Caniglia and Gowen explained that Vatican officials believed Pavelić should only be put on trial by a 'Christian and Democratic Government', regardless of the nature of his crimes, and argued that his arrest and extradition would, 'weaken the forces fighting atheism and aid Communism in its fight against the Church'.[196] Caniglia and Gowen, apparently ignorant of the Ratline's existence, recommended that:

> the VATICAN and Četnik views of PAVELIĆ be appreciated and that no direct police action be taken against him (Pavelić) on the part of the American Military Authorities. Such action would force his extradition to Tito and would bolster the present British anti-American propaganda campaign being waged among the political émigrés in Western Europe.[197]

This was more evidence of the sometimes intense rivalry that existed between American and British occupation forces as well as between the State Department and the Foreign Office. Instead of American action, Caniglia and Gowen proposed that the British relationship with Pavelić be exposed to shame them into arresting and extraditing him. This was a reference to the alleged British involvement in allowing Pavelić to flee from Austria to Italy. If

British cooperation with Pavelić could be proved, London would have no choice but to aggressively act and arrest him. Even though they opposed American involvement, both men realized that some action against Pavelić was necessary 'if the Croat democratic and resistance forces are to ever be recognized by the United States'.[198]

Believing, amazingly, that Pavelić was a low flight risk, the CIC continued to monitor his activities to the best of their abilities. A report dated 12 September 1947 showed no concern about a potential escape to Spain or South America, indicating that American informants and the CIC in Rome were not current on Pavelić's actions or the development of the Ratline or that they had no real interest in preventing an escape. Although the CIC in Italy probably had little or no knowledge of the Ratline, they were in contact with Draganović who provided the CIC officers with information about Pavelić, allegedly through a third source.[199] Caniglia and Gowen entertained the notion of meeting with the Poglavnik outside of Vatican property, hoping that 'the final disposition of Subject's case await the clarification that such an interview [...] could bring'.[200] Although a meeting with Pavelić most likely never occurred, the investigators understood the magnitude of this case noting that 'Pavelić's contacts are so High and his present position is so compromising to the VATICAN, that any extradition of Subject would deal a staggering blow to the Roman Catholic Church'.[201]

From September to November 1947, the Pavelić case apparently languished. On 8 November Lt Colonel G.F. Blunda, assistant chief of staff G-2 MTOUSA, concluded that arresting Pavelić 'would not have been to our best interests as a number of Croats have been used as informers by U.S. Intelligence agencies. A number of such Croats are known to be loyal to Pavelić's anti-Communist activities and Catholic fanaticism.'[202] Action against Pavelić could have jeopardized American operations that utilized Croatian operatives and caused the evaporation of intelligence received from these sources. Even if the United States had wished to arrest Pavelić, it was far from certain as to his whereabouts. Blunda noted that the Poglavnik had not been seen since July 1947, when he was spotted in a monk's clothing on Vatican property. Further complicating any search were persistent rumours that Pavelić had undergone plastic surgery.[203]

Blunda also was sensitive to Pavelić's high-placed friends in the Catholic Church and their efforts to protect him and other Croatian war criminals. 'It is doubtful that any further action will be taken on this case prior to our departure from Italy,' wrote Blunda.[204] 'In view of the implications of Vatican participating in harboring war criminals, I have kept this file in my custody in the safe at G-2 MTOUSA Headquarters.'[205] With the communists threatening to win the upcoming Italian elections, the United States was willing to ignore Pavelić's past to preserve mutual American and Vatican interest in opposing communism. Blunda ended his report with gravitas, remarking that 'this document should not be seen by any British authorities'.[206] Was this because British authorities were interested in arresting Pavelić and American intransigence had been the stumbling block?

American officials made no move to find or arrest Pavelić in 1948. With the Ratline in place and the Cold War growing more frigid, the prospects for Pavelić to escape grew brighter. The key to any successful escape was a valid passport, preferably under an assumed name. Pavelić acquired one from the International Red Cross, which issued thousands of passports after World War II, many unintentionally and some intentionally going to war criminals. Pavelić's ally, Father Draganović, was Croatia's representative to the Red Cross and probably obtained the passport, although there is little hard evidence to support this. Under the assumed name Pablo Aranyos and holding Red Cross passport number 74369, Pavelić left Naples in a disguise aboard the SS *Sestriere*.[207] He arrived in Argentina on 6 November 1948.[208]

CHAPTER 6

HIDING TO THE END

The shores of Argentina must have seemed like heaven to the former Poglavnik as his ship neared his new home over 6,000 miles from Croatia. Pavelić, like many fascists, was eager to blend into the masses immigrating to South America. As he had with Mussolini in the 1930s, Pavelić found another world leader, Juan Peron, interested in protecting him and perhaps using his services. As the Cold War emerged and World War II grew more distant, memories of fascist atrocities faded. Interest was not in the past but the future. Few people wanted to discuss the horrors of concentration camp life and the bloodthirsty executions of the war years. It would take the trial of Adolf Eichmann held in Jerusalem in 1961 to again stimulate interest in quislings and war criminals who had escaped prosecution.

In the late 1940s and early 1950s, Pavelić felt secure enough to reorganize his forces with an eye towards once again taking power in Croatia. He saw no reason for the Ustaše to fold simply because the movement was in exile and tainted by accommodations made with the Nazis. Pavelić knew all about exile from his experiences during the 1930s and appreciated that the path to power was sometimes slow and arduous. He understood what was necessary to keep an organization alive even when it was far removed from its goals.

Although the State Department continually monitored Ustaše elements, especially its activities in Europe, and occasionally expressed interest in Pavelić's whereabouts and actions, it showed little significant concern about Pavelić. The CIA surely gave an occasional look at his movements. Pavelić was seen as a potential asset who could be used to weaken Tito's control over Croatia. After Tito broke with Stalin in 1948, Washington gradually understood that obstinately opposing Yugoslavia's communist government was not a wise policy. By the 1950s, the United States realized that a closer relationship with Tito was a sound strategy for challenging Soviet influence in the Balkans. There was therefore little reason to consider using Pavelić to destabilize Yugoslavia as Mussolini had done.

Safe-haven Argentina

Argentina's strong man, Juan Peron, a great admirer of Benito Mussolini, was eager to exploit Europe's chaotic post-war situation by recruiting as many 'brains' as he could. It was hoped that German or Italian scientists, mathematicians, engineers, or politicians, all fleeing the war-torn continent for reasons they wished better left unsaid, would help industrialize, modernize and strengthen Argentina. Peron benefited from the new bipolar world by offering a third alternative for those not wanting or unable to find sanctuary in the United States or the Soviet Union. His greatest success in post-war immigration came in Italy, where on 21 February 1947 he concluded a treaty with Rome allowing thousands of Italians to immigrate to Argentina.[1] This opened the floodgates for war criminals who could obtain an Italian or Red Cross passport or some type of travel authorization.

The immigration process was further aided by America's decision to restore authority to the new Italian government and to ignore the backgrounds of some quislings and war criminals seeking to enter Argentina. As many former fascists with anti-Communist credentials arrived in South America, the United States believed it was helping form a bulwark against communism to its south. To the thousands of Croatians with questionable pasts milling about Italy, the new American policy was heaven sent. It meant that the Ratline could function with the greatest of freedom. As historian Ronald Newton wrote:

Under the Italo-Argentine agreements, and with the aid of Italian and Croat priests, Argentina received several thousand Croats between November 1946 and April 1947; beginning in March 1947, General Hilldring (assistant secretary of state for occupied Europe) urged Argentina to accept 2,000 Yugoslav 'grays' (and not a few 'blacks') whose future under the Tito regime was uncertain at best. In this fashion, many former Ustachi fascists, including Ante Pavelić and many subordinates in the Croat puppet regime, entered Argentina toward the end of 1947.[2]

Again, Pavelić was the beneficiary of Cold War tensions. The United States was eager for Peron to continue as an anti-communist stalwart in South America, and was tired of fighting the battles over quislings, war criminals and displaced persons. Emigration to Argentina solved two problems at once. No one much minded in 1947 or 1948 if Argentina became the home for a man responsible for hundreds of thousands of deaths.

Arrival and a new life

Using the alias Pablo Aranyos, Pavelić made the journey across the Atlantic with a first-class ticket – Draganović or someone else had spared no expense. It is obvious that the channels had been cleared for Pavelić, because his cartoonish-looking passport photo would have fooled only the dimmest of customs officials. The photo shows Pavelić behind big glasses and a beard that did little to mask his true identity. Nevertheless, it was all he needed. His arrival in Buenos Aires, rumoured for years at this point, received no public fanfare, but it was a source of great happiness to radical sectors of the Croatian community in Argentina. The former Poglavnik was reunited with his family, who had arrived on 3 May 1948, and promptly integrated into the sizable Croatian population in Argentina that had actively supported him since the early 1930s.

A Yugoslav informant in Argentina told American authorities that Krunoslav Draganović had informed Ivica Frković, Vjekoslav Vrančić and Jozo Dumandzic that Pavelić would be arriving on the SS *Sestriere*.[3] All three men had immigrated successfully to Argentina thanks to the Ratline. Frković had served in Pavelić's government from 1941 to 1943 as minister of forestry and mines while Dumandzic, a Lika native, completed a brief stint as justice and religion minister. Vrančić, however, was one of Pavelić's closest associates, having served in several posts in the NDH including minister of labour and deputy foreign minister. After World War II, he had been given quarter at San Girolamo. Another Lika native, Vrančić, who had been deeply involved in the operation of concentration camps, was one of the leading figures among Croatian émigrés, continuing in this role until his death in 1990. Having worked in Latin America in the 1930s, he was an excellent liaison for Pavelić. Vrančić wasted no time acclimatising himself to his new country, even landing a professorship at Buenos Aires University.[4] That these men were already in Argentina was an indication of how effectively Croatian war criminals had been spirited away to Argentina.

The Ratline was working very well. An American informant had even confirmed that Pavelić had been sequestered in a monastery near Castel Gandolfo prior to Draganović's assistance in moving him to Genoa for the journey to Argentina.[5] The informant explained that Pavelić wasted no time establishing the Ustaše in exile, meeting with figures such as Branko Benzon, the former Ustaše minister to Berlin and the editors of a Croatian newspaper in Argentina. Benzon was an important figure in Argentina's Croatian community, one of Juan and Evita Peron's close friends and supporters, certainly someone Pavelić was eager to exploit.[6] Without a doubt, Benzon was influential in facilitating Pavelić's entry and successful assimilation into Argentina. In the final analysis, the anonymous American who penned the report surmised that Pavelić 'plans to become politically active'.[7]

Long before Pavelić rose to power in the NDH, he had sought sympathy and support from Croatian émigrés in Argentina. As we have seen, beginning in the early 1930s, the Croatian community had been fertile ground for the Ustaše. Ante Valenta had organized Domobran cells in Argentina and had published a pro-Pavelić newspaper. Croatians had welcomed visits from Pavelić's supporters such as Archbishop Šarić and Branimir Jelić. Although exact figures are unknown, Ustaše efforts in Argentina provided Pavelić's movement with monetary assistance and carved out a base of support stronger than that found in the United States. During World War II, the State Department and the British Foreign Office had been cognizant of pro-Pavelić influences in Argentina and on occasion expressed concern over the growing influence of pro-Pavelić factions among Croatian-Argentines. Pavelić's South American friends were rewarded for their efforts with daily hour-long broadcasts to Argentina from Radio Rakovica urging them to fervently support the Poglavnik. Ante Valenta, also a leader of the pro-Pavelić forces in the United States during the 1930s, was again a key figure in organizing Croatian-Argentine support for Pavelić.[8] Upon reaching Argentina, Pavelić found himself among friends willing to protect him and aid in the reconstitution of the Ustaše movement.

Although he lived the life of a construction engineer, a profession he had learned from his father, Pavelić was probably connected with Peron's neo-fascist Alianza Libertadora Nacionalista.[9] Established in the 1930s, the Alianza was a fascist organization based on the principles of nationalism, duty, discipline and one-man rule. This fervently nationalistic, pro-Catholic and anti-communist organization was absorbed into the Peronist movement in the 1940s.[10] Such involvement was likely because it matched Pavelić's pedigree and would have offered him the security that he craved. Pavelić was mirroring the desires of Nazi immigrants who also sought government work with the same concerns in mind. He could be confident that as long as he remained useful to Peron, he would be protected from extradition, and could continue to promote his brand of Croatian propaganda without any interference from the Argentine government. Considering that Yugoslavia's secret police, the UDBA, were searching for him, the closer Pavelić could get to Peron the safer he would be.

Croatian-Americans and Pavelić

Although Pavelić had been in Argentina since 1948, the State Department seemed unclear about his whereabouts as late as 1951.

One informant for the State Department, deemed reliable, reported that Pavelić was living in Buenos Aires, although he emphasized a rumour that Pavelić had been residing in Chicago. Another contact stated that there were, 'strong rumors during the past six months to the effect that Ante Pavelić is in the United States and is believed to be in Chicago'.[11] Alarmed by these informants, the State Department and the FBI attempted in the summer of 1951 to determine whether Pavelić had indeed entered the United States, perhaps seeking to organize support there.[12] Certainly, there was fertile soil to be found in Chicago, Youngstown, Cleveland and Akron, because pro-Ustaše groups, some focused around recent Croatian immigrants, were active there in the 1950s. With a circulation of 4,050, *Danica* (*Morning Star*), published by the Croatian Franciscan Fathers, continued to produce nationalistic articles condemning Tito's Yugoslavia and favouring Pavelić and Croatian independence.[13] Pavelić even admitted in a 1955 interview that members of his new movement were found in many places abroad including North America.[14] Support for Croatian independence and for Pavelić was often led by Croatian priests who had fled from Yugoslavia at the end of World War II. Although there is no solid evidence that Pavelić entered the United States, the possibility that he or several of his lieutenants visited America to cultivate financial support from Croatian-Americans cannot be excluded.

The Croatian-American community had been split during the war on whether to support Pavelić's NDH or Yugoslavism.[15] The establishment of Tito's government had done little to reduce the tension between those Croats who favoured independence and those who sought Yugoslavism. Cities such as Chicago and Cleveland were centres for passionate anti-Yugoslav and pro-independence Croatians. Croatian Franciscans, including those who fled Europe for the United States in the late 1940s and early 1950s, remained Pavelić's allies, especially because they hated the reprisals Tito levelled against the Catholic Church and the slaughter of fleeing Croatians conducted at Bleiburg. The Franciscan Order, however, had much to hide, since some of its members had gleefully participated in carrying out the Ustaše's bloodbath.[16]

A good example of the complexity of the Pavelić issue in America occurred in 1949 when the Croatian Fraternal Union (CFU), the largest and oldest Croatian association in the United States, reported to the White House that a meeting of pro-Pavelić Croatians, calling themselves United Croatians, was held on 27 February at the Sherman Hotel in Chicago. Learning that the meeting had featured a statement of support from President Harry Truman, the CFU moved quickly to inform the White House that most of the meeting's supporters were 'staunch and loyal supporters of the infamous Dr Ante Pavelich'.[17] The CFU was eager for the United States government to understand that this meeting, called the Second Croatian Congress, was a gathering of only a fringe element, many participants not even United States citizens.[18] They did not want the White House to believe that Ustaše supporters represented mainstream Croatian opinion. The concerns raised by the CFU had already been voiced to Walworth Barbour, the State Department's chief for Southern European Affairs. Yugoslav Ambassador Sava Kosanović, in statements reminiscent of the 1930s, expressed disappointment that President Truman would issue any kind of support for a group whose main goal was the dismemberment of Yugoslavia, although President Truman had only issued a statement celebrating and recognizing the contributions of Croatian-Americans.[19] Those opposed to Pavelić's idea of an independent Croatia were keen to inform American authorities that the United Croatians did not represent mainstream Croatian-Americans.[20]

Still, this meeting reconfirmed that Pavelić and the Ustaše had active support from some Croatian-Americans. The FBI and the State Department were aware of figures such as Father Silvije Grubusić of Chicago, who had gained control of the United Croatians and turned it into an Ustaše front. Educated in Siroki Brijeg, Herzegovina, Grubusić, a Franciscan, held a powerful pulpit in the Croatian and Franciscan community as editor of the *Croatian Catholic Messenger* from 1942 to 1949 and of the *Croatian Almanac* from 1944 to 1949. Both of these nationalistic publications were produced by the Croatian Franciscans of Chicago. In a 1949 State Department meeting, Dr Branko Peshell, Vladimir Maček's secretary, alerted the United States government to Rev. Grubusić's threat to the Croatian Peasant Party and good order in general declaring that he was 'an avowed supporter of an independent Croatia and his sympathies have been and apparently still are with the Ustashi party'.[21] By 1950, Grubusić held sway over the Croatian American Congress and the Committee of United American Croatians, both organizations reflecting his strongly nationalist, pro-Pavelić positions.[22] Through pro-Pavelić newspapers and organizations like these, Grubusić and his supporters hoped to weaken Vladimir Maček's significance among Croatian-Americans while working to establish an independent Croatia along Ustaše lines. Notable pre-war Pavelić supporters such as Rudolf Erić found a home in this organization and others like it.[23] It appears that Pavelić was at least somewhat knowledgeable of the allies he had within the United States and was probably quite pleased that to them he remained a symbol of Croatian independence.

The Chicago-based United American Croatians did far more than simply publish newspapers. This organization concerned the FBI enough to warrant infiltration by a reliable FBI informant named Anton Klobucar.[24] The United American Croatians favoured Ante Pavelić and operated a refugee assistance organization called Hrvatski Odbor za Izbjeglice (Croatian Committee for Refugees), led by Reverend David Zrno, allegedly a prominent former Domobran who by the late 1940s was leading an organization called Croatian Franciscan Fathers of the United States.[25] Zrno, a native of Bosnia-Herzegovina, a region well known for Ustaše support, was a seminary professor in Mostar before immigrating to the United States in 1930. The organization's mission was to provide an avenue for Croatian refugees to immigrate to the United States, even if they were supporters of Pavelić's government.[26] Their rate of success is unknown.

The CCU of Gary, Indiana continued to favour an independent Croatia and, to no great surprise, was an outspoken opponent of communism and Tito.[27] With a national membership of over 9,000, the CCU had faced criticism from the Croatian Peasant Party and was forced to mitigate some of their effusive praise for Pavelić that had been found in the pages of *Nasa Nada (Our Hope)*.[28] In contrast *Danica*, published by the Croatian Franciscan Fathers, remained a publication devoted to a Croatian nationalist agenda.[29] The FBI summarized the ideological differences among Croatian-Americans saying, 'In the opinion of *Danica*, archbishop Alyosius Stepenac of Zagreb who is in prison, is a national hero of the Independent Croatian state: to *Nasa Nada* he is a martyr, to *Americki Hrvatski Glasnik*, a persecuted priest and to the Titoists, a Nazi-Fascist collaborator'.[30]

By 1951, the Croatian Franciscans appeared to be wavering in their devotion to Pavelić's cause. The FBI learned that some Croatian Franciscans were growing weary of Pavelić, whose commitment to Catholicism was being questioned, and believed that their support for him alienated them from the American government and its citizens.[31] In addition, they were unable to check the continual popularity of the Croatian Peasant Party, which had come to be viewed by most Croatians as the legitimate party for those opposed to Tito's Yugoslavia. According to the FBI, Pavelić bore responsibility for this situation because 'he still will not desist from acting as a tyrant and mixing with neo-Fascists and neo-Nazis'.[32] An unknown FBI official sagely summarized the situation, writing that 'the common error of the Croat rightist is that they cannot see that any national Croat front has to be a coalition of democratic forces and must exclude Pavelić'.[33] It was obvious that Maček was the only Croat in exile with enough standing to lead Croatian-Americans in their efforts to obtain greater freedoms for Croatians.

Croatian gold

Like the Nazis who fled to South America, the Ustaše émigrés needed a great deal of money to provide for their security and to fund a new Croatian liberation movement. As mentioned earlier, Pavelić and his colleagues had fled Croatia with gold and currency looted from the treasury, some of which he had stashed in Switzerland towards the end of World War II. It is unclear how much of it Pavelić and other Ustaše officials were able to transfer out of the country. An American document from 1949 stated that the NDH at the end of the war had assets of 2,500,000 Swiss francs, 1,700 kg of gold and 40,000 kg of silver.[34] In a 1946 report, Treasury Department official Emerson Bigelow declared that his source estimated the Ustaše had 'deposits which apparently amount to between 12 and 16 million Swiss francs'.[35] Although these estimates may not be accurate, they do indicate that Ustaše wealth was considerable immediately after World War II.

The problem Pavelić encountered in Argentina was how to gain access to these deposits. Although some funds may have been used to buy his freedom from British captors, and more had probably ended up in Vatican coffers, Pavelić still retained assets, albeit less than he had hoped. As early as March 1948, there were reports that Ante Godina, one of Pavelić's wartime economic advisors had 'smuggled a large amount of Gold belonging to Pavelić into Argentina'.[36] The exact route that this gold followed was not known to contemporary American officials and, even today, is quite difficult to trace.

Some clues to the movement and amount of Croatian wealth can be gleaned from the travels of former Ustaše economic officials such as Franjo Cvijić, who arrived in Buenos Aires in 1949. As the last president of the Croatian State Bank, Cvijić had been removing funds from Croatia and depositing them in Switzerland at the end of 1944 and into early 1945.[37] His appearance in Argentina meant that Pavelić had greater ability to access Swiss accounts and siphon the stolen Croatian Treasury from Europe to Argentina. The former Poglavnik's financial fortunes were improving.

Keeping an eye on the money, the Central Intelligence Agency (CIA) learned that Pavelić probably sent Ante Godina on a return mission to Europe in October 1951. Godina, also known as Pelivan, and another unnamed colleague were to transfer Croatian gold from Europe to Argentina.[38] The gold in question was alleged to have been secured in a wall near Salzburg in the final days of World War II. Since it has been established that Pavelić fled to Salzburg at the end of the war with a few followers, it is not much of a leap to believe that he had been travelling with gold looted from the Croatian treasury. Although the CIA's source did not know if the gold had arrived in

Argentina, Pavelić was known to have been 'offering to sell on the Buenos Aires market 200 kilograms of gold through his intermediary, Juan Heinrich', the key financier for Croatian immigrants with an Ustaše past.[39] In addition, Pavelić, it was believed, 'transferred five million Swiss francs from Switzerland to Argentina' in January 1952.[40] The CIA informant believed that this money had been part of the Croatian Treasury that disappeared at the end of World War II.

Although American information on Pavelić's financial dealings was slight, it established a clear and logical pattern. The former Poglavnik was financing his lifestyle and planning the re-emergence of the Ustaše with funds removed from Croatia in the last days of World War II. The new Ustaše would be funded with the remnants of the Croatian Treasury which had been bolstered by gold and loot confiscated from Serbians, Jews and Roma who had been killed by the Ustaše. Neither the CIA nor the State Department seemingly made this connection, although it would have been obvious to anyone familiar with Pavelić's past activities. The murky history surrounding Ustaše finances could have received some clarity with a class action lawsuit filed originally in 1999 in Northern California against the Vatican Bank and the Franciscan Order.[41] The case was dismissed, however.

Continuing the fight

In the early 1950s, the United States military and the State Department took a renewed interest in Pavelić, in part because it was becoming apparent that the Ustaše movement was reorganizing in Europe. Although Pavelić remained in exile, there were plenty of Ustaše sympathizers in Europe, especially in Spain and Germany, who hoped to overthrow Tito's regime. As we have seen, Belgrade was forced to deal with Ustaše insurgents, the Krizari, for several years after the conclusion of World War II. Ustaše operatives in Yugoslavia had been squelched, but the movement continued to operate underground in other parts of Europe.

After arriving in Argentina, Pavelić wasted little time fomenting Ustaše ideology and planning the re-emergence of an independent

Croatia. His successful construction company served as a convenient cover for his political ambitions. On 8 June 1956, Pavelić founded the Croatian Liberation Movement (Hrvatski Oslobodilacki Pokret, HOP) in Buenos Aires. Although it is certain that the former Poglavnik wished this neo-Ustaše organization to further the cause of Croatian independence, it may have been designed more to challenge Croatians who were rivals for his leadership than simply to promote the re-establishment of a Croatian state. With the fall of his protector, Juan Peron, in 1955, it would seem odd timing for Pavelić to take a more public role if not for reasons of preserving his personal power. By this time, Pavelić's movement had begun to splinter. Vjekoslav 'Maks' Luburić, formerly one of Pavelić's steadfast lieutenants, organizer of the Ustaše Defense Battalion, commander of the concentration camp system in the NDH and a leading figure in post-war Ustaše activities in Europe, broke ranks with his former commander and established the Croatian National Resistance (Hrvatski Narodni Odpor) in 1955. It was rumoured that Luburić's defection was caused by Pavelić's willingness to abandon historically Croatian territory in exchange for re-establishing an independent Croatia. The split between the long-time allies was a severe blow to Pavelić, in part because Luburić, a close ally since the early 1930s and a former comrade in exile in Italy and Hungary, had commanded the Ustaše's military wing since the end of the war. Enjoying the protection of Franco's Spain and living the life of a publisher, Luburić, the last commander of Ustaše forces during World War II, was severely criticized by Pavelić for establishing this rival organization, and the former Poglavnik moved quickly to isolate him as much as possible.[42] Living thousands of miles from Europe, however, he was in no position to seriously challenge Luburić's activities. In some ways, the Croatian independence movement had moved past the old Ustaše ideas, which were outdated, to a younger generation of nationalists. Luburić spent his later years working for Croatian independence and publishing propaganda tracts until he was cut down by an assassin from the Yugoslav secret service in his Spanish villa in 1969.[43]

The State Department was not very curious about these rival Croatian political organizations. There was little concern about the remnants of the Ustaše or their new front organization HOP. Neither the State Department nor the CIA demonstrated much interest regarding their activities or plans to use terror to achieve their ends. Likewise, Pavelić was rarely mentioned by American agencies, at least not in cables and memos. Surprisingly, perhaps no one in the State Department was certain of his whereabouts as late as 1952. This illustrated a disconnect between intelligence agencies and the State Department. European media outlets possessed better intelligence on Pavelić and the Ustaše than did the CIA or the State Department.

The end of the road

The collapse of Peron's government in September 1955 placed new pressure on Pavelić. Rumours persisted that political events had forced Pavelić to make a quick departure from Argentina to Brazil, although this alleged journey was never confirmed.[44] In the same year, O Jornal, a newspaper in Rio de Janeiro, reported on Ustaše exiles in Argentina including Ante Pavelić, further increasing the pressure on Pavelić and alerting the FBI to the Poglavnik's new predicament.[45] Peron's successor, General Pedro Aramburu, who took the reins of the state in November, allowed greater press freedom, which in turn led to more and more calls for something to be done about Ante Pavelić. With a fresh wind blowing in Buenos Aires, the former Poglavnik had become a political liability and was at the mercy of a new government not too interested in protecting him. Yugoslav officials had consistently pestered Buenos Aires in the 1950s about arresting Pavelić and, as early as 1951, had requested Pavelić's extradition to stand trial in Yugoslavia. Basing their claim on Argentine and Yugoslav law, Yugoslavia issued a formal indictment void of any mention of political crimes, instead hoping to trigger his repatriation based on the allegation that Pavelić was a 'common criminal'.[46] This 1951 extradition request fell on deaf ears, with Peron's government arguing both that Pavelić was not in Argentina and that no extradition treaty existed between Buenos Aires and Belgrade.[47] The Poglavnik wisely shunned any publicity and retired deeper into his role as a kindly, ageing building contractor, although his efforts for an Ustaše renaissance continued. The State Department observed a change in attitude in 1956, noting that the Argentine foreign ministry 'had even gone so far as informally to admit that Pavelić was in fact in Argentina', something that they had refused to do under Peron.[48] But Buenos Aires was not ready to move against him. Nevertheless, newspapers in Argentina escalated their calls for the government to expel Pavelić, who was deemed an embarrassment to the country.[49]

On the night of 10 April 1957, Ante Pavelić was returning home from celebrating the sixteenth anniversary of the NDH's founding. He was standing at the entrance of his home at 643 calle Jean-Mermoz when six shots rang out from a 0.32-calibre pistol. Pavelić crashed to the ground, having received two bullets; one hit his chest and the other struck him between the first and second vertebrae.[50] The assassin eluded authorities and was never captured. Pavelić was rushed by passers-by to a local hospital where he was treated for the wounds and, surprisingly, released the next day. Although his wounds were serious, they were not sufficiently debilitating to prevent him from giving interviews and posing for photographs the following day.[51]

In the interviews, Pavelić, acquiring the persona of a saintly old gentleman victimized by powerful vindictive forces, alleged that the Yugoslav government, in particular the UDBA, was responsible for the assassination attempt.[52] Most likely, this was the case; however, Belgrade would have been wise to show a bit more patience. The prospects for extradition were improving despite the lack of an extradition treaty between Argentina and Yugoslavia. The Aramburu government had admitted Pavelić's presence on Argentine soil and stressed that they had no relationship with the quisling. By waiting another year or two, Yugoslavia might have been in a position to whisk Pavelić back to Belgrade to stand trial for his actions. Another theory is that exiled Četniks, attempting to settle old scores, were the perpetrators of the attack on Pavelić. It is also possible that a dissatisfied Ustaše member committed the act. One could even nominate the Israeli government to the pantheon of potential candidates. With news of the assassination attempt widespread in

Argentina, and Argentine newspapers urging Pavelić's arrest, Belgrade renewed its request that the Argentine government arrest and extradite him. Pressure was building on Buenos Aires to act, even though some believed that Pavelić was 'being protected by the Roman Catholic hierarchy and by some Argentine military leaders'.[53] The United States was more concerned about how the potential extradition would affect the Andrija Artuković case than about Pavelić's status. There was not much interest in determining who had attempted the assassination. As Yugoslavia sought Pavelić, the United States government haggled over Belgrade's request for Artuković's extradition. Artuković, a NDH minister and the author of Croatia's anti-Serb and anti-Semitic legislation, had been living in California since 1948, having immigrated under an assumed name. Although he had entered the country illegally and was clearly a war criminal, the United States was far from eager to extradite him to Yugoslavia. Because of legal manoeuvring and lobbying campaigns from the Knights of Columbus and other organizations, Artuković was allowed to remain in the United States until his deportation to Yugoslavia in 1986.[54] By that time, the extradition was rather meaningless, considering that Artuković was a senile old man. Washington wished for the crisis over Pavelić to fade rapidly so as to avoid any more bad publicity regarding Artuković.

Although under police surveillance and still weakened from his wounds, Pavelić disappeared from his home on 28 April 1957. Under pressure from Belgrade and public opinion, the Argentine government had ordered the arrest of Pavelić on 26 April.[55] It would be safe to say that Pavelić's escape from Argentina was assisted by compliant figures within the Argentine government. Rumours abounded about his fate and whether or not the Argentine government had assisted in his disappearance. The American Embassy in Buenos Aires suggested that 'the disappearance of Pavelích may be something of a blessing to the Argentine Government, since the question of his extradition is believed to pose practical political headaches beyond the legal issues involved'.[56] Some of the 'political headaches' referred to the Aramburu government's wish to ask Chile to extradite six key Peronists who had escaped to Chile in the previous month. It would be difficult to demand the extradition of these men from Chile but not comply with Yugoslavia's request. Pavelić's disappearance relieved the Argentine government of this problem.

So, where was the aged dictator? There are few clues available from the State Department or any other United States government agency, because Washington was less curious about his whereabouts than in 1934. Other than the Israeli government, few states in 1957 were interested in finding any quislings or criminals from World War II. Although rumoured to have escaped to Paraguay or Bolivia, he probably travelled with a small entourage across the Andes to Chile in a Volkswagen. According to his son-in-law, he spent time in Punta Arenas and Santiago, both cities that possessed significant Croatian émigré populations. Pavelić tried not to draw attention to himself or his entourage. Most likely, the assassins continued to follow his trail. After several months in Chile, the situation grew more perilous, and it was decided he would flee to the safety of old fascist friends. Pavelić flew from Chile to an unknown location in the Middle East. From this unknown destination, he boarded another plane to Spain.[57]

Pavelić and his family must have been greatly relieved to arrive in Spain, where many Ustaše friends from the past, such as Archishop Šarić of Sarajevo, had found sanctuary. Although Pavelić did not have a close relationship with Francisco Franco, living under a fascist government provided him with a great sense of comfort and relief. It was now well into 1958 and the former Poglavnik was a tired and weak man, still suffering from the wounds inflicted upon him a year earlier. Under Franco's security, Pavelić lived quietly, avoiding publicity.

Ante Pavelić's sordid sojourn ended in Madrid on 29 December 1959. He died, somewhat ironically, in the German Hospital from complications caused by the wounds he had received two years earlier. In his hands rested one of his treasured possessions, a crucifix presented to him by Pope Pius XII upon his first visit to Rome as Poglavnik. Reuters quoted Pavelić's former chaplain, Reverend Rafhal Medić, as saying, 'Pavelić was a good Catholic and he died consoled by the sacraments. He was a fighter all his life for freedom from tyranny for the Croatian people.'[58] Pavelić's remains were interred in a large, distinguished, granite tomb featuring a prominent crucifix at Cementerio Sacramental de San Isidro in Madrid. He was 70 years old.[59]

The news of Pavelić's death did not produce a stir in Washington. There were no dispatches from Madrid or Belgrade or anywhere else that mentioned the former dictator's demise or reactions within Croatian émigré organizations. There was no official statement from any branch of the American government. One wonders whether the State Department received any notice of Pavelić's death except the obituaries found in major newspapers like the *New York Times*. The lack of notice echoed the time before 1934 when Pavelić was unknown to the United States government. Pavelić's relationship with Washington had come full circle.

Pavelić's legacy

Pavelić's death did not mean the end for the Ustaše. The movement, having splintered already, evolved into several different organizations, with its strongest cells in Australia.[60] These splinter groups reprised Pavelić's strategy of the 1930s, conducting terrorist operations throughout the 1960s and 1970s, trying to cause havoc and destabilize Yugoslavia. They were especially active in the early 1970s, killing Vladimir Rolović, the Yugoslav Ambassador to Sweden and hijacking a Swedish aeroplane. One of their more notorious actions was the 1972 bombing of a Yugoslav Airlines DC-9 in the skies over Czechoslovakia, killing 27 passengers and crew members.[61] Croatian terrorist attacks even reached American shores with the hijacking of a TWA Boeing 727 out of La Guardia on 11 September 1976, diverting the flight to Paris. The hijackers claimed to have bombs on board the plane, although they did not. The mastermind of the hijacking, Zvonko Bušić, had placed a bomb in Grand Central Station that exploded and killed New York City policeman Brian J. Murray while an attempt was being made to defuse it.[62] Although none of these terrorist acts were effective in establishing an independent Croatia, Ustaše-inspired organizations were sustaining the violent revolutionary activity as condoned by Ante Pavelić.[63]

When civil war engulfed Yugoslavia in the early 1990s, memories of Pavelić and the Ustaše were dredged up as a rallying cry for the Croatians. Pavelić's image began to reappear on posters and graffiti as a symbol of Croatian independence. Ustaše 'U' nostalgia was very popular, with depictions seen occasionally on the walls of bars and sometimes along city streets. Even Ustaše-inspired clothing such as t-shirts and sweatshirts was in vogue (and remain so today among a fringe element). The memory of Ustaše atrocities galvanized some Serbs to kill Croatians and convinced some Croatians to revive the policies of 1941. Both sides drew inspiration from Pavelić's NDH, either to celebrate it or castigate it.[64] Revenge crept into all quarters of the former Yugoslavia.

The Ustaše lost its chief reason for existence when an independent Croatia was established in 1992. With the goal of an independent state reached, an uneasy relationship developed between modern Croatia and its Ustaše past. Not content to disappear from the political landscape, Ustaše supporters and their institutions returned from exile to Croatia and continued their xenophobic agenda. Their ultra-nationalist ambitions were steeped in a rehabilitation and celebration of the NDH. Hoping to connect the present state with the NDH, they made great efforts to salute Pavelić and World War II Croatia through publications like the newspaper *Nezavisna Hrvatska Država*, which moved its offices from Toronto to Zagreb. The paper excelled in hagiography, painting Pavelić as something akin to a saint. Efforts were made to change street names so that former Ustaše leaders would be revered and honoured. The new Croatia announced that its currency would be called the Kuna, the same as in the NDH, and adopted the red checkerboard (*šahovnica*) – a medieval emblem – used by Pavelić's government. Some young Croatians, infatuated with Croatia's World War II experience, began to sport tattoos with the Ustaše 'U' or other images of Pavelić's regime. Croatian rock star Marko Perković, known as Thompson, has gained a following that often parades Ustaše symbols and chants Ustaše slogans at his concerts. His association with Ustaše sentiment is perhaps best illustrated by his hit song 'Jasenovac i Gradiška Stara', which revels in World War II assaults on Serbs, linking them with the conflicts of the early 1990s. Although Thompson, who enjoys rabid fan support, maintains that he is a Croatian patriot interested in promoting God and family, some of his fans find within his music a glorification of the Croatian past, especially the Pavelić era.

The efforts by Croatian ultra-nationalists to rehabilitate Pavelić have led to embarrassing moments for Croatia, especially in the eyes of foreign observers. In the 1990s, Croatian President Franjo Tudjman, an apologist for the NDH, was in the forefront of rehabilitating the NDH, commemorating the state and its actions in World War II while diminishing its role in the execution of Serbs, Jews and Roma. Another example, since repeated, occurred in 1999, when Father Vjekoslav Lasić delivered a Mass in Croatia for Pavelić at the request of his relatives. After an investigation into the matter, Lasić's superior, Master of Dominicans Father Timothy Radcliffe, in a letter to Lasić said, 'he did not know what was said at the Mass, but it was not appropriate to use the liturgy for political purposes'.[65] President Tudjman echoed these sentiments.[66] Unfortunately, these types of event continue to this day and damage the attempts by moderate Croatians to integrate the state into mainstream Western European society.

The current Croatian government is anxious to quell any of these memorials for fear that they will damage Croatia's relationship with the European Union as well as foment internal turmoil. But squelching pro-Ustaše demonstrations has been difficult. Over the past few years there have been marches to honour Pavelić and other notable Ustaše. Annually, the small town of Bleiburg becomes a pilgrimage site for pro-Ustaše elements honouring the anniversary of the 1945 massacre. Monuments have been erected, although quickly removed by the government, to notorious Ustaše figures such as Mile Budak and Jure Francetić. The NDH continues to cast a long shadow over Croatian affairs, especially since the political far right persists in exalting the Ustaše. These efforts to reinterpret the past in no way rehabilitate modern Croatia as the actions of the NDH cannot be rehabilitated.

These incidents and many similar ones might have been avoided had the United States not failed to abide by its World War II era promises to arrest and extradite quislings and war criminals. The United States failed – when it had the chance – to draw suitable attention to the crimes of Pavelić and his regime. Focused on Cold War concerns, the CIC was more interested in protecting its assets and, allowing Pavelić to escape in order to pursue its own purposes. American military authorities never arrested Pavelić, because the Ratline was too important and their dislike for Tito and communist Yugoslavia too great. These policy decisions undermined America's moral authority and heightened tensions between Washington and Belgrade. American inaction also made it possible for Croatian ultra-nationalists and, later, impressionable Croatians to conclude that Pavelić must not have been too bad if the United States, the supposed moral force remaining at the end of World War II, did so little to arrest him. Thus his legacy continues to be troublesome.

Any examination of Pavelić's career would be inadequate if some judgement was not offered about his life. Pavelić was not a mad man, a phrase too often associated with dictators. He was clever, calculating and cunning. Pavelić was not a drifter ready to latch on to any dogma that fit his needs. Indeed, he was a well-educated lawyer and former member of the Yugoslav Parliament, as well as a devoted Catholic. Somehow, however, the respectable institutions of the law, the state and the Church did not restrain him as he pursued his nightmarish vision for achieving an independent Croatia. In this he was like Mussolini and Hitler. Unlike them, he enjoyed little popular support and came to power only through the intervention of others, and he maintained only a brief and tenuous rule over his country. Yet long after Hitler and Mussolini were gone, Pavelić remained at large, still committed to reigniting the Ustaše movement and returning it to power, and still beyond the reach of justice.

NOTES

Chapter 1   Ante Pavelić and the Emergence of the Ustaše

1. Although the name Yugoslavia was not used until 1929, for the sake of clarity, it will be employed instead of the original name, the Kingdom of Serbs, Croats and Slovenes.
2. The United States elevated its mission to embassy rank during World War II.
3. Vladimir Petrov, *A Study in Diplomacy: The Story of Arthur Bliss Lane* (Chicago: Henry Regnery, 1971), p. 104.
4. United States Department of Commerce, *Foreign Commerce Yearbook, 1932–1939* (Washington: USGPO, 1932–1942).
5. Martin Weil, *A Pretty Good Club: The Founding Fathers of the U.S. Foreign Service* (New York: W.W. Norton, 1978), pp. 75–6.
6. Later in his career, Wallace Murray served as ambassador to Iran from 1945 to 1946.
7. Petrov, *A Study in Diplomacy*, p. 104.
8. There are numerous sources of excellent quality on the complicated political scene between Croatians and Serbians in the late 1920s and early 1930s. See John R. Lampe, *Yugoslavia as History: Twice there was a Country* (Cambridge: Cambridge University Press, 1996); Sabrina Ramet, *The Three Yugoslavias: State Building and Legitimation, 1918–2005* (Bloomington: Indiana University Press, 2006); Jill A. Irvine, *The Croat Question: Partisan Politics in the Formation of the Yugoslav Socialist State* (Boulder: CO: Westview Press, 1993); Marcus Tanner, *Croatia: A Nation Forged in War* (New Haven: Yale University Press, 1997); Ivo Goldstein, *Croatia: A History*, trans. Nikolina Jovanović (London: Hurst, 1999); L.S. Stavrianos, *The Balkans since 1453* (New York: Holt, Rinehart and Winston, 1958).

9. There is considerable debate on when the Ustaše was established. While 7 January may not be the exact date, the Ustaše appears to have been in existence by the end of the month and was a functioning body by the latter stages of 1929.

10. Ladislaus Hory and Martin Broszat, *Der Kroatische Ustascha-Staat, 1941–1945* (Stuttgart: Deutsche Verlags-Anstalt, 1964), pp. 13–15.

11. Ramet, *The Three Yugoslavias*, pp. 117–18.

12. According to Italian Foreign Minister Galeazzo Ciano, Mussolini was furious at Pavelić's statement indicating Goth ancestry. Mussolini saw this as a tactic for bringing Croatia more into Germany's orbit. See Galeazzo Ciano, *The Ciano Diaries, 1939–1943*, ed. Hugh Gibson (Garden City: NJ: Garden City Publishing, 1947), p. 401.

13. The relationship between Catholicism and the Ustaše is complicated by religious and national frictions in the 1920s and 1930s and those that have manifested themselves within the historiography of the era. For a thorough explanation of these intricacies see Mark Biondich, 'Religion and Nation in Wartime Croatia: Reflections on the Ustaše Policy of Forced Religious Conversions, 1941–1942', *Slavonic and East European Review* 83 (January 2005), pp. 71–116 and Pedro Ramet, 'From Strossmayer to Stepinac: Croatian National Ideology and Catholicism', *Canadian Review of Studies in Nationalism* 12 (Spring 1985), pp. 123–39. For a compelling theological explanation of the issue that examines why a Christian can justify the use of violence, see Miroslav Volf, *Exclusion and Embrace: A Theological Exploration of Identity, Otherness, and Reconciliation* (Nashville: Abingdon Press, 1996). Volf, an influential Croatian theologian who fought against the Serbs in 1992, sought a theological answer to the question of violence and Christianity when asked by a colleague if he could, 'embrace a Četnik'.

14. Vladko Maček, *In the Struggle for Freedom*, trans. Elizabeth and Stjepan Gazi (University Park: PA: Pennsylvania State University Press), p. 245.

15. Fitzroy MacLean, *The Heretic: The Life and Times of Josip Broz – Tito* (New York: Harper, 1957), p. 46.

16. Sabrina Ramet, 'Vladko Maček and the Croatian Peasant Defence in the Kingdom of Yugoslavia', *Contemporary European History* 16/2 (May 2007), p. 221–22. Maček's concern about Ustaše influence in and Belgrade violence against the Croatian public forced him to create two militias to compete with the Ustaše.

17. For a discussion of Ustaše targets and strategies in this period see James J. Sadkovich, 'Terrorism in Croatia, 1929–1934', *East European Quarterly* 22/1 (March 1988), pp. 55–79.

18. R.J. Crampton, *A Short History of Modern Bulgaria* (Cambridge: Cambridge University Press, 1987), pp. 90–112.

19. Bennett Kovrig, 'Mediation by Obfuscation: The Resolution of the Marseille Crisis, October 1934 to May 1935', *The Historical Journal* 19 (March 1976), p. 194.

20. *The New York Times* had mentioned the existence of Croatian camps in Italy as early as 10 October 1934.

21. Letter to the Secretary of State from Charles S. Wilson, Belgrade, 3 April 1934 (NAMP, M1203, Roll 2, File 860H.00/673). Of the three assassins put on trial, Petar Oreb and Josib Begović were convicted and executed. The third, Ante Podgorelats, had his sentence commuted to life in prison.

22. Vladeta Milićević, *A King Dies in Marseilles: The Crime and its Background* (Bad Godesberg: Hohwacht, 1959), p. 32.

23. For a detailed discussion of the assassination see Allen Roberts, *The Turning Point: The Assassination of Louis Barthou and King Alexander I of Yugoslavia* (New York: St Martin's, 1970); Francois Broche, *Assassinat de Alexandre Ier et Louis Barthou, Marseille, le 9 Octobre 1934* (Paris: Balland, 1977); and Joseph Bornstein, *The Politics of Murder* (New York: William Sloane, 1950). For a sympathetic portrayal of Aleksandar see Stephen Graham, *Alexander of Yugoslavia: The Story of the King Who Was Murdered at Marsailles* (New Haven: Yale University Press, 1939). For more information on Ivan Mihailov see Antonio Pitamitz, '55 Years after the Marseilles Attack the Conspirator Rediscovered', *Soria Illustrata* (1990), pp. 46–51.

24. Memo to John Dyneley Prince from Paul Bowerman, Zagreb, 12 January 1931 (NAMP, M1203, Roll 1), letter to the Secretary of State from John Dyneley Prince, Belgrade, 20 February 1931 (NAMP, M1203, Roll 1, File 860H.00/474), letter to the Secretary of State from John Dyneley Prince, Belgrade, 16 April 1931 (NAMP, M1203, Roll 1, 860H.00/474), letter to the Secretary of State from Charles Wilson, 3 April 1934, Belgrade (NAMP, M1203, Roll 2, File 860H.00/673). Other documents to this effect are found in this collection.

25. Wallace Murray, Department of State, Division of Near Eastern Affairs, Daily Report, 'The Assassination of King Alexander of Yugoslavia', 10 October 1934 (NAMP, M1203, Roll, 5, 860H.00AL2/67).

26. Ibid.

27. Wallace Murray, Department of State, Division of Near Eastern Affairs, Daily Report, 12 October 1934 (NAMP, M1203, Roll 5, 860H.001AL2/123).

28. 'Through Donations, American Croatians Financing Defense of Croatians Arrested in France', *Croatiapress* (April 1935), p. 2.

29. Telegram to the Secretary of State from Long, Rome, 23 October 1934 (NARA, RG 59, Box 2319, File 860H.001AL2/87).

30. Ibid.

31. Letter to the Secretary of State from Breckinridge Long, Rome, 24 October 1934 (NAMP, M1203, Roll 5, File 860H.001 AL 2/125).

32. Memo to the Secretary of State from Breckinridge Long, Rome, 26 October 1934 (NAMP M1203, Roll 5, File 860H.001AL2/127).

33. Ibid.

34. Ibid.

35. Telegram to the Secretary of State from Interim Chargé Alexander Kirk, Rome, 2 November 1934 (NARA, RG 59, Box 4319, File 860h.001 Al 2/129.
36. Kovrig, 'Mediation by Obfuscation', pp. 196–8.
37. Ibid., pp. 195–7.
38. FBI Memo, 'Croatian Activities in United States – Ustaše', by D. Dilillo, 11 May 1942 (NARA, RG 65, Box 165, File 30311).
39. Ibid. It was not until 1942 that the FBI learned about Croatian-Americans financially supporting these defendants. The information was obtained after searching the residence of Karlo Krompotich, a treasurer for the Domobrans. Documents obtained by Alex Dragnich during World War II tell a slightly different story. They indicate that the Croatian National Representation raised $9,419.38 to help with criminal defense costs. The majority of the funds totalling $6,222.79 was sent to George Desbons and Saint Auban. See 'The Croatian People: A New Epoch', published in the 1941 *Croatian Home Defender's Yearbook* (ADP, Box 32, Folder 5).
40. Ibid.
41. Letter to the Secretary of State from Alexander Kirk, Rome 9 November 1934 (NAMP, M1203, Roll 5, File 860H.001 AL 2/148).
42. Memo to the Secretary of State from Charles S. Wilson, Belgrade, 14 November 1934 (NAMP, M1203, Roll 5, File 860H.001AL2/180).
43. Ibid.
44. Ibid.
45. Telegram to Secretary of State from Alexander Kirk, Rome, 26 November 1934 (NAMP, M1203, Roll 5, File 860H.001AL20138).
46. Letter to Secretary of State from Charles S. Wilson, Belgrade, 4 May 1936 (NAMP, M1203, Roll 3, File 860h.00/862).
47. Report by Wallace Murray, 19 May 1936 (NAMP, M1203, Roll 3, File 860h.00/864).
48. Vladeta Milićević, *A King Dies in Marseilles*, p. 98.

Chapter 2   Investigating Domobrans

1. Letter to the State Department from Serge de Tucich, 15 October 1934 (NAMP, M1203, Roll 4, File 860H.00 Croatian Activities in the US).
2. Ibid. For more information about Jelić's time in the United States see Jere Jareb, *Političke uspomene i rad dra Branimira Jelića* (Cleveland: Mirko Šamija, 1982), pp. 86–97. In Yugoslavia, it was customary to use the title 'Doctor' for lawyers, which Jelić was.
3. Ibid.
4. Memo to the District Director of Immigration and Naturalization, 10 September 1934 (NARA, RG 65, Box 161, File 30311).

5. Letter to the State Department from Serge de Tucich.

6. 'Chronology' (Alex Dragnich Papers, Box 32, Folder 5).

7. Ibid.

8. FBI Report on Branimir Jelić, 16 August 1934, Jelić File.

9. 'Croat Leader Hails Killing', *Youngstown Daily Vindicator* (10 October 1934), p. 1.

10. Ibid.

11. FBI Memo on Jelić, 3 March 1943, Jelić File. Information about the establishment and operation of Domobran chapters is limited. Most of the documentation either never existed or has been lost. The best information is found in newspaper reports, Domobran proclamations, and in the documents of various United States agencies.

12. James J. Sadkovich, *Italian Support for Croatian Separatism, 1927–1937* (New York: Garland, 1987), p. 191. Jelić's activities in South America were exceedingly successful. He established a strong network of pro-Pavelić Croatians connected through newspapers and fraternal groups.

13. Letter to Cordell Hull from Yugoslav Charge d'Affaires, 22 November 1934 (NAMP, M1203, Roll 4, File 860H.00 Croatian Activities in U.S./2).

14. FBI Memo, 'Branimir Drazorvic Jelić', 15 March 1943 (NARA, RG 65, Box 166, File 30311).

15. Ibid.

16. Department of Commerce, Bureau of the Census, *Abstract of the Fourteenth Census of the United States, 1920* (Washington: United States Government Printing Office, 1923), pp. 386, 392–5.

17. Joseph Kraja, 'The Croatian Circle, 1928–1946', *Journal of Croatian Studies* 5–6 (1964–5), pp. 146–8.

18. Ibid., pp. 150–2.

19. Ibid., pp. 165–7.

20. Ibid., p. 198.

21. 'Resolutions Adopted by All Croatian Congress in Youngstown, Receives Full Acknowledgment of Croats in Homeland', *Croatiapress* (January 1935), p. 2.

22. Manifesto of the Croatian National Representation for Independence of Croatia, 29 November 1934 (NAMP, M1203, Roll 4, File 860H.00 Croatian Activities in U.S./3).

23. Memo by Wallace Murray, 8 December 1934 (NAMP, M1203, Roll 4, File 860H.00 Croatian Activities in U.S./3).

24. Letter to Cordell Hull from Yugoslav Chargé d'Affaires, 22 November 1934 (NAMP, M1203, Roll 4).

25. Ibid.

26. Jure Krišto, 'Čuvari svoje braće: policijsko nadgledanje američkih Hrvata tijekom Drugoga svjetskoga rata', *Časopis za suvremenu povijest* 35 (2003), p. 414.

27. Extracts from Ante Doshen's Diary, 1937–41 (ADP, Box 33, Folder 4). Because the Hoover Institution, like many news outlets of the period, uses the

Anglicized spelling of Ante Došen's name, it will be used when referring to his diary collection in the Dragnich Papers.

28. FBI Memo, 'Hrvatski Domobran', by William C. Leonard, 1 May 1944 (NARA, RG 65, Box 167, File 30311).

29. Extracts from Ante Doshen's Diary, 1937–41 (ADP, Box 33, Folder 4).

30. Letter to T.M. Milligan from John J. Farrell, 26 November 1934 (NAMP, M1203, Roll 4, File 860H.00 Croatian Activities in U.S./6).

31. Ibid.

32. Ibid.

33. Ibid.

34. Ibid.

35. Letter to T.M. Milligan from John J. Farrell, 4 December 1934 (NAMP, Roll 4, File 860H.00).

36. 'Seek Freedom for 2 Peoples', *Youngstown Daily Vindicator* (30 November 1934), p. 10.

37. 'Ask Plebiscite for Croatians', *Youngstown Daily Vindicator* (8 December 1934), p. 10.

38. Letter to T.M. Milligan from John J. Farrell, 4 December 1934 (NAMP, Roll 4, File 860H.00).

39. 'City Feels 'Repercussions' of Yugoslavian Troubles', *Youngstown Daily Vindicator* (9 December 1934), A:11.

40. FBI and State Department files accuse Budak of unsavoury activities related to the Poland Country Club. The first such charge appeared in Letter to T.M. Milligan from John J. Farrell, 4 December 1934 (NAMP, M1203, Roll 4, File 860H.00 Croatian Activities in U.S./10).

41. Transcript of a talk by Ante Valenta, 4 December 1934 (NAMP, M1203, Roll 4, File 860H.00 Croatian Activities in U.S./9).

42. Ibid.

43. Ibid.

44. Memo to the Secretary of State from Wallace Murray, 8 December 1934 (NAMP, M1203, Roll 4, File 860H.001/AL2/174).

45. Ibid.

46. Ibid.

47. Eckhardt played a significant role in Hungarian politics during the 1930s, leading the Small Holders Party. He immigrated to the United States in 1941, working closely with the State Department during World War II. He tirelessly laboured for Hungarian independence until his death in 1972.

48. Ibid.

49. Letter to R.C. Bannerman from John J. Farrell, 9 December 1934 (NAMP, M1203, Roll 4, File 860H.00 Croatian Activities in the U.S./11).

50. 'Deny Charge that Plot to Kill Jugoslav King was Known Here', *Youngstown Telegram*, 7 December 1934, p. 1.

51. Ibid., p. 2.

52. Letter to R.C. Bannerman from John J. Farrell, 9 December 1934 (NAMP, M1203, Roll 4, File 860H.00 Croatian Activities in the U.S./11).

53. Ibid.

54. To Mr Phillips from Wallace Murray, 11 December 1934 (NAMP, Roll4, File 860H.00 Croatian Activities in U.S./14).

55. Memo by the Foreign Nationalities Branch to the Director of Strategic Services, 'Foreign Nationality Groups in the United States', 28 June 1944, www.pavelićpapers.com/documents/oss/oss011.html (accessed on 22 February 2006).

56. Department of State Memo, 'Activities in the United States of Alleged Croatian Revolutionaries', 11 December 1934 (NAMP, M1203, Roll 4, File 860H.00 Croatian Activities in U.S./15).

57. Ibid.

58. Memo by the Foreign Nationalities Branch.

59. George J. Prpic, *The Croatian Immigrants in America* (New York: Philosophical Library, 1971), p. 275.

60. The largest collection of *Nezavisna Država Hrvatska* is found scattered through FBI and State Department files at the National Archives in College Park, Maryland.

61. Alex Dragnich, 'Memorandum for James R. Sharp, Chief, Foreign Agents Registration Section', 26 February 1944 (ADP, Box 32, Folder 5), p. 3.

62. Ibid., p. 4.

63. Ibid., pp. 4–6. Dragnich developed a detailed chronology that demonstrated that Došen and Grbić printed Pavelić's speeches and other articles on order from Ustaše in Europe. See 'Chronology' (ADP, Box 32, Folder 5).

64. 'Hrvatski Domobran', *Croatiapress*, August 1936, p. 2.

65. *Croatipress* Article, February 1937, quoted in 'Memorandum for James R. Sharp...' by Alex Dragnich (ADP, Box 32, Folder 5), pp. 7–8.

66. 'The Traits of Serbian Crown Prince Peter', *Croatiapress*, October 1938, p. 6.

67. 'Activities in the United States of Alleged Croatian Revolutionaries', Division of Near Eastern Affairs, 11 December 1934 (NAMP, M1203, Roll 4, File 860H.00 Croatian Activities in the U.S./15).

68. Telegram to Secretary of State from Charles Wilson, 8 December 1934 (NAMP, M1203, Roll 5, File 860H.001AL2/168).

69. Memo to Colonel McIntyre, Assistant Secretary to the President from James Clement Dunn, 12 December 1934 (NAMP, M1203, Roll 5, File 860H.001AL2/168).

70. 'Archbishop Says US Poverty Equals Europe's Prosperity', *Youngstown Daily Vindicator*, 10 December 1934, p. 16.

71. Extracts from Ante Doshen's Diary, 1937 (ADP, Box 33, Folder 4).

72. Ibid.

73. Ibid.

74. Ibid.

75. To Secretary of State from Wallace Murray, 9 December 1935 (NAMP M1203, Roll 4, File 860H.00 Croatian Activities in the U.S./29).
76. To the Secretary of State from Constantin Fotitich, 6 February 1936 (NAMP M1203, Roll 4, File 860H.00 Croatian Activities in U.S./41) and 'Memorandum of Conversation with the Yugoslav Minister, 7 February 1936 (NAMP M1203, roll 4, file 860H.00 Croatian Activities in U.S./42).
77. To James A. Farley From Cordell Hull, 17 February 1936 (NAMP M1203, Roll 4, File 860H.00 Croatian Activities in U.S./43).
78. 'Memorandum of Conversation with Mr. Parrish, of the Department of Justice, relative to the complaint against the "Independent State of Croatia" and its editor, Ante Došen', 18 May 1936 (NAMP, M1203, Roll 4, File 860H.00 Croatian Activities in U.S./49).
79. To Frances Perkins from Cordell Hull 3 July 1936 (NAMP, M1203, Roll 4, File 860H.00 Croatian Activities in U.S./60).
80. To Secretary of Labor Frances Perkins from Wallace Murray, 2 July 1936 (NAMP, M1203, Roll 4, File 860H.00 Croatian Activities in U.S./60).
81. Letter to Frances Perkins from Cordell Hull, 3 July 1936 (NAMP, M1203, Roll 4, File 860H.00 Croatian Activities in U.S./60).
82. Letter to the Secretary of State from Assistant Attorney General Brien McMahon, 23 November 1937 (NAMP, M1203, Roll 4, File 860H.00 Croatian Activities in U.S./77).
83. Letter to the Secretary of State from Brien McMahon, 23 November 1937 (NAMP, M1203, Roll 4, File 860H.00 Croatian Activities in U.S./77).
84. Ibid.
85. Department of State Memo from H. Tittmann, 28 May 1938 (NAMP, M1203, Roll 4, File 860H.00 Croatian Activities in U.S./86). Vladimir Rybar levelled this accusation after noting that several Yugoslav citizens and Americans of Yugoslav ancestry had been convicted of counterfeiting.
86. Letter to Attorney General Homer S. Cummings from Acting Secretary Sumner Welles, 28 December 1938 (NAMP, M1203, Roll 4, File 860H.00 Croatian Activities in U.S./96).
87. Ibid.
88. Ibid.
89. Extracts from Ante Doshen's Diary, 1937–39 (ADP, Box 3, File 4).
90. Department of State Memo, 8 March 1939 (NAMP, M1203, Roll 4, File 860H.00 Croatian Activities in the U.S./106).
91. 'Protest from the Official Organs of the Croatian Independence Movement', *Croatiapress*, June 1937, p. 5.
92. Rudolf Erić, 'Lance sramotnog ropstva treba kidati', *Godisnjak (Croatian Almanac)* 1940 (Pittsburgh: Hrvatski Domobran, 1940), p. 195.
93. Ante Pavelić, 'Oslobodjenje', *Godišnjak (Croatian Almanac)* 1940 (Pittsburgh: Hrvatski Domobran, 1940), pp. 20–22.
94. FBI Memo on Branimir Jelić, 3 March 1943, Jelić File.
95. Ibid.

96. Ibid.

97. Ibid.

98. FBI Memo on Jelić, 5 September 1939, Jelić File.

99. Ibid.

100. Extracts from Ante Doshen's Diary, 1938–39 (ADP, Box 3, File 4). Došen's diary entries portray him as a victim of hateful, vindictive and power-hungry men such as Frank Budak, Rudolf Erić and Luka Grbić.

101. Letter to the Secretary of State from Frank R. McNinch, 3 March 1939 (NAMP, M1203, Roll 4, File 860H.00 Croatian Activities in U.S./105).

102. Letter to J. Edgar Hoover from Arthur M. Thurston, 28 January 1943, FBI File.

103. FBI Memo, 'Croatian Activities in United States', 11 May 1942.

104. Sadkovich, *Italian Support for Croatian Separatism, 1927–1937*, pp. 265–7, 269.

105. Jure Krišto, 'Communist Penetration of Croatian American Organizations during World War II', *Review of Croatian History* 5 (2009), pp. 182–3.

Chapter 3   Unlikely Victory

1. Telegram to the Secretary of State from Morris, Berlin, 9 April 1941 (NAMP, M1203, Roll 16, File 860J.00/1280).

2. H. James Burgwyn, *Italian Foreign Policy in the Interwar Period, 1918–1940* (Westport: CT: Praeger, 1997), pp. 155–6. Burgwyn provides excellent context for understanding Italian diplomatic maneuvering in relation to Yugoslavia and the Great Powers.

3. Memo to Arthur Bliss Lane from John J. Meily, 11 October 1938 (NAMP, M1203, Roll 3, File 860H.00/966). Albeit highly critical of Serbian politicians and early wartime decisions and rather defensive regarding Croatian fault, a thorough examination of American–Yugoslav relations prior to World War II is found in Ivo Tasovac, *American Foreign Policy and Yugoslavia, 1939–1941* (College Station: TX: Texas A&M Press, 1990).

4. Telegram to the Secretary of State from Arthur Bliss Lane, 16 March 1939 (NAMP, M1203, Roll 3, File 860J.00/901).

5. Meily's career was cut short when he was killed in a plane crash on 21 September 1944. He was travelling to Recife, Brazil, where he was to serve as consul-general.

6. Telegram to the Secretary of State from Arthur Bliss Lane, 28 February 1940 (NAMP, M1203, Roll 16, File 860H.00/1131).

7. Letter to the Secretary of State from Arthur Bliss Lane, 2 March 1940 (NAMP, M1203, Roll 16, File 860H.00/1150). From 1944 to 1947, Lane served as ambassador to Poland where he became disenchanted with Allied policy towards Warsaw.

8. Ibid.

9. Ibid.

10. Telegram to the Secretary of State from Arthur Bliss Lane, 11 March 1940 (NAMP, M1203, Roll 16, File 860H.00/1136).

11. Telegram to the Secretary of State from Arthur Bliss Lane, 4 November 1940, (NAMP, M1203, Roll 16, File 860H.00/1213).

12. Vladko Maček, *In the Struggle for Freedom*, trans. Elizabeth and Stjepan Gazi (University Park: PA: Pennsylvania State University Press), p. 204.

13. Richard Dunlop, *Donovan: America's Master Spy* (Chicago: Rand McNally, 1982), p. 249.

14. Ibid., pp. 256–7.

15. Anthony Cave Brown, *The Last Hero: Wild Bill Donovan* (New York: Times Books, 1982), p. 156. Also see Peter B. Lane, *The United States and the Balkan Crisis of 1940–1941* (New York: Garland, 1988), pp. 98–136, and Tasovac, *American Foreign Policy and Yugoslavia, 1939–1941*, pp. 79–92. Donovan struggled to convince Balkan leaders that the United States would stand behind Great Britain and ultimately them. In particular, Donovan could not convince Tsar Boris of Bulgaria to remain outside of Hitler's sphere.

16. Dunlop, *Donovan*, p. 256. See also Cordell Hull, *The Memoirs of Cordell Hull*, vol. II (New York: Macmillan, 1940), pp. 925–30. Hull provides a basic discussion of American attempts to convince Prince Paul to oppose Nazi aggression.

17. Telegram to the Secretary of State from Arthur Bliss Lane, 18 February 1941, *FRUS 1941*, Vol. II *Europe* (Washington: USGPO, 1959), p. 946.

18. Telegram to Arthur Bliss Lane from the Acting Secretary of State, 21 March 1941, ibid., p. 961.

19. Prior to World War II, the Yugoslav military had 165 generals of whom all but four were Serb.

20. Telegram to the Secretary of State from Arthur Bliss Lane, 21 March 1941, ibid., p. 962.

21. For a thorough examination of American attitudes toward the Balkans prior to the German invasion see Lane, *The United States and the Balkan Crisis of 1940–1941*, pp. 141–210.

22. Telegram to Arthur Bliss Lane from the Acting Secretary of State, 27 March 1941, *FRUS 1941*, p. 969.

23. Ibid., p. 969.

24. Ulrich von Hassell, *The Von Hassell Diaries, 1938–1944* (London: Hamish Hamilton, 1948), p. 160. Many of von Hassell's experiences were contradictory to those of Meily.

25. Even as late as 10 April, Maček rejected all German attempts to woo him.

26. For a good examination of German policy see Norman Rich, *Hitler's War Aims: The Establishment of the New Order*, vol. II (New York: W.W. Norton, 1974), pp. 273–82. Slavko Kvaternik's connections with extremist politics in Croatia were deeper than most. His wife was the daughter of Josip Frank, the well-known Croatian nationalist and one of the intellectual founders of the Ustaše.

27. Malcolm Muggeridge (ed.), *Ciano's Diary, 1939–1943* (London: William Heinemann, 1950), p. 201.

28. Ciano met with Pavelić several times and discussed briefly some of these meetings in his memoirs.

29. Ian Kershaw, *Hitler, 1936–1945: Nemesis* (New York: Norton, 2000), p. 366.

30. Telegram to Arthur Bliss Lane from the Secretary of State, 6 April 1941, *FRUS 1941*, Vol. II, *Europe* (Washington: USGPO, 1959), p. 975.

31. For an in-depth examination of Lane's policies and his retreat from Yugoslavia, see Petrov.

32. Jozo Tomasevich, *War and Revolution in Yugoslavia: Occupation and Collaboration* (Stanford: Stanford University Press, 2001), pp. 47–58. Tomasevich offers a detailed description of Pavelić's negotiations with Italy and his path to power in Croatia.

33. Ivo Goldstein, 'Ante Pavelić, Charisma and National Mission in Wartime Croatia', *Totalitarian Movements and Political Religions* 7 (June 2006), pp. 225–7.

34. 'Free Croat State Reported Formed,' *New York Times*, 11 April 1941, p. 1.

35. 'The Balkans,' *Time*, 21 April 1941, p. 42.

36. 'Crowns that Fade,' *New York Times*, 19 May 1941, p. 16.

37. Editor, 'Free Croatia' *The Washington Evening Star* (12 April 1941) in *A Nations Fight for Survival: The 1941 Revolution and War in Yugoslavia as Reported by the American Press* (n.p., 1944), p. 203.

38. *Nezavisna Hrvatska Država*, 17 May 1941, p. 1.

39. Ibid.

40. Ibid., 17 May 1941, 24 May 1941, 31 May 1941.

41. Ibid.

42. H. James Burgwyn, *Empire on the Adriatic: Mussolini's Conquest of Yugoslavia, 1941–1943* (New York: Enigma, 2005), p. 160.

43. Galeazzo Ciano, in his diary, referred to Pavelić's followers as 'cutthroats'.

44. Stevan K. Pavlowitch, *Unconventional Perceptions of Yugoslavia, 1940–1945* (New York: East European Monographs, 1985), pp. 109–12, and Herbert L. Matthews, 'Croats Visit Italy to Tender Crown', *New York Times*, 18 May 1941, p. 24. For a thorough discussion of Italian–NDH relations, see Burgwyn, *Empire on the Adriatic*.

45. Herbert L. Matthews, 'Croats Get Spoleto as King; Dalmatia is Given to Italy', *New York Times*, 19 May 1941, p. 1.

46. Telegram to the Secretary of State from Phillips, 19 May 1941, (NAMP, M1203, Roll 19, File 860H.01/325 Section 1).

47. Ibid.

48. Anthony Rhodes, *The Vatican in the Age of the Dictators, 1922–1945* (London: Hodder and Stoughton, 1973), p. 326.

49. Ibid., p. 326.

Chapter 4   Carnage

1. Telegram to the Secretary of State from MacMurray, 6 May 1941 (NAMP, M1203, Roll 16, File 860J.00/1289). Many thanks to the University of Toronto Press for allowing me to reproduce portions of my article 'The United States' Response to Genocide in the Independent State of Croatia, 1941–1945' *Genocide Studies and Prevention* 3 (2008), pp. 75–98.

2. There is heated debate over the exact number of Serbs, Jews and Roma killed by the Ustaše, with nationalism and political ambitions permeating and exaggerating statistics. A full discussion of this issue is well beyond the scope of this book. With many records missing, it is very difficult to obtain precise figures devoid of bias. These are statistics recognized by the United States Holocaust and Memorial Museum as the best available at this time, but they are in no way definitive. Complementary to this issue is the question of genocide. Although some figures have denied genocide in Croatia during World War II, there is considerable research that supports calling the NDH government's policies and actions genocide. See Leo Kuper, *Genocide: Its Political Use in the Twentieth Century* (New Haven: CT: Yale University Press, 1981); Ben Kiernan, 'Twentieth Century Genocides: Underlying Ideological Themes from Armenia to East Timor', in Robert Gellately and Ben Kiernan (eds), *The Specter of Genocide: Mass Murder in Historical Perspective* (Cambridge: Cambridge University Press, 2003), p. 29–51; Robert Melson, 'Paradigms of Genocide: The Holocaust, the Armenian Genocide, and Contemporary Mass Destructions', *Annals of the American Academy of Political and Social Science* 548 (1996), pp. 156–68; Helen Fein, *Accounting for Genocide: National Responses and Jewish Victimization during the Holocaust* (New York: Free Press, 1979); Bette Dinich, 'Dismembering Yugoslavia: Nationalists Ideologies and the Symbolic Revival of Genocide', *American Ethnologist* 21 (1994), pp. 367–90; Robert Hayden, 'Recounting the Dead: The Rediscovery and Redefinition of Wartime Massacres in Late- and Post-Communist Yugoslavia', in Rubie S. Watson (ed.), *Memory and Opposition under State Socialism* (Santa Fe: NM: School of American Research, 1993), pp. 167–84, 176–7; Michael Sells, 'Kosovo Mythology and the Bosnian Genocide', in Omer Bartov and Phyllis Mack (eds), *In God's Name: Genocide and Religion in the Twentieth Century* (New York: Berghahn Books, 2001), pp. 180–205, p. 185.

3. Ilija Jukić, *The Fall of Yugoslavia*, trans. Dorian Cooke (New York: Harcourt, Brace, Jovanovich, 1974), p. 290.

4. Vladimir Dedijer, *The Yugoslav Auschwitz and the Vatican: The Croatian Massacre of the Serbs During World War II* (Buffalo: NY: Prometheus, 1992), pp. 129–76; Edmond Paris, *Genocide in Satellite Croatia, 1941–1945*, trans. Lois Perkins (Chicago: American Institute for Balkan Affairs, 1961), p. 59; and Jukić, *The Fall of Yugoslavia*, p. 97. For an excellent account of Ustaše racial policies and the justification for them as well as the NDH government's genocidal behaviour see Sabrina Ramet, *The Three Yugoslavias: State Building*

and Legitimation, 1918–2005 (Bloomington: Indiana University Press, 2006), pp. 116–20. Dedijer's account, extensive in documentation and emotional due to having personally witnessed atrocities in the NDH, focuses on Catholicism's role in the slaughter and does not provide a thorough history of events. Paris's work is highly emotional as well as prone to innuendo and exaggeration and therefore must be treated carefully. Most of the studies pertaining to genocide in the NDH are flawed by nationalism, political leverage and anti-Catholic sentiment. There remains to be written a dispassionate and careful study of the atrocities committed by the NDH government.

5. Srdjan Trifković, *Ustaša: Croatian Separatism and European Politics, 1929–1945* (London: The Lord Byron Foundation for Balkan Studies, 1998), pp. 139–41. Also see Raphael Lemkin, *Axis Rule in Occupied Europe* (Carnegie Endowment for International Peace, 1944), pp. 620–6.

6. Ibid., 626–7.

7. Jozo Tomasevich, *War and Revolution in Yugoslavia: Occupation and Collaboration* (Stanford: Stanford University Press, 2001), p. 383. Also see N. Dinko Šuljak, *Croatia's Struggle for Independence: A Documentary History* (Arcadia: CA: Croatian Information Service, 1977), p. 177.

8. Ibid., 384. Also see Trifković, *Ustaša*, p. 139

9. Ibid., p. 137.

10. Ibid., p. 138–9.

11. Harriet Pass Freidenreich, *The Jews of Yugoslavia: A Quest for Community* (Philadelphia: The Jewish Publication Society of America, 1979), pp. 191–2 and United States Holocaust Memorial Museum, *Historical Atlas of the Holocaust* (New York: Macmillan, 1996), pp. 171–7. Also see Tomasevich, *War and Revolution in Yugoslavia*, pp. 592–7.

12. Bela Vago, 'The Reaction to the Nazi Anti-Jewish Policy in East-Central Europe and in the Balkans', in Francois Furet (ed.), *Unanswered Questions: Nazi Germany and the Genocide of the Jews* (New York: Schocken Books, 1989), pp. 199–251, 207–08, 216–18.

13. Tomasevich, *War and Revolution in Yugoslavia*, pp. 106–8.

14. For a full discussion see Ivo Goldstein, *Holokaust u Zagrebu* (Zagreb: Zidovska opcina Zagreb, 2001); Ivo Goldstein, 'The Independent State of Croatia in 1941: On the Road to Catastrophe', in Sabrina Ramet (ed.), *The Independent State of Croatia 1941–1945* (London: Routledge, 2007), pp. 19–29; Barry M. Lituchy, *Jasenovac and the Holocaust: Analyses and Survivor Testimonies* (New York: Jasenovac Research Institute, 2006); Dedijer, *The Yugoslav Auschwitz and the Vatican*; Marjan Jurjevic, *Ustasha under the Southern Cross* (Published by the author, 1973), p. 20.

15. Dedijer, *The Yugoslav Auschwitz and the Vatican*, pp. 231–67.

16. Richard West, 'Death Camp Capture Revives Croat Shame', *The Sunday Telegraph*, 7 May 1995, p. 25.

17. Zvi Loker, 'The Testimony of Dr Edo Neufeld: The Italians and the Jews of Croatia', *Holocaust and Genocide Studies* 7 (Spring 1993), p. 69.

18. Press Statement by James B. Foley, Deputy Spokesman United States Department of State, 'United States Welcomes Croatia's Extradition Request to Prosecute Dinko Sakić for Crimes Committed During the Holocaust and Swift Action by Argentina to Arrest Sakić', 1 May 1998.

19. *Hrvatski List* quoted in West, 'Death Camp Capture Revives Croat Shame', p. 88. As has been mentioned by other historians, Budak never spelled out such a policy in writing.

20. Jonathan Steinberg, *All or Nothing: The Axis and the Holocaust, 1941–1943* (London: Routledge), p. 30.

21. The USHMM possesses a significant and moving collection of photographs and records that detail this type of Ustaše behaviour. Some evidence is also found at the National Archives in Washington and the Public Record Office in London.

22. Constantin Fotitch, *The War We Lost* (New York: Viking, 1948), pp. 121–2. In the media and in United States government documents, there was great variation in the spelling of Fotić's name.

23. Letter to Ambassador Richard Patterson from Stoyan Pribichevich, 8 November 1946, *FRUS 1945–49* (NARA, Roll 3, File 860H.00/11–646).

24. Letter to the Secretary of State from K.L. Rankin with enclosure 14 August 1941 (NAMP, M1203, Roll 16, File 860H.00/1322).

25. Ibid.

26. Letter to the Secretary of State from Samuel Honaker, 28 August 1942 (NAMP, M1203, Roll 16, File 860H.00/1410) and a telephone interview with an anonymous survivor, 23 May 2001.

27. Svetlana Isaković (ed.), *Genocide Against the Serbs* (Belgrade: Museum of Applied Arts, 1992), p. 11.

28. Fotitch, p. 123–4.

29. Stella Alexander, *Church and State in Yugoslavia since 1945* (Cambridge: Cambridge University Press, 1979), p. 30.

30. Mark Biondich, 'Religion and Nation in Wartime Croatia: Reflections on the Ustaše Policy of Forced Religious Conversions, 1941–1942', *Slavonic and East European Review* 83 (January 2005), pp. 71–116, 91.

31. West, 'Death Camp Capture Revives Croat Shame'.

32. Dedijer, *The Yugoslav Auschwitz and the Vatican*, pp. 88–9, 268–83.

33. 'Interrogation of Siegfried Kasche', 10 July 1945, (RG 319, IRR XE 002491, Box 473). The interrogation was conducted by the British Army.

34. Dedijer, *The Yugoslav Auschwitz and the Vatican*, pp. 97–100.

35. Quoted in Trifković, *Ustaša*, pp. 142–3.

36. Anthony Rhodes, *The Vatican in the Age of the Dictators, 1922–1945* (London: Hodder and Stoughton, 1973), p. 324.

37. Stepinac had become archbishop in 1939, having been a priest for a mere nine years. He had never served in a parish. For a stinging indictment of Stepinac, see Dedijer's *The Yugoslav Auschwitz and the Vatican*.

38. Mark Biondich, 'Controversies Surrounding the Catholic Church in Wartime Croatia, 1941–1945', in *The Independent State of Croatia, 1941–1945*, ed. by Sabrina Ramet (London: Routledge, 2007), pp. 42–4.

39. Alexander, *Church and State*, pp. 34–8.

40. Quoted in Trifković, *Ustaša*, pp. 146–7. Glaise von Horstenau survived the war but was arrested by the Allies and committed suicide on 20 July 1946.

41. After World War II, Siegfried Kasche was arrested by the Allies and returned to Yugoslavia to stand trial for war crimes. He was convicted and executed in 1947.

42. Ivo Omrčanin, *The Pro-Allied Putsch in Croatia in 1944 and the Massacre of Croatians by Tito's Communists* (Philadelphia: Dorrance, 1975), p. 13. Omrčanin was a key cog in the Ratline, working in Pontifical Assistance in the late 1940s. Even with his dodgy background, Omrčanin immigrated to the United States in the 1950s, later working as a history professor at Indiana University of Pennsylvania.

43. 'Illegal Act Charged to US Aide in Croatia', *New York Times*, 31 August 1941, 11:3, 'Espionage is Charged to US Aide in Croatia', *New York Times*, 1 September 1941, 6:4, 'US Consul is Accused Again in the Italian Press', *New York Times*, 4 September 1941, 14:5. Ivo Tasovac in *American Foreign Policy and Yugoslavia, 1939–1941* (College Station: TX: Texas A&M Press, 1990) is prone to believe Lorković's position, arguing that keeping the consulate open was in line with Roosevelt's policy of splintering Yugoslavia. Roosevelt and the State Department, however, believed that Yugoslavia was an area of British interest and at this point in the war were unwilling, most likely, to unnecessarily cause difficulties for the British by ignoring their will and keeping the consulate open. Likewise, recognition of a state led by a man with two death sentences looming above him would have been a difficult public relations battle for the US government.

44. Telegram to the Secretary of State from Arthur Bliss Lane, 17 May 1941 (NAMP M1203, Roll 19, File 860H.01/328).

45. Telegram to the Secretary of State from Boucher, 7 June 1941 (NAMP, M1203, Roll 16, File 860H.00/1304).

46. Letter to the Secretary of State from Consul K.L. Rankin, 14 August 1941 (NAMP, M1203, Roll 16, File 860H.00/1322).

47. Enclosure, ibid.

48. Enclosure, ibid.

49. Ibid.

50. Walter R. Roberts, *Tito, Mihailović and the Allies, 1941–1945* (Durham: NC: Duke University Press, 1987), p. 19.

51. Letter to the American Embassy in Rome from Cordell Hull, 29 September 1941 (NAMP, M1203, roll 16, 860H.00/1327CF).

52. Fotitch, pp. 116–18.

53. Memo from G. Wadsworth in Rome, 'Conditions in Croatia', 2 December 1941 (NAMP, M1203, Roll 16, File 860H.00/1331).

54. Ibid.

55. Fotitch, p. 179.

56. Ibid., p. 179.
57. Ibid., pp. 179–80.
58. Letter to the Secretary of State from A.J. Drexel Biddle, Jr, 9 September 1942, *FRUS, 1942, Europe* (Washington: USGPO, 1961), pp. 812–13.
59. Kenneth S. Davis, *FDR: The War President, 1940–1943* (New York: Random House, 2000), p. 727.
60. Ibid., p. 728. Also see Henry L. Feingold, *The Politics of Rescue: The Roosevelt Administration and the Holocaust, 1938–1945* (New Brunswick: Rutgers University Press, 1970).
61. Feingold, *The Politics of Rescue*, p. 170.
62. For a more detailed look at Breckinridge Long's positions see Sara Peck, 'The Campaign for an American Response to the Nazi Holocaust, 1943–1945', *Journal of Contemporary History* (April 1980), pp. 367–70 and Fred L. Israel (ed.), *The War Diary of Breckinridge Long* (Lincoln: University of Nebraska Press, 1966).
63. 'Massacres Laid to Croat Ustashi', *New York Times*, 11 October 1941, 3:6.
64. James MacDonald, 'Serbian Prelate Charges Killing of 180,000 in Nazi-Invaded Croatia', *New York Times*, 3 January 1942, 8:6.
65. Telegram to the Secretary of State from Huddle, 9 March 1942, (NAMP, M1203, Roll 16, File 860H.00/1376).
66. Letter to Mr Atherton from A.J. Biddle Jr, 31 July 1942 (NAMP, M1203, Roll 16, File 860H.00/14041/2).
67. Ibid.
68. Department of State Memo, 30 July 1942 (NAMP, M1203, Roll 16, File 860H.00/14041/2).
69. Telegram to King Petar II from President Roosevelt, 3 August 1942, *FRUS, 1942, Europe* (Washington: USGPO, 1961), p. 806.
70. 'Statement of the President of the United States', no date (NAMP, M1203, Roll 16, File 860H.00/1404 $\frac{1}{2}$).
71. Department of State Memo, 'Regarding the Serb-Croat Dispute', 27 May 1942 (NAMP, M1203, Roll 20).
72. Ibid.
73. Ibid. Also see George J. Prpic, *The Croatian Immigrants in America* (New York: Philosophical Library, 1971).
74. FBI Quarterly Report, 'Croatian Activities in the United States', 4 May 1942 (NARA, RG 65, Box 160, File 30311).
75. FBI Memo, 'Croatian Activities in the United States – Ustaše', by A.J. Rafferty, 3 September 1941 (NARA, RG 65, Box 160, File 30311).
76. FBI Memo, 'Defenders of Croatia', by W.W. Gregory, 15 September 1941 (NARA, RG 65, Box 160, File 30311).
77. Prpic, *The Croatian Immigrants in America*, p. 298.
78. FBI Memo, 'Croatian Activities in the United States – Ustaše', by E.J. Rose, 19 June 1941 (NARA, RG 65, Box 159, File 30311).
79. FBI Memo, 'Charged, Ante Marko Doshen', by E.J. Rose, 11 December 1941 (NARA, RG 65, Box 161, File 30311).

80. Ibid.
81. Ibid.
82. OSS Memo, 'Re: Ante Doshen', 31 March 1942, www.pavelić papers.com/
    documents/oss/oss001.html, accessed on 20 February 2006.
83. FBI Memo, 'Charged, Ante Marko Doshen'.
84. Ibid. Stanley Todd Karran, known as S.K., provided the FBI with considerable
    information about Došen, whom he had befriended, and other Croatians and
    Nazis in the United States. According the Yugoslav Consul in Pittsburgh,
    Karran was an agent for the Yugoslav, British and American governments.
    Karran had informed the Americans that he was a British agent. The FBI had
    reason to believe Karran's information in part because Mitchell Solomon,
    special inspector of the Bureau of Immigration and Naturalization, had
    praised Karran for being invaluable to the Došen investigation.
85. FBI Memo, 'Croatian Activities in the United States – Ustaše', by T.H.
    Council, 28 October 1941 (NARA, RG 65, Box 161, File 30311).
86. 'Croat Leader Goes to Jail', *The Pittsburgh Press*, 23 March 1943, p. 5.
87. FBI Memo, 'Croatian Activities in the United States – Ustaše'.
88. Ibid.
89. FBI Memo, 'Croatian Activities in the United States – Ustaše', by C.R.
    Monticone, 30 October 1941; FBI Memo, 'Croatian Activities in the United
    States – Ustaše', by John H. Wilson, 15 November 1941; FBI Memo,
    'Croatian Activities in the United states – Ustaše', by T.H. Council, 28
    October 1941 (NARA, RG 65, Box 161, File 30311).
90. Ibid.
91. Ibid.
92. FBI Memo, 'Croatian Activities in the United States – Ustaše', by W.H. Cole
    (NARA, RG 65, Box 161, File 30311).
93. Ibid.
94. FBI Memo, 'Croatian Activities in the United States – Ustaše', by E.L. Boyle
    (NARA, RG 65, Box 161, File 30311).
95. FBI Memo, S.K. 31 March 1942 (NARA, RG 65, Box 161).
96. FBI Memo, 'Croatian Activities in the United States – Ustaše', by E.L. Boyle.
97. FBI Memo, 'Croatian Activities in the United States – Ustaše', by C.L.
    Johnson, 8 December 1941 (NARA, RG 65, Box 161, File 30311).
98. FBI Memo, 'Croatian Activities in the United States – Ustaše', by D.J.
    Williams, 14 January 1941 (NARA, RG 65, Box 161, File 30311).
99. Ibid. Also see FBI Memo, S.K., 4 May 1942.
100. OSS Memo, 'Axis Propagandists within the Croatian Catholic Union', 9 May
    1942, www.pavelićpapers.com/documents/oss/oss005.html (accessed on 21
    February 2006).
101. FBI Memo, 3 May 1942. Obtained under FOIA by Jon Levy.
102. FBI Memo, 'Croatian Activities in the United States – Ustaše', by Clarence
    E. Clay, 16 April 1942 (NARA, RG 65, Box 165, File 30311).
103. FBI Memo, S.K., 4 May 1942 (NARA, RG 65, Box, 165, File 30311).

104. Ibid.
105. FBI Memo, 3 May 1942.
106. Letter to Mr Elmer Davis from Francis X. Kolander, 3 October 1942, (NARA, RG 208, Entry 221, Box 1070).
107. Letter to Mr John Birek from Rt. Rev. Msgr. M.G. Domladovac, Ibid.
108. FBI Memo, 'Croatian Activities in the United States – Ustaše', by D.J. Williams.
109. Ibid.
110. FBI Memo, 'Croatian Activities in United States – Ustaše', by E.L. Boyle (NARA, RG 95, Box 161, File 30311).
111. Ibid.
112. Letter to Charles F. Uhl from J.E. Thornton, 4 January 1942 (NARA, RG 65, Box 161, File 30311).
113. Ibid.
114. FBI Memo, 'Croatian Activities in the United States', 25 April 1942 (NARA RG 65, Box 165, File 30311).
115. Ibid.
116. Ibid.
117. Ibid.
118. 'Action', *Youngstown Vindicator*, 20 June 1943, p. 40.
119. 'Budaks Jailed by Federal Men as Parole Violators', *Youngstown Vindicator*, 23 October 1948, p. 1. The editors of the newspaper were overjoyed that Budak was behind bars, hailing his imprisonment as a major step in helping clean up the city.
120. Memo to Attorney General Wendell Berge from J. Edgar Hoover, 20 March 1942 (NARA, RG 65, Box 153, File 30311).
121. Ibid.
122. Raids also were conducted in San Francisco, Chicago, Des Moines, Detroit, Indianapolis, Kansas City, Los Angeles, Milwaukee, New York, Philadelphia, St Louis, St. Paul, Butte, Akron and some small Ohio towns.
123. Wallace Murray, Department of State Memo, 6 July 1942 (NAMP, M1203, Roll 19, File 860H.01/396).
124. 'Foreign Nationality Groups in the United States', (NAMP, M1203, Roll 20, File 860H.01/486).
125. FBI Memo, 'Croatian Activities in United States', by William J. Jovick, 18 December 1942 (NARA, RG 65, Box 166, Entry 30311).
126. Ibid.
127. Ibid. The important and trusted FBI contact T-9 was State Senator William Boyd of Ohio. Boyd, who the FBI believed harboured communist sympathies and had deep connections in the Croatian community, especially with the Croatian Fraternal Union.
128. State Department Memo by Wallace Murray, 6 July 1942 (NAMP, M1203, Roll 19, File 860H.01/396).
129. State Department Memo, 25 June 1942 (NAMP, M1203, Roll 16, File 860H.00/1402 $\frac{1}{2}$).

130. State Department Memo by A.A. Berle Jr, 25 September 1942 (NAMP, M1203, Roll 17, File 860H.00/1417).

131. FBI Memo, William J. Jovick

132. Rakovica is a suburban area of Belgrade.

133. Letter to J. Edgar Hoover from James Lawrence Fly, 24 December 1942 (NARA, RG 65, Box 166, File 30311).

134. Memo to Mr DeWitt Poole and Mr L.M.C. Smith from Alan Cranston, 26 April 1943 (DDEL, Sturman Papers, Box 4, File 3, Yugoslavia). Emphasis is in the original.

135. Ibid.

136. Ibid.

137. OWI Memo to Alan Cranston from Paul Sturman with enclosure, 1 February 1943 (DDEL, Sturman Papers, Box 4, File 3).

138. Ivan Čizmić, *History of the Croatian Fraternal Union of America, 1894-1994* (Zagreb: Goldent, 1994), p. 278.

139. OWI Memo to Alan Cranston from Paul Sturman with enclosure.

140. Čizmić, *History of the Croatian Fraternal Union of America*, p. 281.

141. Croatian Catholic Union, 'American Croatian Catholics' Plea for Justice', 18 April 1945 (NAMP, M1203, Roll 10, File 860H.01/4–1845).

142. Ibid.

143. Telegram to Secretary of State from Phillips, 19 September 1941 (NAMP, M1203, Roll 16, File 860H.00/1327).

144. Ray Brock, 'Yugoslavia Chaotic Under Axis; Nazi Reinforcements Face Fights', *New York Times*, 4 May 1942, 4:5.

145. Office of Strategic Services Report, 'The Situation in Croatia', 21 August 1942 (NARA, RG 226 Entry 16, #19956).

146. Srdjan Trifković, 'Rivalry Between Germany and Italy in Croatia, 1942–1943', *The Historical Journal* 36 (1993), pp. 879–904, p. 893.

147. These reports, chiefly from Istanbul, are found in NAMP, M1203, Rolls 17 and 18.

148. Burton Y. Berry, 'Address by Dr Pavelićh, Croatian Chief of State Before the Final Session of Parliament', 1 February 1943 (NAMP, M1203, Roll 17, File 860H.00/1446).

149. Milovan Djilas, *Memoir of a Revolutionary*, trans. Drenka Willen (New York: Harcourt, Brace, Jovanovich, 1973), p. 131.

150. Report to the Secretary of State from Burton Y. Berry, 'Croatian Affairs, According to a Private Source', 14 July 1943, (NARA, M1203, Roll 17, File 860J.00/1517), Report to the Secretary of State from Burton Y. Berry, 'Further Information from Croatia', 29 June 1943 (NARA, M1203, Roll 17, File 860H.00/1511).

151. Report to the Secretary of State from Burton Y. Berry, 'The Political Situation in Croatia According to a Private Source', 26 May 1943 (NARA, M1203, Roll 17, File 860H.00/1497).

152. Norman Rich, *Hitler's War Aims: The Establishment of the New Order*, vol. II (New York: W.W. Norton, 1974), p. 281.
153. Memo to President Roosevelt from William J. Donovan, 21 October 1943 (NARA, M1203, Roll 17, File 860H.00/1551).
154. Ibid.
155. Ibid.
156. Memo to President Roosevelt from Edward R. Stettinius, Jr, 1 November 1943 (NARA, M1203, Roll 17, File 860H.00/1551).
157. Ibid.
158. Fotitch, pp. 189–90. Also see Jukić, *The Fall of Yugoslavia*, p. 132.
159. Robert E. Sherwood, *Roosevelt and Hopkins: An Intimate History* (New York: Harper & Brothers, 1948), pp. 708–11 and Jukić, *The Fall of Yugoslavia*, p. 168.
160. United States, *FRUS 1943*, vol. I, *General* (Washington: USGPO, 1963), p. 543.

Chapter 5   The Escape

1. For more information see Alan Clark, *Barbarossa: The Russian-German Conflict, 1941–45* (New York: William Morrow, 1965); John Erickson, *The Road to Berlin*, vol. II (New Haven: Yale University Press, 1999); and Albert Seaton, *The Russo-German War, 1941–45* (New York: Praeger, 1971).
2. OSS, 'Yugoslavia – Political', 22 November 1944 (NARA, RG 226, Entry 16, Box 1221, File 108483).
3. Ibid.
4. OSS Report, 24 February 1945 (NARA, RG 226, Entry 16, Box 1334, File 116989).
5. Srećko Pšeničnik, interview by author, 16 July 1999.
6. See the Bedell Smith Cable Log at the DDEL, Walter Bedell Smith Papers, Boxes 23–27.
7. OSS Report, 17 April 1945 (NARA, RG 226, Entry 16, Box 1415, File 123575).
8. Vladko Maček, *In the Struggle for Freedom*, trans. Elizabeth and Stjepan Gazi (University Park: PA: Pennsylvania State University Press, 1957).
9. Jerome Jareb and Ivo Omračanin (eds), 'Croatian Government's Memorandum to the Allied Headquarters Mediterranean May 4, 1945', *The Journal of Croatian Studies*, 21 (1980), p. 143.
10. Stephen Clissold, *Whirlwind: An Account of Marshal Tito's Rise to Power* (London: Cresset, 1949), pp. 224–6. Also see Fitzroy MacLean, *The Heretic: The Life and Times of Josip Broz – Tito* (New York: Harper, 1957), p. 257.
11. E.W. Annan, 'First Detailed Interrogation Report on SA Obergruppenfuehreh Kasche, Siegfried', 10 July 1945 (PRO, WO 204/12811). Kasche was a long-time admirer of Pavelić who often found himself defending the Poglavnik

from his many detractors in Berlin. Kasche's escape attempt was short lived. He was captured near Wolfsberg on 12 May 1945, interrogated by the Allies and extradited to Yugoslavia. Kasche was convicted of war crimes and hanged on 7 June 1947.

12. Srečko Pšeničnik, interview by author, and Marcus Tanner, *Croatia: A Nation Forged in War* (New Haven: Yale University Press, 1997), pp. 166–7. Ironically, Dragutin Došen later worked for the British government in Naples, although he was known to have killed Serbs during the war. In the NDH, he served as a member of Pavelić's bodyguard, the Poglavnikova Tjelesna Bojna.

13. OSS Report, 'Reign of Terror in Zagreb', 8 May 1945 (NARA, RG 153, Box 576, File 25–20).

14. Stella Alexander, *Church and State in Yugoslavia since 1945* (Cambridge: Cambridge University Press, 1979), p. 55.

15. Tomislav Dulić, 'Tito's Slaughterhouse: A Critical Analysis of Rummel's Work on Democide', *Journal of Peace Research* 41 (January 2004), pp. 87–100. Dulić provides a thorough and convincing discussion of the difficulties that abound when examining the Bleiburg incident.

16. Mark Wyman, *DPs: Europe's Displaced Persons, 1945–1951* (Ithaca: Cornell University Press, 1998), pp. 156–7.

17. Bogdan Krizman, *Pavelić u Bjekstvu* (Zagreb: Globus, 1986), pp. 165–221. Krizman provides a good look at Pavelić's movements from 1945 to 1948.

18. Report by Major Owen Reed, 14 May 1945 (PRO, WO 202/301).

19. Robert Clayton Mudd, CIC Report, 'Present Whereabouts and Past Background of Ante Pavelić, Croat Quisling', 30 January 1947, Pavelić Dossier (NARA, IRR, RG 319, Box 17). Celovec was the Slovenian name for Klagenfurt.

20. Srečko Pšeničnik, interview by author.

21. Memo by E.W. Annan (PRO, WO 204/12811).

22. G-2 Memo, 'Apprehension of Croat Quislings', 5 June 1945, Pavelić Dossier (NARA, IRR, RG 319, Box 17).

23. The refugee problem in Austria was mentioned repeatedly in American Army intelligence reports. It was estimated on 15 August 1945 that the American zone in Austria was home to approximately 400,000 displaced persons. This was a serious problem which overwhelmed the United States Army. A similar circumstance confronted British forces.

24. '100,000 Yugoslavs Reported Captives', *New York Times*, 31 August 1945, pp. 1 and 10.

25. Richard West, *Tito: And the Rise and Fall of Yugoslavia* (New York: Carroll & Graf, 1994), p. 205.

26. Report to Central Registry, Counter-Intelligence Branch, G-2 Division from Colonel C.B. Mickelwait, Deputy Theater Judge Advocate's Office, 5 November 1945 (NARA, HICOG, RG 466, Box 176, File 101–08, Pavelić Extradition File). Also See West, *Tito*, p. 205.

27. Ibid.

28. Srečko Pšeničnik, interview by author.

29. Memo to War Crimes Branch from Harold W. Sullivan, War Crimes Branch Liaison Officer, 15 November 1945 (NARA, HICOG, RG 466, Box 176, File 101–08).

30. Letter to Commanding Officer, Yugoslav War Crimes Liaison Detachment from Colonel C.B. Mickelwait, 19 February 1946 (NARA, HICOG, RG 466, Box 176, File 101–08). Several American documents allege that British authorities aided Pavelić's escape. One of the more complete versions of these allegations – albeit most of these allegations are vague – is found in a CIC document dated 29 August 1947 located in the Pavelić Dossier at the National Archives.

31. Telegram to the Foreign Office from British Diplomatic Representative in Austria, 11 February 1946 (PRO, FO 371/59401/2234).

32. 'Yugoslavs Protest Allies' Behavior', *New York Times*, 16 August 1946, p. 5.

33. Control, 'Present Whereabouts of Former Ustaschi Officials, 11 October 1946 (NARA, RG 263, Box 63, Entry ZZ-19, Ustasha Activities).

34. Ibid.

35. Ibid.

36. Nick Fielding, 'Nazi "Bribed the British with Looted Gold"', *Mail on Sunday*, 14 June 1998, p. 6. Also see Stephen Dorril, *MI6: Inside the Covert World of Her Majesty's Secret Intelligence Service* (New York: Touchstone, 2000), p. 338. Dorril argues that MI6 was deeply involved in protecting Pavelić in and around Klagenfurt.

37. 'Transfer of Croatian Gold to Argentina', CIA Report, 16 April 1952. Obtained through FOIA request.

38. Ibid.

39. William Z. Slany, 'US and Allied Wartime and Postwar Relations and Negotiations with Argentina, Portugal, Spain, Sweden, and Turkey on Looted Gold and German External Assets and U.S. Concerns About the Fate of the Wartime Ustasha Treasury' (Washington: The State Department, 1997).

40. 'The Organization of the Ustashies Abroad', 30 October 1946 (NARA RG 263, Box 63, Entry ZZ-19, Ustasha Activities). Yugoslav authorities after the war accused Pečnikar of having killed Serbs and Jews with his own hands. Also see Mark Aarons and John Loftus, *Unholy Trinity: The Vatican, The Nazis, and the Swiss Banks* (New York: St Martin's, 1989), pp. 124–8.

41. Ibid. Also see letter to Acting Secretary of State from the Yugoslav Embassy, 19 August 1946 (NAMP, Roll 2, File 860H.00/8–1946) as well as Department of State Memo, 2 April 1947 (NAMP, Roll 4, File 860H.00/4–247).

42. 'Request for Delivery of a Person Desired for Trial for a War Crime, Ante Pavelić', 31 October 1945 (NARA, HICOG, RG 466, Box 176, File 101–08).

43. Ibid.

44. Lieutenant General Morgan, 'Policy towards Yugoslavs', 16 November 1945, ACC-Italy HQ (NARA, RG 331, Box 222, File 10000/109/535).

45. For information about United States operatives in wartime Yugoslavia see Frank Lindsay, *Beacons in the Night* (Stanford: Stanford University Press, 1996).

46. One need only look at Patterson's memos sent to the State Department to get a clear indication of his distaste for Tito's government and communism in general. His reports are far from neutral.

47. John R. Lampe, *Yugoslavia as History: Twice there was a Country* (Cambridge: Cambridge University Press, 1996), p. 236. For a more thorough explanation see *FRUS 1947* Vol. IV.

48. *Yearbook of the United Nations, 1947–48* (Lake Success: NY: Department of Public Information, 1949), p. 220.

49. Ibid.

50. G.L. Warren, State Department Position Paper for the United Nations General Assembly, 'War Criminals, Traitors, and Quislings', 12 September 1947 (NARA, RG 153, Box 576, File 25–20).

51. Ibid.

52. Ibid.

53. United States Mission to the United Nations, 'War Criminals, Traitors, and Quislings', 29 September 1947 (NARA RG 84, Box 85).

54. Ibid., p. 222.

55. David L. Larson, *United States Foreign Policy toward Yugoslavia, 1943–1963* (Washington: University Press of America, 1979), p. 89.

56. The State Department saw so much mail related to the Mihailović trial that it composes almost an entire roll in *State Department Papers Relating to the Internal Affairs of Yugoslavia, 1944–1949*.

57. There are numerous accounts of the trial and the publicity that surrounded it. See David Martin, *Patriot or Traitor: The Case of General Mihailovich* (Stanford: Hoover Institution Press, 1978); Walter Roberts, *Tito, Mihailović, and the Allies* (Durham: Duke University Press, 1987); and Milovan Djilas, *Rise and Fall*, trans. John Fiske Loude (New York: Harcourt Brace Jovanovich, 1985).

58. There are several works which deal with Stepinac's controversial career. See Stella Alexander's *The Triple Myth: A Life of Archbishop Alozije Stepinac* (New York: Columbia University Press, 1987) and *Church and State in Yugoslavia*. An official account was published by the Embassy of the Federal Peoples Republic of Yugoslavia, *The Case of Archbishop Stepinac* (Washington: Federal Peoples Republic of Yugoslavia, 1947). For a sympathetic opinion see Richard Patte's *The Case of Cardinal Aloysius Stepinac* (Milwaukee: Bruce, 1953).

59. Stepinac was released from prison in 1951 and lived under house arrest. Though Tito would have been happy to ship him off to the Vatican, Stepinac remained in Yugoslavia until his death in 1960.

60. American newspapers thoroughly covered the downing of the planes and consequently the crises that followed. In particular see 'Byrnes Summons Yugoslav Envoy', *New York Times*, 23 August 1946, p. 3; '12 from US Plane Held by Yugoslavs', *New York Times*, 13 August 1946, p. 4; 'Turk Wounded in Attack

on Plane is Free to Leave Yugoslavs Say', *New York Times*, 28 August 1946, p. 3; and 'Released Airmen Talk with Byrnes', *New York Times* 25 August 1946, p. 3.

61. John M. Cabot, 'Current Situation in Yugoslavia', Cabot Papers, Part 2: *Europe*, Reel 6.

62. Military Intelligence Division, 'War Criminals in Croatia', Source, Dr Benson (Former Minister from Croatia to Berlin) 24 April 1945 (NARA, RG 153, Box 577, File 25–27).

63. Telegram to Alex Kirk from James Byrnes, 11 October 1945. *FRUS, 1945* Vol. V, *Europe*, 1967, pp. 1265–6.

64. Letter to Political Advisers from Brigadier General M.S. Lush, 14 June 1945, ACC-Italy HQ (NARA, RG 331, Box 221, File 10000/109/553).

65. Letter to Brigadier Lush from H. Hopkinson, 15 June 1945, ACC-Italy HQ (NARA, RG 331, Box 221, File 10000/109/553).

66. Ibid.

67. Ibid.

68. Arieh, J. Kochavi, *Post-Holocaust Politics: Britain, the United States and Jewish Refugees, 1945–1948* (Chapel Hill: University of North Carolina Press, 2001), pp. 242–4.

69. Letter to G-5 Section, Allied Force Headquarters from Rear Admiral Ellery W. Stone, 23 July 1946, ACC-Italy HQ (NARA, RG 331, Box 211, File 10000/109/360).

70. Letter to Rear Admiral Ellery W. Stone from A.L. Hamblen, 22 August 1946, ACC-Italy HQ (NARA, RG 331, Box 211, File 10000/109/360).

71. Letter to the Earl of Halifax from the Foreign Office, 6 March 1946 (PRO, FO 371/59380/3505).

72. Ibid.

73. Minute to Executive Commissioner from Brigadier General M. Carr, 3 September 1946 (NARA, RG 331, Box 211, File 10000/109/360).

74. Letter to Dr Sloven J. Smodlaka from Rear Admiral Ellery W. Stone, 10 September 1946, ACC-Italy HQ (NARA, RG 331, Box 211, File 10000/109/360).

75. Minute #19 by J. Wesley Jones, ACC-Italy HQ (NARA, RG 331, Box 211, File 10000/109/360).

76. Letter to Supreme Allied Commander, Mediterranean Theatre (General Lee) from Dr Sloven Smodlaka, 15 January 1947, ACC-Italy HQ (NARA, RG 331, Box 259, File 10000/109/1093).

77. Ibid.

78. Ibid.

79. Ibid.

80. Ibid.

81. Telegram to Secretary of State from Homer Byington, 24 January 1947 (NARA, RG 59, Box 3621, File 740.00116EW/1–2447).

82. Ibid.

83. Telegram to Caserta from George Marshall, 30 January 1947 (NARA, RG 59, Box 3621, File 740.00116 EW/1–2447).

84. Ibid.

85. Telegram to Caserta from George C. Marshall, 30 January 1947 (NARA, RG59, Box 3621, File 740.00116EW?1–2447).

86. Letter with enclosure to the Secretary of State from T.J. Hohenthal, 4 August 1948 (NARA, roll 6, file 860H.00/8–448). The enclosure was a translation of a 14 July 1948 article in *Vjesnik*. Ljubo Miloš was executed on 27 August 1948 for his role in conducting executions in Ustaše-run camps.

87. William Gowen, interview by author, 9 March 1999, telephone.

88. No Title, Italian Document in CIC file obtained through FOIA request.

89. Robert Clayton Mudd, report titled, 'Present Whereabouts and Past Background of Ante Pavelić, Croat Quisling', 30 January 1947 (NARA, Pavelić Dossier, IRR, RG 319, Box 17).

90. Control, 'Present Whereabouts'.

91. Robert Clayton Mudd, 'Present Whereabouts and Past Backgrounds'.

92. Ibid.

93. Ibid.

94. Louis S. Caniglia and George A Zappala, Counter Intelligence Corps Report, 15 March 1947 (NARA, Pavelić Dossier, IRR, RG 319, Box 17).

95. Ibid.

96. Gowen, interview by author.

97. Gowen, interview by author. The British material mentioned by Gowen is not found in the NARA or the PRO.

98. William Gowen, Report on Ante Pavelić, 22 January 1947 (NARA, Pavelić Dossier, IRR, RG 197, Box 17).

99. Ibid.

100. Mudd, Report.

101. Ibid.

102. Ibid.

103. Robert Clayton Mudd, 'Father Krunoslav Draganović, Past Background and Present Activity', 12 February 1947 (NARA, RG 263, Box 28, Entry ZZ–18, Draganović File).

104. Ibid.

105. Ibid.

106. Ibid.

107. Gowen, interview by author.

108. 'Jugoslav Refugees', *The Economist*, 1February 1947, p. 189.

109. Ibid.

110. Memo to Secretary of State from Cabot, 25 February 1947, *FRUS 1947* Vol. IV, *Eastern Europe: The Soviet Union* (Washington: USGPO, 1972), p. 766. John M. Cabot enjoyed a long career in foreign service capped by serving as ambassador to the newly-established Pakistan from 1952 to 1953.

111. General Milan Nedić, a former officer in the Yugoslav army, ran the Nazi puppet state in Serbia. After the war, he was arrested and later executed by Yugoslav authorities on 4 February 1946.

112. Ibid., p. 768.

113. John Moors Cabot, *First Line of Defense: Forty Years' Experiences of a Career Diplomat* (Washington: School of Foreign Service, Georgetown University, n.d.), 29. Cabot's memoirs provide a brief but candid look at his trying tenure in Yugoslavia.

114. Lorraine M. Lees, *Keeping Tito Afloat: The United States, Yugoslavia, and the Cold War* (University Park, PA: The Pennsylvania State University Press, 1997), p. 28. For more information about Patterson's tumultuous period as ambassador see pp. 1–28. For a full examination of Patterson's tenure, see the Richard Patterson Papers at the Harry S. Truman Presidential Library.

115. Telegram to the Secretary of State from Cabot, 26 February 1947 (NARA, RG 84, Box 85).

116. The Diplomatic Papers of John Moors Cabot (HSTL, Part 4, *Diaries*, Reel 18).

117. Ibid.

118. Ibid.

119. Ibid.

120. Memo to the Embassy in Yugoslavia from the Acting Secretary of State Dean Acheson, *FRUS 1947* Vol. IV *Eastern Europe: The Soviet Union* (Washington: USGPO, 1972), p. 779.

121. Telegram to Belgrade Embassy from Dean Acheson, 11 March 1947 (NARA, RG 84, Box 85).

122. Ibid.

123. Telegram to Secretary of State from Cabot, 12 March 1947 (NARA, RG 84, Box 85; Telegram to Belgrade Embassy from Secretary of State, 13 March 1947 (NARA, RG 84, Box 85); Telegram to Secretary of State from Cabot, 19 March 1947 (NARA, RG 84, Box 85).

124. Memo to the Embassy in Yugoslavia from Acting Secretary of State Dean Acheson, *FRUS*, Footnote #3.

125. Ibid., p. 779.

126. *Yearbook of the United Nations, 1947–1948* (Lake Success: NY: Department of Public Information, 1949), p. 220.

127. Enclosure 1 to Dispatch 783, 9 April 1947 (NARA, RG 84, Box 85).

128. Memo from Yugoslav Government to the American Embassy in Belgrade, 17 April 1947 (NARA, RG 84, Box 85).

129. Ibid.

130. Ibid.

131. Ibid.

132. Memo to the Secretary of State from Cabot, 23 April 1947, *FRUS 1947* Vol. IV, p. 791.

133. Memo to the Secretary of State from John Cabot, 'Release of War Criminals to Yugoslavia', 12 March 1947 (NAMP, M1203, Roll 4, File 860H.00/3–1247). The memo included articles from the 8 March and 11 March issues of *Borba*.

134. Ibid.

135. Ibid.

136. Telegram to Secretary of State from John Cabot, 30 April 1947 (NAMP, M1203, Roll 4, File 860H.00).

137. Telegram to Belgrade from Secretary of State Marshall, 2 May 1947 (NARA, RG 84, Box 85).

138. Telegram to the Secretary of State from Dunn, 29 May 1947, *FRUS* 1947, Vol. IV, pp. 804–5.

139. Telegram to the Secretary of State from Cabot, 15 May 1947, *FRUS* 1947, Vol. IV, 799.

140. Ibid., 799.

141. Ibid., 800.

142. Ibid., 800.

143. Ibid., 799.

144. Cypher to Rome from Caserta, 23 February 1947 (PRO, FO 371/67372/R2518).

145. Letter to Walworth Barbour from Peter Solly-Flood, 5 May 1947 (NARA, RG 84, Box 85).

146. Ibid.

147. Ibid.

148. Ibid.

149. Ibid.

150. Walworth Barbour, a native of Cambridge, Massachusetts, was promoted to chief of the Division of South European Affairs in 1947 and served in the post until 1949. He was a distinguished American diplomat who capped his career serving in Moscow and London before being named as ambassador to Israel from 1961 to 1973.

151. Letter to Peter Solly-Flood from Walworth Barbour, 19 May 1947 (NARA, RG 84, Box 85).

152. Ibid. This was a restating of the position often repeated by Ambassador Patterson in 1946.

153. Ibid.

154. Memo to the Department of State and the British Embassy from the Combined Chiefs of Staff, 29 May 1947, *FRUS 1947* Vol. IV, p. 803.

155. Ibid., p. 803.

156. Telegram to the Secretary of State from Cabot, 7 June 1947, *FRUS 1947* Vol. IV, p. 807.

157. Telegram to the Secretary of State from Cabot, 11 June 1947, *FRUS 1947* Vol. IV, p. 812. Complete document obtained through FOIA request.

158. Ibid.

159. Ibid.

160. Telegram to Secretary of State from Cabot, 25 June 1947 (NARA, RG 84, Box 85).

161. Ibid.

162. Ibid.

163. Caniglia and Zappala Report, 15 March 1947.

164. Captain Marion H. Scott, Counter Intelligence Corps Report, 18 April 1947 (NARA, Pavelić Dossier, IRR RG 319, Box 17).

165. Ibid.

166. G-2 Report (NARA, Pavelić Dossier, IRR, RG 319, Box 17). Unfortunately, this report was sanitized and sensitive information was deleted. There is some reason to believe that the information about Pavelić's passports and other information about his whereabouts came from OZNA.

167. 'Krunoslav Stjepan Dragonovic', 28 November 1951 (NARA, RG 263, File ZZ–18, Box 28).

168. Memo to AFHQ for Lee From AGWAR from CCS, 28 May 1947 (NARA, Pavelić Dossier, IRR, RG 319, Box 17).

169. Ibid.

170. Memo from Bernard J. Grennan to Supervising Agent, CIC, Zone Five, APO 528, 7 July 1947 (NARA, Pavelić Dossier, IRR, RG 319, Box 17).

171. Ibid.

172. Ibid.

173. Sam Pope Brewers, 'Peron's Wife is Hailed in Madrid', *New York Times*, 9 June 1947, p. 1.

174. Gowen, interview by author.

175. For a detailed discussion defending the Ratline see James V. Milano and Patrick Brogan, *Soldiers, Spies, and the Rat Line: America's Undeclared War Against the Soviets* (Washington: Brassey's, 1995). Also see Aarons and Loftus, *Unholy Trinity*.

176. Aarons and Loftus, *Unholy Trinity*, p. 97.

177. CIC Documents obtained from FOIA requests.

178. 'Krunoslav Stjepan Dragonovic.'

179. Memo, 'Ratline from Austria to South America' by Paul Lyon, 12 July 1948, in Allan A. Ryan Jr, *Klaus Barbie and the United States Government: The Report, with Documentary Appendix, to the Attorney General of the United States* (Frederick, MD: University Publication of America, 1984), tab. 95.

180. Milano and Brogan, *Soldiers, Spies*, p. 53.

181. Ryan, Jr, *Klaus Barbie*, p. 47.

182. Ibid., pp. 47–8.

183. Telegram to the American Embassy in Rome from George C. Marshall, 28 July 1947 (NARA, RG 59, Box 3624, File 740.00116EW/7–2847).

184. Telegram to Foreign Office from Washington, 25 July 1947 (PRO, FO 371/67387/10228).

185. Ibid.

186. To A/SACMED from P.W. Scarlett, British Political Adviser, 2 August 1947 (Pavelić Dossier, IRR, RG 197, Box 17).

187. Ibid.

188. Cypher from Foreign Office to Rome, 30 July 1947 (PRO, FO 371/67387).

189. Cypher from Foreign Office to Office of British Political Advisor to Supreme Allied Commander Mediterranean, 30 July 1947 (PRO, FO 371/67387).

190. Informal Routing Slip, Headquarters MTOUSA (Pavelić Dossier, IRR, RG 197, Box 17). Later in 1947, Jaynes commanded the withdrawal of American troops from Italy.

191. 'Ante Pavelić and other Ustasha Personalities' (Pavelić Dossier, IRR, RG 197, Box 17).

192. Louis S. Caniglia and William E.W. Gowen, Memo on Ante Pavelić, CIC, 29 August 1947 (Pavelić Dossier, IRR, RG 197, Box 17).

193. Ibid.

194. Ibid.

195. Ibid.

196. Ibid.

197. Ibid.

198. Ibid.

199. Louis S. Caniglia and William E.W. Gowen, Memo on Ante Pavelić, 12 September 1947, CIC (Pavelić Dossier, IRR, RG 197, Box 17).

200. Ibid.

201. Ibid.

202. Memo to Colonel Carl F. Fritzsche from Lt. Colonel G.F. Blunda, 8 November 1947 (Pavelić Dossier, IRR, RG 319). Obtained through the Department of Justice, Criminal Division, FOIA Office.

203. Ibid.

204. Ibid.

205. Ibid.

206. Ibid.

207. Uki Goni, *The Real Odessa: Smuggling the Nazis to Peron's Argentina* (London: Granta, 2002), p. 224. Goni offers a detailed discussion of how the Red Cross passport may have been obtained.

208. Ibid. Also see Krizman, *Pavelić u Bjekstvu*, p. 225. Krizman notes that Pavelić was bold enough to list his proper birth year on his passport.

Chapter 6 Hiding to the End

1. Ronald C. Newton, *The 'Nazi Menace' in Argentina, 1931–1947* (Stanford: Stanford University Press, 1992), pp. 373–5.

2. Ibid., p. 377.

3. 'Reported Arrival of Ante Pavelić in Argentina', 2 December 1948 (NARA, RG 263, ZZ–18, Draganović File, Box 28).

4. Uki Goni, *The Real Odessa: Smuggling the Nazis to Peron's Argentina* (London: Granta, 2002), p. 214.

5. 'Reported Arrival of Ante Pavelić in Argentina'.

6. Goni, *The Real Odessa*, pp. 111, 215.

7. 'Reported Arrival of Ante Pavelić in Argentina'.

8. State Department Memo to Cordell Hull from Arthur Biddle Jr, 31 October 1942 (NARA, RG 59, File 800.20210/1403).

9. John J. Mannion, 'Ante Pavlic "Ustachis"', FBI Memo, 27 October 1955 (NARA, RG 65, File 30311, Box 168).

10. Michael Goebel, 'A Movement from Right to Left in Argentine Nationalism? The Alianza Libertadora Nacionalista and Tacuara as Stages of Militancy', *Bulletin of Latin American Research*, 26 (2007), pp. 359–60.

11. State Department Memo to Reinhardt from Nicholson, 10 October 1951. Obtained through FOIA request.

12. FBI Memo to Director from SAC, LA, 'Ante Pavelić', 3 July 1951 and FBI Memo to Donald L. Nicholson from J. Edgar Hoover, 'Ante Pavelić', 25 July 1951 (NARA, RG 65, File 30311, Box 168). There are several other documents in this record group that refer to concern regarding Pavelić's potential entry into the United States.

13. FBI Memo to J. Edgar Hoover from SAC, New York, 'National Committee for Free Europe, Information Gathering', 5 October 1950 (NARA, RG 65, File 30311, Box 168).

14. Indro Montanelli, 'Pavelić', *Corriere Della Sera*, 19 July 1955, p. 7.

15. Ibid.

16. Some post-World War II Croatian Franciscan immigrants played a significant role in developing pro-Ustaše sentiment within the United States. At present, no work has examined the numbers who were involved or the dodgy wartime history of some of the Franciscans who entered the United States after World War II.

17. Letter to President Harry Truman from V.I. Mandich and John Badovinać, 2 March 1949 (NAMP, M1203, Roll 6, File 860H.00/3–249).

18. Ibid.

19. State Department Memo, 'Message from the President to the Secretary of the United Croatian Organization', 24 February 1949 (NAMP, Roll 6, File 860H.00/2–2449). Kosanović was a long-time Serbian politician who, interestingly, was Nikola Tesla's nephew.

20. Ibid.

21. Department of State Memo, 'Dissolution of original "United Croatians" organization in Chicago and usurpation of its name and convocation of "Second United Croatians Congress" by Croatian Ustashi (Fascist) elements in US', 4 February 1949 (NAMP, M1203, Roll 6, File 860H.00/12–2248).

22. FBI Memo, 'National Committee'.

23. Department of State Memo, 'Dissolution of Original'.
24. Memo from SAC, Chicago to FBI Director, 'Ante Pavelić, Internal Security – YU', 15 October 1951 (NARA, RG 65, Box 168, File 30311). Anton Klobucar served as vice-president of the United American Croatians.
25. FBI Memo, 'National Committee'.
26. Ibid. Little is known about this organization or its effectiveness.
27. Ibid.
28. Ibid.
29. Ibid.
30. Ibid.
31. FBI Memo, 'Croat Activities in the United States', 13 September 1951 (NARA, RG 65, Box 168, File 30311).
32. Ibid.
33. Ibid.
34. Sanitized document dated 17 June 1949 regarding Franjo Cvijic, the last president of the Croatian State Bank in Zagreb. Obtained through a FOIA request. For more information about Ustaše finances see William Z. Slany *United States and Allied Wartime and Postwar Relations and Negotiations with Argentina, Portugal, Spain, Sweden, and Turkey on Looted Gold and German External Assets and United States Concerns about the Fate of the Wartime Ustasha Treasury*, U.S. Government Printing Office June 1998.
35. Memo to L.C. Houck from Emerson Bigelow, 18 July 1946. Obtained through a FOIA request.
36. Central Intelligence Agency, 'Ustashi Activities in Argentina, 28 September 1951. Obtained through a FOIA request.
37. Central Intelligence Agency Memo, 17 June 1949. Obtained through a FOIA request.
38. Central Intelligence Agency, 'Transfer of Croatian Gold to Argentina', 16 April 1952. Obtained through a FOIA request.
39. Ibid.
40. Ibid.
41. United States District Court for Northern California, Alperin v. Vatican Bank and Franciscan Order, Case C-99-4941 MMC (EDL).
42. Mark Aarons, *Sanctuary: Nazi Fugitives in Australia* (Port Melbourne: William Heinemann Australia, 1989), pp. 250–1 and Marjan Jurjevic, *Ustasha under the Southern Cross* (Published by the author, 1973), pp. 26–7.
43. Tomislav Dulić, 'Tito's Slaughterhouse: A Critical Analysis of Rummel's Work on Democide', *Journal of Peace Research* 41 (January 2004), p. 92.
44. John J. Mannion, FBI Memo, 'Ante Pavelić, Ustaschis', 27 October 1955 (NARA, RG 65, File 30311, Box 168).
45. FBI Memo, 'Ante Pavelić, Ustachis' 27 October 1955 (NARA, RG 65, Box 168, File 30311).
46. 'Pavelić Extradition Sought', *The Times*, 22 April 1957. Also see 'Yugoslav Protest to Argentina', *The Times*, 24 May 1951, p. 3.

47. Ibid.
48. Letter to the Department of State from Robert G. Hooker, 27 September 1956 (NARA, RG 59, Entry 250).
49. Ibid.
50. Srečko Pšeničnik, interview by the author.
51. Jean-Marc Sabathier, 'Un fait divers ressuscite le diable oustachi', *Paris Match* (25 May 1957), pp. 16–25. Letter to the State Department from James F. O'Connor, Jr, American Embassy, Buenos Aires, 22 April 1957. There are numerous newspaper reports describing the assassination attempt on Pavelić. Most of the coverage, however, was limited to Latin American and European press outlets.
52. Ibid.
53. 'Croat Fugitive in Argentina', *The Times*, 23 April 1957, p. 11.
54. Allan A. Ryan, Jr, *Klaus Barbie and the United States Government: The Report, with Documentary Appendix, to the Attorney General of the United States* (Frederick, MD: University Publication of America, 1984), pp. 144–55. Artuković died in prison on 16 January 1988.
55. 'Order for Arrest of Pavelić, *The Times*, 26 April 1957, p. 6.
56. Memo to the Department of State from James F. O'Connor, Jr in the Buenos Aires Embassy, 2 May 1957 (NARA, RG 59, Entry 250).
57. Telephone interview with Srečko Pšeničnik. Except for the plane trip to the Middle East, Vladimir Dedijer confirms Pšeničnik's account. Although omitting the Middle East sequence as well, Bogdan Krizman essentially substantiates this chronology of events in *Pavelić u Bjekstvu* (Zagreb: Globus, 1986).
58. 'Rites for Ante Pavelić', *New York Times*, 1 January 1960, p. 19.
59. 'Ante Pavelić Dies in Madrid at 70', *New York Times*, 30 December 1959, 21:1.
60. For a full discussion of Ustaše influenced organizations in Australia see Mark Aarons, *Sanctuary: Nazi Fugitives in Australia* (Port Melbourne: William Heinemann), 1989.
61. 'Yugoslavia Accuses Croatian Nationalists of Killing 27 in Airliner Bomb Explosion', *The Times*, 28 January 1972, p. 1.
62. Al Baker, 'Croatian Leader of 1976 Hijacking is Granted Parole, but Faces Deportation', *New York Times*, 19 July 2008, p. 17. Bušić was released from prison in 2008. He lives in Croatia where he is celebrated as a hero.
63. For a detailed examination of Croatian émigré activity in the 1960s and 1970s see Paul Hockenos, *Homeland Calling: Exile Patriotism and the Balkan Wars* (Ithaca: Cornell University Press, 2003).
64. Sabrina Ramet, *The Three Yugoslavias: State Building and Legitimation, 1918– 2005* (Bloomington: Indiana University Press, 2006), pp. 399–400. Also see Sabrina P. Ramet, 'The NDH – An Introduction', in Sabrina Ramet (ed.), *The Independent State of Croatia, 1941–1945* (London: Routledge, 2007), pp. 3–4.
65. 'Bad News', *US Catholic*, April 1999, p. 9.
66. Ramet, 'The NDH', p. 4.

BIBLIOGRAPHY

Archives and private papers

Alex N. Dragnich Papers, Hoover Institution Archives, Stanford University.
Branimir Jelic File, Federal Bureau of Investigation, FOIA.
John Moor Cabot Papers, Harry S. Truman Library, Independence, Missouri.
Louis Adamic File, Federal Bureau of Investigation, FOIA.
Paul Sturman Papers, Dwight D. Eisenhower Library, Abilene, Kansas.
Robert Patterson Papers, Harry S. Truman Library, Independence, Missouri.
Walter Bedell Smith Papers, Dwight D. Eisenhower Library, Abilene, Kansas.

United Kingdom, Public Record Office

FO 371, *Foreign Office Papers, General Correspondence from 1906.*
FO 1020, *Allied Commission for Austria, Headquarters and Regional Files.*
WO 202, *War Office Papers, British Military Missions in Liaison with Allied Forces, Second World War.*
WO 204, *Allied Forces, Mediterranean Theatre: Military Headquarters Papers, Second World War.*

US National Archives and Record Administration

Department of State, *Records of the Department of State Relating to Internal Affairs of Yugoslavia, 1930–1944 and 1945–1949.*
RG 59, *General Records of the Department of State*
RG 65, *Records of the Federal Bureau of Investigation*
RG 84, *State Department Records Post Files*
RG 153, *Records of the Office of the Judge Advocate General (Army)*
RG 208, *Office of War Information*
RG 226, *Records of the Office of Strategic Services*
RG 263, *Records of the Central Intelligence Agency*

RG 319, *Records of the Army Staff*
RG 331, *Records of Allied Operational and Occupation Headquarters, World War II*
RG 466, *Records of the United States High Commissioner for Germany*

Published documents

Beljo, Ante, *Genocide: A Documented Analysis*, trans. D. Sladojević-Šola (Sudbury, MA: Northern Tribune Publishing, 1985).

Ciano, Galeazzo, *The Ciano Diaries, 1939–1943*, ed. Hugh Gibson (Garden City, NJ: Garden City Publishing, 1947).

Cowgill, Anthony, Lord Brimelow and Christopher Booker, *The Repatriations from Austria in 1945: The Report of an Inquiry* (Bury St Edmunds, Suffolk: Sinclair-Stevenson, 1990).

Gantenbein, James W. (ed.), *Documentary Background of World War II, 1931 to 1941* (New York, NY: Columbia University Press, 1948).

General Accounting Office, *Nazis and Axis Collaborators Were Used to Further US Anti-Communist Objectives in Europe – Some Immigrated to the United States*, 28 June 1985.

Lemkin, Raphael, *Axis Rule in Occupied Europe* (Carnegie Endowment for International Peace, 1944).

Petersen, Neal H. (ed.), *From Hitler's Doorstep: The Wartime Intelligence Reports of Allen Dulles, 1942–1945* (University Park, PA: Pennsylvania State University Press, 1996).

Report by the Comptroller General of the United States, *Nazis and Axis Collaborators were used to further U.S. Anti-Communist Objectives in Europe – Some Immigrated to the United States* (Washington, WA: General Accounting Office, 1985).

Sherwood, Robert E., *Roosevelt and Hopkins: An Intimate History* (New York, NY: Harper & Brothers, 1948).

Suljak, N. Dinko, *Croatia's Struggle for Independence: A Documentary History* (Arcadia, CA: Croatian Information Service, 1977).

United Nations. *Yearbook of the United Nations*, 1946–1948 (Lake Success, NY: Department of Public Information, 1947–1949).

United Nations War Crimes Commission. *History of the United Nations War Crimes Commission and the Development of the Laws of War* (London: His Majesty's Stationery Office, 1948).

United States Department of Commerce, *Foreign Commerce Yearbook, 1932–1939* (Washington, WA: USGPO, 1932–1942).

United States Department of Commerce, Bureau of the Census, *Abstract of the Fourteenth Census of the United States, 1920* (Washington, WA: United States Government Printing Office, 1923).

United States Department of State, *Foreign Relations of the United States 1945*, vol. V, *Europe* (Washington, WA: United States Government Printing Office, 1967).

_____ *Foreign Relation of the United States 1947*, vol. IV, *Eastern Europe: the Soviet Union* (Washington, WA: United States Government Printing Office, 1974).

United States Holocaust Memorial Museum, *Historical Atlas of the Holocaust* (New York, NY: Macmillan, 1996).

von Hassell, Ulrich, *The Von Hassell Diaries, 1938–1944* (London: Hamish Hamilton, 1948).

Interviews

Dr Srečko Pšeničnik, Zagreb.
Mr William Gowen, New York City.
Rev. Msg. Andrew Landi, New York City.

Newspapers

CroatiaPress, 1934–38.
Corriere Della Sera, 1955.
Daily Telegraph, 1999–2002.
Deutsche Presse-Agentur, 2002.
New York Times, 1933–59.
The Times (London), pp. 1933–59.
Youngstown Vindicator, 1933–37.

Secondary sources

Aarons, Mark, *Sanctuary: Nazi Fugitives in Australia* (Port Melbourne: William Heinemann Australia, 1989).

———— and John Loftus, *Unholy Trinity: The Vatican, The Nazis, and the Swiss Banks* (New York, NY: St Martin's, 1989).

Alexander, Stella, *Church and State in Yugoslavia since 1945* (Cambridge: Cambridge University Press, 1979).

———— *The Triple Myth: A Life of Archbishop Alozije Stepinac* (New York, NY: Columbia University Press, 1987).

Armstrong, John A., 'Collaborationism in World War II: The Integral Variation in Eastern Europe', *The Journal of Modern History* 40 (September 1968), pp. 396–410.

Biondich, Mark, 'Religion and Nation in Wartime Croatia: Reflections on the Ustaše Policy of Forced Religious Conversions, 1941–1942', *Slavonic and East European Review* 83 (January 2005), pp. 71–116.

Bokun, Branko, *Spy in the Vatican, 1941–1945* (New York, NY: Praeger, 1973).

Bornstein, Joseph, *The Politics of Murder* (New York, NY: William Sloane, 1950).

Broche, Francois, *Assassinat de Alexandre Ier et Louis Barthou, Marseille, le 9 Octobre 1934* (Paris: Balland, 1977).

Brock, Ray, *Nor Any Victory* (New York, NY: Reynal & Hitchcock, 1942).

Brown, Anthony Cave, *The Last Hero: Wild Bill Donovan* (New York, NY: Times Books, 1982).

Bulajić, Milan, *The Role of the Vatican in the Break-up of the Yugoslav State* (Belgrade: Ministry of Information of the Republic of Serbia, 1993).

Burgwyn, H. James, *Empire on the Adriatic: Mussolini's Conquest of Yugoslavia, 1941–1943* (New York, NY: Enigma, 2005).

———— *Italian Foreign Policy in the Interwar Period, 1918–1940* (Westport, CT: Praeger, 1997).

Butler, Hubert, *The Sub-prefect Should Have Held his Tongue and other Essays* (London: Allen Lane, 1990).

Cabot, John Moors, *First Line of Defense: Forty Years' Experiences of a Career Diplomat* (Washington, WA: School of Foreign Service, Georgetown University, n.d.).

Cheles, Luciano, Ronnie Ferguson and Michalina Vaughan (eds), *The Far Right in Western and Eastern Europe* (London: Longman, 1995).

Chesnoff, Richard Z., *Pack of Thieves: How Hitler and Europe Plundered the Jews and Committed the Greatest Theft in History* (New York, NY: Doubleday, 1999).

Čizmić, Ivan, *History of the Croatian Fraternal Union of America, 1894–1994* (Zagreb: Goldent, 1994).

_____ Ivan Miletić and George J. Prpić, *From the Adriatic to Lake Erie: A History of Croatians in Greater Cleveland* (Eastlake, OH: American Croatian Lodge 'Cardinal Stepinac', 2000).

Clark, Alan, *Barbarossa: The Russian-German Conflict, 1941–45* (New York, NY: William Morrow, 1965).

Clissold, Stephen, *Whirlwind: An Account of Marshal Tito's Rise to Power* (London: Cresset, 1949).

_____ 'Croat Separatisim: Nationalism, Dissidence and Terrorism', *Conflict Studies* (January 1979), pp. 3–19.

_____ 'The Marseilles Murders, 1934', *History Today* 29 (October 1979), pp. 631–8.

Cornwell, John, *Hitler's Pope: The Secret History of Pius XII* (New York, NY: Viking, 1999).

Crampton, R.J., *A Short History of Modern Bulgaria* (Cambridge: Cambridge University Press, 1987).

Creel, George, *War Criminals and Punishment* (New York, NY: Robert M. McBride, 1944).

Davis, Kenneth S., *FDR: The War President, 1940–1943* (New York, NY: Random House, 2000).

Dedijer, Vladimir, *Tito* (New York, NY: Simon & Schuster, 1953).

_____ *The Yugoslav Auschwitz and the Vatican: The Croatian Massacre of the Serbs During World War II* (Buffalo, NY: Prometheus, 1992).

Deschner, Karlheinz, *Mit Gott und den Faschisten: Der Vatikan im Bund mit Mussolini, Franco, Hitler, und Pavelic* (Stuttgart: Hans E. Gunther, 1965).

Dinich, Bette, 'Dismembering Yugoslavia: Nationalists Ideologies and the Symbolic Revival of Genocide', *American Ethnologist* 21 (1994), pp. 367–90.

Djilas, Aleksa, *The Contested Country: Yugoslav Unity and Communist Revolution, 1919–1953* (Cambridge, MA: Harvard University Press, 1991).

Djilas, Milovan, *Memoir of a Revolutionary*, trans. Drenka Willen (New York, NY: Harcourt, Brace, Jovanovich, 1973).

_____ *Wartime*, trans. Michael B. Petrovich (New York, NY: Harcourt, Brace, Jovanovich, 1977).

_____ *Rise and Fall*, trans. John Fiske Loude (New York, NY: Harcourt Brace Jovanovich, 1985).

Dorril, Stephen, *MI6: Inside the Covert World of Her Majesty's Secret Intelligence Service* (New York, NY: Touchstone, 2000).

Došen, Ante M. (ed.), *Godišnjak (Croatian Almanac) 1938, 1940* (Pittsburgh, PA: Hrvatski Domobran, 1938, 1940).

Dulić, Tomislav, 'Tito's Slaughterhouse: A Critical Analysis of Rummel's Work on Democide', *Journal of Peace Research* 41 (January 2004), pp. 85–102.

Dunlop, Richard, *Donovan: America's Master Spy* (Chicago, IL: Rand McNally, 1982).

Embassy of the Federal Peoples Republic of Yugoslavia, *The Case of Archbishop Stepinac* (Washington, WA: Federal Peoples Republic of Yugoslavia, 1947).

Erić, Rudolf, 'Lance sramotnog ropstva treba kidati', *Godisnjak (Croatian Almanac)* 1940 (Pittsburgh, PA: Hrvatski Domobran, 1940).

Erickson, John, *The Road to Berlin*, vol. II (New Haven, CT: Yale University Press, 1999).

Fein, Helen, *Accounting for Genocide: National Responses and Jewish Victimization during the Holocaust* (New York, NY: Free Press, 1979).

Feingold, Henry L., *The Politics of Rescue: The Roosevelt Administration and the Holocaust, 1938–1945* (New Brunswick: Rutgers University Press).

Ford, Kirk Jr, *OSS and the Yugoslav Resistance, 1943–1945* (College Station, TX: Texas A&M University Press, 1992).

Freidenreich, Harriet Pass, *The Jews of Yugoslavia: A Quest for Community* (Philadelphia, PA: The Jewish Publication Society of America, 1979).

Furet, Francois, *Unanswered Questions: Nazi Germany and the Genocide of the Jews* (New York, NY: Schocken Books, 1989).

Gaddis, John Lewis, *The United States and the Origins of the Cold War, 1941–1947* (New York, NY: Columbia University Press, 1972).

Glenny, Misha, *The Balkans: Nationalism, War and the Great Powers, 1804–1999* (New York, NY: Viking, 2000).

Goebel, Michael, 'A Movement from Right to Left in Argentine Nationalism? The Alianza Libertadora Nacionalista and Tacuara as Stages of Militancy', *Bulletin of Latin American Research*, 26 (2007), pp. 356–77.

Goldstein, Ivo, *Croatia: A History*, trans. Nikolina Jovanović (London: Hurst, 1999).

———— *Holokaust u Zagrebu* (Zagreb: Zidovska opcina Zagreb, 2001).

———— 'Ante Pavelić, Charisma and National Mission in Wartime Croatia', *Totalitarian Movements and Political Religions* 7 (June 2006), pp. 225–34.

———— 'The Independent State of Croatia in 1941: On the Road to Catastrophe', in Sabrina Ramet (ed.), *The Independent State of Croatia 1941–1945* (London: Routledge, 2007), pp. 19–29.

Goni, Uki, *Peron y los Alemanes* (Buenos Aires: Editorial SudAmericana, 1998).

———— *The Real Odessa: Smuggling the Nazis to Peron's Argentina* (London: Granta, 2002).

Govorchin, Gerald Gilbert, *Americans from Yugoslavia* (Gainesville, FL: University of Florida Press, 1961).

Graham, Stephen, *Alexander of Yugoslavia: The Story of the King Who Was Murdered at Marsailles* (New Haven, CT: Yale University Press, 1939).

Grubišić, Slavko (ed.), *Ein Teil der blutigen Geschichte* (Silverdalen: Hrv. Radnicki-Savez, 1976).

Gumz, Jonathan E., 'Wehrmacht Perceptions of Mass Violence in Croatia, 1941–1942', *The Historical Journal* 44 (2001), pp. 1015–38.

Hockenos, Paul, *Homeland Calling: Exile Patriotism and the Balkan Wars* (Ithaca, NY: Cornell University Press, 2003).

Hefer, Stjepen, *Croatian Struggle for Freedom and Statehood* (Argentina: Croatian Information Service, 1979).

Heuser, Beatrice, *Western 'Containment' Policies in the Cold War: The Yugoslav Case, 1948–1953* (London: Routledge, 1989).

Hory, Ladislaus and Martin Broszat, *Der Kroatische Ustascha-Staat, 1941–1945* (Stuttgart: Deutsche Verlags-Anstalt, 1964).

Hull, Cordell, *The Memoirs of Cordell Hull*, vol. II (New York, NY: Macmillan, 1940).

Irvine, Jill A., *The Croat Question: Partisan Politics in the Formation of the Yugoslav Socialist State* (Boulder, CO: Westview Press, 1993).

Isaković, Svetlana (ed.), *Genocide Against the Serbs* (Belgrade: Museum of Applied Arts, 1992).

Israel, Fred L. (ed.), *The War Diary of Breckinridge Long* (Lincoln, NA: University of Nebraska Press, 1966).

Jareb, Jere, *Političke uspomene i rad dra Branimira Jelića* (Cleveland, OH: Mirko Šamija, 1982).

Jareb, Jerome and Ivo Omrčanin (eds), 'Croatian Government's Memorandum to the Allied Headquarters Mediterranean May 4, 1945', *The Journal of Croatian Studies*, 21 (1980), pp. 120–43.

Judah, Tim, *The Serbs: History, Myth and the Destruction of Yugoslavia* (New Haven, CT: Yale University Press, 1997).

Jukic, Ilija, *The Fall of Yugoslavia*, trans. Dorian Cooke (New York, NY: Harcourt, Brace, Jovanovich, 1974).

Jurjevic, Marjan, *Ustasha under the Southern Cross* (Published by the author, 1973).

Kalijarvi, Thorsten V., 'Central-Eastern European Minorities in the United States', *Annals of the American Academy of Political and Social Science* 232 (March 1944), pp. 148–54.

Kershaw, Ian, *Hitler, 1936–1945: Nemesis* (New York, NY: Norton, 2000).

Kiernan, Ben, 'Twentieth Century Genocides: Underlying Ideological Themes from Armenia to East Timor', in Robert Gellately and Ben Kiernan (eds), *The Specter of Genocide: Mass Murder in Historical Perspective* (Cambridge: Cambridge University Press, 2003), pp. 29–51.

Kljakić, Slobodan, *A Conspiracy of Silence: Genocide in the Independent State of Croatia and Concentration Camp Jasenovac* (Belgrade: The Ministry of Information of the Republic of Serbia, 1991).

Kochavi, Arieh J., *Post-Holocaust Politics: Britain, the United States and Jewish Refugees, 1945–1948* (Chapel Hill, NC: University of North Carolina Press, 2001).

Kossutitch, August, 'The Croatian Problem', *International Affairs* 12 (January 1933), pp. 79–106.

Kostich, Lazo M., *The Holocaust in the Independent State of Croatia: An Account Based on German, Italian and other Sources* (Chicago, IL: Liberty, 1981).

Kovrig, Bennett, 'Mediation by Obfuscation: The Resolution of the Marseille Crisis, October 1934 to May 1935', *The Historical Journal* 19 (March 1976), pp. 191–221.

Kraja, Joseph, 'The Croatian Circle, 1928–1946', *Journal of Croatian Studies* 5–6 (1964–65), pp. 145–204.

Krippendorff, Ekkehart (ed.), *The Role of the United States in the Reconstruction of Italy and West German, 1943–1949* (Berlin: John F. Kennedy-Institut fur Nordamerikastudien, 1981).

Krišto, Jure, 'Čuvari svoje braće: policijsko nadgledanje američkih Hrvata tijekom Drugoga svjetskoga rata', *Časopis za suvremenu povijest* 35 (2003), pp. 407–30.

———— 'Communist Penetration of Croatian American Organizations during World War II', *Review of Croatian History* 5 (2009), pp. 169–88.

Krizman, Bogdan, *Ante Pavelić i Ustaše* (Zagreb: Globus, 1978).

———— *Pavelić u Bjekstvu* (Zagreb: Globus, 1986).

Kuper, Leo, *Genocide: Its Political Use in the Twentieth Century* (New Haven, CT: Yale University Press, 1981).

Lampe, John R., *Yugoslavia as History: Twice there was a Country* (Cambridge: Cambridge University Press, 1996).

Lampe, John R., Russell O. Prickett and Ljubisa S. Adamovic, *Yugoslav-American Economic Relations* (Durham, NC: Duke University Press, 1990).

Lane, Peter B., *The United States and the Balkan Crisis of 1940–1941* (New York, NY: Garland, 1988), pp. 98–136.

Laqueur, Walter (ed.), *The Second World War: Essays in Military and Political History* (London: Sage, 1982).

Larson, David L., *United States Foreign Policy toward Yugoslavia, 1943–1963* (Washington, WA: University Press of America, 1979).

Lees, Lorraine M., *Keeping Tito Afloat: The United States, Yugoslavia, and the Cold War* (University Park, PA: The Pennsylvania State University Press, 1997).

Lindsay, Frank, *Beacons in the Night* (Stanford, CA: Stanford University Press, 1996).

Linklater, Magnus, Isabel Hilton and Neal Ascherson, *The Nazi Legacy: Klaus Barbie and the International Fascist Connection* (New York, NY: Holt, Rinehart and Winston, 1984).

Lituchy, Barry M. (ed.), *Jasenovac and the Holocaust: Analyses and Survivor Testimonies* (New York, NY: Jasenovac Research Institute, 2006).

Loker, Zvi, 'The Testimony of Dr Edo Neufeld: The Italians and the Jews of Croatia', *Holocaust and Genocide Studies* 7 (Spring 1993), pp. 67–76.

Macdonald, David Bruce, *Balkan Holocausts? Serbian and Croatian Victim-Centred Propaganda and the War in Yugoslavia* (Manchester, Manchester University Press, 2002).

Maček, Vladko, *In the Struggle for Freedom*, trans. Elizabeth and Stjepan Gazi (University Park, PA: Pennsylvania State University Press).

Martin, David, *Patriot or Traitor: The Case of General Mihailovich* (Stanford, CA: Hoover Institution Press, 1978).

McCormick, Robert B., 'The United States' Response to Genocide in the Independent State of Croatia, 1941–1945', *Genocide Studies and Prevention* 3 (Spring 2008), pp. 75–98.

McLynn, Frank, *Fitzroy MacLean* (London: John Murray, 1992).

Melson, Robert, 'Paradigms of Genocide: The Holocaust, the Armenian Genocide, and Contemporary Mass Destructions', *Annals of the American Academy of Political and Social Science* 548 (1996), pp. 156–68.

Mendelsohn, John (ed.), *The History of the Counter Intelligence Corps*, vols 11 and 12 (New York, NY: Garland, 1989).

Milano, James V. and Patrick Brogan, *Soldiers, Spies, and the Rat Line: America's Undeclared War Against the Soviets* (Washington, WA: Brassey's, 1995).

Milićević, Vladeta, *A King Dies in Marseilles: The Crime and its Background* (Bad Godesberg: Hohwacht, 1959).

Miller, Nicholas, *Between Nation and State: Serbian Politics in Croatia Before the First World War* (Pittsburgh, PA: University of Pittsburgh Press, 1997).

Miller, Sally M. (ed.), *The Ethnic Press in the United States: A Historical Analysis and Handbook* (New York, NY: Greenwood Press, 1988).

Mirkovich, Nicholas, 'Jugoslavia's Choice', *Foreign Affairs* 20 (October 1941), pp. 131–51.

Morgenstern, Felice, 'Asylum for War Criminals, Quislings and Traitors', *British Year Book of International Law* 25 (1948), pp. 382–6.

Muggeridge, Malcolm (ed.), *Ciano's Diary, 1939–1943* (London: William Heinemann, 1950).

Newton, Ronald C., *The 'Nazi Menace' in Argentina, 1931–1947* (Stanford, CA: Stanford University Press, 1992).

Ognyanova, Irina. 'Nationalism and National Policy in Independent State of Croatia (1941–1945)', in Dorothy Rogers, Joshua Wheeler, Marina Zavacka and Shawna Casebier (eds), *Topics in Feminism, History and Philosophy, IWM Junior Visiting Fellows Conferences*, vol. 6 (Vienna: IWM, 2000).

Omrčanin, Ivo, *The Pro-Allied Putsch in Croatia in 1944 and the Massacre of Croatians by Tito's Communists* (Philadelphia, PA: Dorrance, 1975).

_____ *Dramatis Personae and Finis of the Independent State of Croatia in American and British Documents* (Bryn Mawr, PA: Dorrance, 1983).

Paris, Edmond, *Genocide in Satellite Croatia, 1941–1945*, trans. Lois Perkins (Chicago, IL: American Institute for Balkan Affairs, 1961).

Patte, Richard, *The Case of Cardinal Aloysius Stepinac* (Milwaukee, WI: Bruce, 1953).

Pavelić, Ante, 'Oslobodjenje', *Godišnjak (Croatian Almanac) 1940* (Pittsburgh, PA: Hrvatski Domobran, 1940).

Pavlowitch, Stevan K., *Unconventional Perceptions of Yugoslavia, 1940–1945* (New York, NY: East European Monographs, 1985).

Peck, Sarah E., 'The Campaign for an American Response to the Nazi Holocaust, 1943–1945', *Journal of Contemporary History* (April 1980), pp. 367–400.

Peter II. *A King's Heritage: The Memoirs of King Peter II of Yugoslavia* (London: Cassell, 1955).

Petrov, Vladimir, *A Study in Diplomacy: The Story of Arthur Bliss Lane* (Chicago, IL: Henry Regnery, 1971).

Phayer, Michael, *The Catholic Church and the Holocaust, 1930–1965* (Bloomington, IN: Indiana University Press, 2000).

Pitamitz, Antonio, '55 Years after the Marseilles Attack the Conspirator Rediscovered', *Soria Illustrata* (1990), pp. 46–51.

Prcela, John and Stanko Guldescu (eds), *Operation Slaughterhouse: Eyewitness Accounts of Postwar Massacres in Yugoslavia* (Philadelphia, PA: Dorrance, 1970).

Presseisen, Ernst L., 'Prelude to "Barbarossa": Germany and the Balkans, 1940–1941', *The Journal of Modern History* 32 (December 1960), pp. 359–70.

Pribichevich, Stoyan, 'Fratricide in Yugoslavia', *Fortune* 27 (June 1943), pp. 148–53, 162–8.

Prpic, George J., *The Croatian Immigrants in America* (New York, NY: Philosophical Library, 1971).

Ramet, Pedro, 'From Strossmayer to Stepinac: Croatian National Ideology and Catholicism', *Canadian Review of Studies in Nationalism* 12 (Spring 1985), pp. 123–39.

Ramet, Sabrina, *The Three Yugoslavias: State Building and Legitimation, 1918–2005* (Bloomington, IN: Indiana University Press, 2006).

_____ (ed.), *The Independent State of Croatia, 1941–1945* (London: Routledge, 2007).

_____ 'Vladko Maček and the Croatian Peasant Defence in the Kingdom of Yugoslavia', *Contemporary European History* 16/2 (May 2007), pp. 221–2.

Rhodes, Anthony, *The Vatican in the Age of the Dictators, 1922–1945* (London: Hodder and Stoughton, 1973).

Rich, Norman, *Hitler's War Aims: The Establishment of the New Order*, vol. II (New York, NY: W.W. Norton, 1974).

Rivelli, Marco Aurelio, *Le Genocide Occulte: Etat Independent de Croatie, 1941–1945*, trans. Gaby Rousseau (Paris: L'age d'homme, 1998).

Roberts, Allen, *The Turning Point: The Assassination of Louis Barthou and King Alexander I of Yugoslavia* (New York, NY: St Martin's, 1970).

Roberts, Walter R., *Tito, Mihailović and the Allies, 1941–1945* (Durham, NC: Duke University Press, 1987). Originally published in 1973 by Rutgers University Press.

Roucek, Joseph S., 'Foreign Politics and Our Minority Groups', *Phylon.* 2 (First Quarter 1941), pp. 44–56.

Ryan, Allan A. Jr, *Klaus Barbie and the United States Government: The Report, with Documentary Appendix, to the Attorney General of the United States* (Frederick, MD: University Publication of America, 1984).

Sabathier, Jean-Marc, 'Un fait divers ressuscite le diable oustachi', *Paris Match* (25 May 1957), pp. 16–25.

Sadkovich, James J., *Italian Support for Croatian Separatism, 1927–1937* (New York, NY: Garland, 1987).

_____ 'Terrorism in Croatia, 1929–1934', *East European Quarterly* 22/1 (March 1988), pp. 55–79.

De Santis, Hugh, *The Diplomacy of Silence: The American Foreign Service, the Soviet Union, and the Cold War, 1933–1947* (Chicago, IL: University of Chicago Press, 1979).

Sayer, Ian and Douglas Botting, *America's Secret Army: The Untold Story of the Counter Intelligence Corps* (New York, NY: Franklin Watts, 1989).

Schmitz, David F., *Thank God They're on Our Side: The United States and Right-Wing Dictatorships, 1921–1965* (Chapel Hill, CA: University of North Carolina Press, 1999).

Seaton, Albert, *The Russo-German War, 1941–45* (New York, NY: Praeger, 1971).

Sells, Michael, 'Kosovo Mythology and the Bosnian Genocide', in Omer Bartov and Phyllis Mackp (eds), *In God's Name: Genocide and Religion in the Twentieth Century* (New York, NY: Berghahn Books, 2001), pp. 180–205.

Sereni, Angelo Piero, 'The Status of Croatia under International Law', *The American Political Science Review* 35 (December 1941), pp. 1144–51.

Seton-Watson, R.W., 'The Yugoslav Dictatorship', *International Affairs* 11 (January 1932), pp. 22–39.

_____ 'King Alexander's Assassination: Its Background and Effects', *International Affairs* 14 (January–February 1935), pp. 20–47.

_____ 'Yugoslavia and the Croat Problem', *Slavonic Review* 16 (1937), pp. 102–12.

Shoup, Paul, *Communism and the Yugoslav National Question* (New York, NY: Columbia University Press, 1968).

Simpson, Christopher, *Blowback: America's Recruitment of Nazis and its Effects on the Cold War* (New York, NY: Weidenfeld & Nicolson, 1988).

_____ The Splendid Blond Beast: Money, Law, and Genocide in the Twentieth Century (New York, NY: Grove Press, 1993).

Stavrianos, L.S., The Balkans since 1453 (New York, NY: Holt, Rinehart and Winston, 1958).

Stehle, Hansjakob, Eastern Politics of the Vatican, 1917–1979, trans. Sandra Smith (Athens, OH: Ohio University Press, 1981).

Steinberg, Jonathan, All or Nothing: The Axis and the Holocaust, 1941–1943 (London: Routledge, 2002).

Tasovac, Ivo, American Foreign Policy and Yugoslavia, 1939–1941 (College Station, TX: Texas A&M Press, 1990).

Tanner, Marcus, Croatia: A Nation Forged in War (New Haven, CT: Yale University Press, 1997).

Tella, Guidodi and D. Cameron Watt (eds), Argentina Between the Great Powers, 1939–46 (Pittsburgh, PA: University of Pittsburgh Press, 1990).

Tomasevich, Jozo, War and Revolution in Yugoslavia: Occupation and Collaboration (Stanford, CA: Stanford University Press, 2001).

Trifković, Srdjan, 'Rivalry Between Germany and Italy in Croatia, 1942–1943', The Historical Journal 36 (1993), pp. 879–904.

_____ 'Yugoslavia in Crisis: Europe and the Croat Question, 1939–41', European History Quarterly 23 (1993), pp. 529–61.

_____ Ustaša: Croatian Separatism and European Politics, 1929–1945 (London: The Lord Byron Foundation for Balkan Studies, 1998).

Vago, Bela, 'The Reaction to the Nazi Anti-Jewish Policy in East-Central Europe and in the Balkans', in Francois Furet (ed.), Unanswered Questions: Nazi Germany and the Genocide of the Jews (New York, NY: Schocken Books, 1989), pp. 199–251.

Van Creveld, Martin L., Hitler's Strategy 1940–1941: The Balkan Clue (Cambridge: Cambridge University Press, 1973).

Volf, Miroslav, Exclusion and Embrace: A Theological Exploration of Identity, Otherness, and Reconciliation (Nashville, TN: Abingdon Press, 1996).

Watson, Rubie S. (ed.), Memory and Opposition under State Socialism (Santa Fe, NM: School of American Research, 1993), pp. 167–84.

Weil, Martin, A Pretty Good Club: The Founding Fathers of the United States Foreign Service (New York, NY: Norton, 1978).

West, Richard, Tito: And the Rise and Fall of Yugoslavia (New York, NY: Carroll & Graf, 1994).

Wyman, Mark, DPs: Europe's Displaced Persons, 1945–1951 (Ithaca, NY: Cornell University Press, 1998).

INDEX

Acheson, Dean, 145–46
Akron, Ohio, Ustaše investigation, 99,
 101
Albania, 55
Aleksandar I (king of Yugoslavia)
 assassination attempts, 14–17,
  34–35
 assassination co-conspirators, 37, 47
 Croatian independence and, 24–26,
  48
 funeral and aftermath of death,
  18–22
 Pavelić role in assassination, 31–33,
  50, 69
 seizure of power, 4–6, 11
 See also Photo insert: Figs. 4–5
Alexander, Harold, 116
Alexander, Stella, 81
Alianza Libertadora Nacionalista, 169
All Croat Congress (Croatian National
 Conference), 28–29
Alt-Gradiska (concentration camp), 78
American isolationism, 1, 3, 62–63, 70
American Slav (magazine), 95
American Srbobran (newspaper), 94
Americki Hrvatski Glasnik (newspaper),
 173
Anderson (British general), 161
Angleton, James, 143

anti-Semitism, 75–76, 90
Aramburu, Pedro, 177
Aranyos, Pablo (Pavelić alias), 167
Ardas (Croatian priest), 99
Argentina
 encouragement of immigration,
  166–67
 establishing Ustaše presence, 29,
  33–35, 39, 175–77
 immigration of war criminals,
  135–36, 157–58
 Pavelić assassination attempt, 177–79
 Pavelić relocation to, 155–69
 Pavelić relocation to Chile, 179–80
 Peron government collapse, 177
 post-war immigration to Argentina,
  166–68
 protection of war criminals, 153
 support for Pavelić, 47
 transfer of Ustaše gold, 173–75
 See also South America
Artuković, Andrija, 30, 40, 45, 116,
 125, 129, 179, 216n54
Austro-Hungarian Compromise of
 1867 (Ausgleich), 8

Balkans
 American trade and diplomatic
  presence, 2